Doing Business with Germany

In association with

Deutsch-Britische
ndustrie- und Handelskammer

German-British
Chamber of Industry & Commerce

PRICEWATERHOUSE COOPERS 🏠

EVERSHEDS

Business Lawyers in Europe

Consultant Editors:
Jonathan Reuvid and Roderick Millar

BUILDING VALUE ACROSS EUROPE

PricewaterhouseCoopers is the world's leading professional services organisation. Drawing on the knowledge and skills of 150,000 people in 150 countries, we help our clients solve complex business problems and measurably enhance their ability to build value, manage risk and improve performance.

Working in conjunction with the German member firm PwC Deutsche Revision AG, we use specialist industry knowledge and experience of German business to provide cross-border advisory services to companies seeking to do business in Germany and German companies working in the UK.

For advice on how to maximise the value of your interests in Germany, please contact:

Morag McLean, PwC Deutsche Revision AG, New-York-Ring 13 D-22297 Hamburg, Germany.
Telephone: 00 49 40 6378 1617.

Douglas Paterson, PricewaterhouseCoopers, Southwark Towers, 32 London Bridge Street, London SE1 9SY.
Telephone: 44 (0)171 212 4572.

www.pwcglobal.com

Doing Business with
Germany

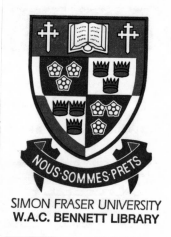

SIMON FRASER UNIVERSITY
W.A.C. BENNETT LIBRARY

First published 1997
This second edition published 1999

Kogan Page Ltd
120 Pentonville Road
London N1 9JN
E-mail: kpinfo@kogan-page.co.uk

© Kogan Page 1999

British Library Cataloguing Data

A CIP record for this book is available from the British Library

ISBN 0 7494 2951 8

Typeset by JS Typesetting, Wellingborough, Northants
Printed and bound in Great Britain by Bell & Bain Limited, Glasgow

Anglo-German Legal Solutions

Eversheds is Europe's second largest law firm with around 1500 top flight lawyers situated in 19 locations across Britain and Europe. Each office provides a wide range of services to the business and financial community as well as to the public sector, combining extensive local market knowledge with an international perspective. As Germany establishes itself as the United Kingdom's most important trading partner, Eversheds has given special attention to the Anglo-German business community by offering a full German and English legal service to its clients. Staffed by five bilingual German lawyers (four dually qualified as German Rechtsanwälte and English Solicitors), the London-based Anglo-German group's work covers all aspects of international commercial activity.

For further information contact:
Dr Michael H Carl
Head of Anglo-German Group
Eversheds
Senator House
85 Queen Victoria Street
London EC4V 4JL
Tel: +44 171 919 4500
Fax: +44 171 919 4919
E-mail: carlm@eversheds.com

 EVERSHEDS

London • Birmingham • Bristol • Cambridge • Cardiff • Derby
Ipswich • Leeds • Manchester • Newcastle • Norwich • Nottingham • Teesside
Brussels • Copenhagen* • Monaco • Moscow • Paris • Sofia*
* Associated offices

Contents

PART THREE: FINANCE AND BANKING ISSUES

PART FOUR: CORPORATE FINANCE ISSUES

PART FIVE: ACCOUNTING AND TAXATION ISSUES

PART SIX: LEGAL ISSUES

APPENDICES

FIRST CLASS
DELIVERY

List of Contributors

Professor Dr Horst Albach is Professor of Business Administration at the Humboldt University in Berlin, and Managing Director of the Research Unit IV, Market Processes and Corporate Development at the Science Centre, Berlin.

Dr Lazslo Alex is the Director of the Federal Institute for Vocational Training in Bonn. This is the research and development body for vocational training.

Dr Eberhard Braun is the senior partner of Schultze & Braun, a law and accountancy firm specialising in pre-bankruptcy advice, turn-arounds, workouts and formal bankruptcy proceeding work. In July 1998 the firm joined the Coopers & Lybrand Deutsche Revision group, now PricewaterhouseCoopers.

Dr Braun is now the German head of Business Recovery Services, the centre of competence for restructuring and insolvency in Germany. He has acted as a trustee in bankruptcy proceedings since 1980 and is a member of the *Institut der Wirtschaftsprüfer AKSI* (workgroup for reconstruction and insolvency), the *Insolvenzrechtsausschuß des Deutschen Anwaltsvereins* (Insolvency Law Board of the German Solicitors Union) and the AEPPC *Europäische Insolvenzverwaltervereinigung* (European Insolvency Administration Union). He has lectured for several years and has published three books on the new German insolvency law.

Anita Davisson is the partner and head of the German Mergers and Acquisitions department of PricewaterhouseCoopers Corporate Finance Beratung, based in Frankfurt. She has been working with Pricewater-houseCoopers since 1986, when she started in London. In 1997, after some years in Berlin she became Partner in Frankfurt. She specialises in the automotive industry, private equity and retail.

Eversheds (Anglo-German Group)
Dr Michael H Carl is a barrister and solicitor, specialising in corporate, banking and commercial law, as well as commercial litigation. He has worked in this field for 25 years and was involved in the first hostile take-over by a German company in the UK, as well as many other take-overs and joint ventures. On the litigation front, he has lead teams dealing with large insurance claims, product liability and art law.
Babette Märzheuser-Wood is a barrister and solicitor. She has full training in English as well as German law, together with a wide experience of Anglo-German company and commercial law. She has assisted many German and UK companies in setting up their businesses and cross-border trading respectively.
Carsten Rumberg is a barrister and solicitor specialising in Anglo-German commercial law, including commercial litigation.
Constanze Randelzhofer is a German barrister and solicitor, specialising in Anglo-German labour law and general corporate matters.

Dr Andreas Freiling joined PricewaterhouseCoopers in 1989 and is qualified as a German Certified Public Accountant. He is based in the Frankfurt office and works as audit partner in ABAS Financial Services. He specialises in the accounting of new financial instruments, the internal control of market risks and new issues of the banking and the insurance supervisory authorities. He is responsible for the audit of insurance clients and head of both Information Systems and Marketing within the German Financial Services sector.

The **German-British Chamber of Industry & Commerce** in London is one of the German Chambers Abroad which form a world-wide network under the auspices of the Association of German Chambers of Industry & Commerce in Germany. Its mission is to promote trade and investment between the United Kingdom and Germany.
Ulrich Hoppe is the Director General of the German-British Chamber of Industry & Commerce in London.
Angelika Baumgarte heads the Legal Department of the German-British Chamber of Industry & Commerce in London. She has held this position since 1982. She advises German and British companies on the legal aspects of doing business in or with the other country.

John Harper is an Investment Manager for HSBC Private Equity GmbH and is based in Düsseldorf. He was a founder member of the office in 1997, having previously worked for HSBC in London. His responsibility is to source and execute private equity transactions such as management buyouts and buy-ins and recapitalisations of privately owned companies.

Dr Wolfgang Lecher studies in Sociology, Economics and Philosophy with the main subject of Industrial and Organisational Sociology in Tübingen and Frankfurt am Main.

Eric Lynn is Managing Director of LCT Consultants in Nuremberg. He has been living and working in Germany since 1984. He is an experienced facilitator of international integration processes and also specialises in preparing German executives for specific assignments in English speaking countries and non-German executives for work in Germany.

Morag McLean is a qualified Chartered Accountant. She specialises in transaction services for PwC Deutsche Revision AG, in Hamburg. Her main clients are subsidiaries of UK, US and Scandinavian parents. As well as being part of the German firm's specialist group on international accounting, she is also part of the UK Business Network Group in Germany. She has worked in Germany since 1982, and joined PricewaterhouseCoopers in 1994.

Roderick Millar is an experienced financial editor and writer specialising in foreign trade, development economics and business start-ups.

Prof Dr Peter Oberender has been Professor of Economics at the University of Bayreuth since 1980, and is a member of the *Wissenschaftsrat*.

Jonathan Reuvid graduated in PPE from Oxford University and is an experienced international business development manager, having worked in many of the EU member countries in senior line and staff management positions. Alongside management consultancy he has pursued a parallel career in publishing as a writer and editor of international business books.

He is Managing Director of the Management Consultancy Business School which, in collaboration with the University of Surrey, offers the first European Master of Science degree in Management Consultancy.

Jens A Roennberg is a Partner of PricewaterhouseCoopers and based in London. Before he relocated to London he worked as an Audit Partner for PricewaterhouseCoopers in Frankfurt. He specialises in the audit and consulting of major German financial institutions with international activities.

Dr Hans Christoph von Rohr is Chairman of the Executive Board of the New German Länder Industrial Investment Council (IIC) in Berlin – the inward investment agency of eastern Germany. He was previously

CEO of Klöckner-Werke AG in Duisburg, and globally active in the machinery, automotive components and plastic processing industries. Before that, he gained considerable experience in international business as Member of the Executive Board of Klöckner & Co, one of the largest German trading companies.

He graduated from the University of Bonn in 1967, completing his PhD in Law and the German legal examinations. He was a Fulbright scholar at the Woodrow Wilson School of Public and International Affairs, Princeton University, USA.

He is a member of various supervisory boards and chairman of the Competition Commission at the Federation of German Industries (BDI).

Sven Rosorius is a Senior Audit Manager for German and international clients at PricewaterhouseCoopers Deutsche Revision in Hamburg. He joined Coopers & Lybrand in 1988, after completing his Diploma in Economics at the University of Hamburg. He has worked as a tax consultant since 1993 and a chartered accountant since 1996.

Dr Christof Schiller is a lawyer and has worked with Schultze & Braun since 1995. He studied in Heidelberg, and has benefited from extended stays in Israel, France and the USA.

Wolfram Schmerl is Assistant Director in the Mergers and Acquisitions team of PricewaterhouseCoopers Corporate Finance Beratung. He has been working for PricewaterhouseCoopers since 1992 and specialises in private equity, public company and the packaging industry.

Astrid Schmidt is a manager in the Mergers and Acquisitions team of PricewaterhouseCoopers Corporate Finance Beratung in Frankfurt. Since joining PricewaterhouseCoopers in 1995 she has worked on several transactions in Germany and cross-border. She specialises in the food and drink industry.

Prof Dr Hermann Schmidt is a professor at the University of Duisburg. He was President of the Federal Institute for Vocational Training until 1998, when he left and took up his current position.

Christoph Schreiber is a German Tax Partner on assignment to PricewaterhouseCoopers New York where he manages the German country programme. He specialises in cross-border tax planning for multinational companies, mergers and acquisitions and tax treaty issues. Over the past 12 years he has been involved in many significant transactions and tax planning projects.

He received his Law degree from the University of Göttingen in Germany. He was admitted to the German Bar in 1988 and has been a certified tax advisor since 1992. Previous foreign assignments include a traineeship with the law firm Walter, Conston, Alexander & Green in New York as well as his work with the Transfer Pricing Group at PricewaterhouseCoopers Chicago.

He is the designated leader of the European Tax Group at Pricewater-houseCoopers New York and chairs the US–German Tax Specialist Committee – a group of US experienced tax professionals formed by PricewaterhouseCoopers Germany. Christoph is also a frequent speaker at seminars.

Wolfgang Suchanek is an Audit Partner responsible for international clients at PricewaterhouseCoopers Deutsche Revision in Hamburg. He completed his Diploma in Economics in 1968 at the University of Hamburg, and became a tax consultant in 1972. That same year he joined Coopers & Lybrand and qualified as a Chartered Accountant in 1976. He worked for PricewaterhouseCoopers in Australia from 1981-1983 and became a partner in 1985.

Walter Tacke is a management consultant and a former president of the Association for German Market and Social Researchers (BVM) in Germany.

Frank Viecens is an attorney at law and has worked for Pricewater-houseCoopers Financial Services in Frankfurt since 1997. He specialises in German regulatory acts for banks and insurance companies.

Adrian Yeeles is an international tax partner with Pricewaterhouse-Coopers, based in London. He specialises in international tax planning with particular emphasis on Germany and is a regular writer and speaker on the subject.

John M Zindar is Director International Strategy at the New German Länder Industrial Investment Council (IIC) – the official inward investment agency for eastern Germany. The IIC provides free professional support to firms throughout the investment cycle. Previously he worked in economic and business development in both Europe and Latin America as well as government relations in Washington DC. A former US Army intelligence officer, he holds an MA from The Johns Hopkins University, Baltimore.

Introduction

There have been many significant changes in Europe and the European Union since the beginning of 1997 when the first edition of *Doing Business with Germany* was published. The economies of EU members have wrestled with economic downturns and, in some cases, the possibility of recession. Although cyclical factors have been at play, the Asian financial crisis and the meltdown of Russia's economic system were strong influencing elements. The political pendulum in the EU has continued to swing from right to left with Germany joining France and Britain in the election of social democrats to government.

The much-heralded eleven member launch of the Economic and Monetary Union (EMU) on 1 January 1999 was managed smoothly and the new European Central Bank (ECB) has shown its mettle during an extended period of weakness by sticking to its non-intervention policy. The Euro-zone economy registered modest economic growth in the first quarter of 1999 with GDP growth rising by 0.4 per cent over the final quarter of 1998. The Euro-zone has also maintained a healthy balance on current account in its first four months and a favourable trade balance during the first quarter. Although the US is still expanding faster than the Euro-zone, mainly because of the weak growth in Germany and Italy, published data this month, including the latest reading of the Ifo index, suggest that the German economy has turned the corner.

During the six month period of its EU Presidency, Germany has taken centre stage. The crisis of confidence arising from the European Parliament's rejection of the European Commissioner's management performance was handled decisively with the rapid appointment of Romano Prodi as the new EC President. Germany has taken a prominent and unprecedented role in the NATO military action in Kosovo and in the resolution of the conflict with Serbia. In the economic field, the common German and British agenda for economic reform, articulated by Chancellor Gerhard Schröder and Prime Minister Tony Blair, has redefined left-of-centre ideology and signals a commitment by the German government to continuing structural and fiscal reform. For the

SDP, a party which has clung to many traditional socialist doctrines, the reformation of the social security support system causes much heart-searching and will be politically difficult, requiring more stamina than the previous centre-right German government demonstrated on both social support and taxation issues.

However, in German-British economic and business relationships much remains the same, with Germany, the largest country in the EU, offering a wide range of business opportunities to British companies as the UK's biggest trading partner. As we enter the millennium, each country will continue to play a major role in each other's economic life, irrespective of the timing of Britain's entry or non-entry into the EMU. At the same time, German industry is expanding its global involvement and cross-border integration with EU partners, all of which will affect the outlook for British companies in the longer term.

As before, this book is intended both for those who are relatively ignorant of economic and business conditions, business practices and development issues in Germany, and for those already doing business there who need to develop a deeper understanding of finance and banking, accounting, taxation and legal issues. The editors are indebted to the German-British Chamber of Industry and Commerce for its active role in the development of the book's contents and in the identification of authors for Parts One and Two; to PricewaterhouseCoopers London and German offices for their editorial contributions, including the whole of Parts Four and Five and to the London partners of Eversheds for Part Six. Our thanks are also due to the individual authors whose particular contributions have provided both the background material and informed opinion which, we hope, will make this book a useful business guide, and an interesting overview of the German business scene.

Jonathan Reuvid and Roderick Millar
London, June, 1999

Part One

Economic and Business Conditions

Political Analysis

1

The Federal Government and the Face of Politics

Jonathan Reuvid

The political landscape of Germany was changed dramatically by the national elections of 1998 that brought to an abrupt end the 16-year Chancellorship of Helmut Kohl and the successive governments of the Christian Democratic Union (CDU) and its political partner, the Christian Socialist Union (CSU). Significant changes in policy have resulted too, on which this book comments through other chapters in Part One.

Many readers of *Doing Business with Germany* will have a more than passing knowledge of the German political system and how federal government is organised, but for those business people wishing to refresh their background knowledge this chapter provides an overview.

THE FEDERAL GOVERNMENT

The German federal assembly is bicameral, consisting of a lower house (*Bundestag*) and an upper house (*Bundesrat*). There are 662 seats in the *Bundestag*, of which 328 are directly elected from individual constituencies and 334 are elected through party lists in each state (*Land*) so as to achieve proportional representation. By contrast, the *Bundesrat* consists of members elected by the 16 *Länder* governments. National *Bundestag* elections are held every four years.

The head of state is the president, elected for a maximum of two five-year terms by an electoral college comprised of members of the *Bundestag* and representatives of the *Länder* legislatures. Elected on 23 May 1999, the current president is Johannes Rau (68), who was formerly premier of North Rhine Westphalia, the most populous *Land*, for 20 years. His resignation in 1998 emphasised the change of generation in the leadership of the Social Democratic Party (SPD) in preparation for last September's national election. He is the second Social Democrat to have served as president after Gustav Heineman (1969–1974), to whom he is linked through his wife, who is former President Heineman's granddaughter.

The chief executive of the federal government is the chancellor, elected by the *Bundestag* on the nomination of the president. Generally the chancellor is the leader of the party in government with the largest number of seats in the *Bundestag*, currently Gerhard Schröder, leader of the SPD–Green coalition government appointed on 27 October 1998. At the time, the chairman of the SPD was Oskar Lafontaine, who resigned from active politics in March 1999 and was succeeded in April as chairman by Mr Schröder.

THE MAIN POLITICAL PARTIES

Represented in the *Bundestag* are:

- Social Democratic Party of Germany (SPD);
- Green Party;
- Christian Democratic Union (CDU); not present in Bavaria;
- Christian Social Union (CSU); present only in Bavaria;
- Free Democratic Party (FDP);
- Party of Democratic Socialism (PDS).

The SDP and the Greens are the present coalition government. The CDU and the CSU form a joint group in parliament.

Not represented in the *Bundestag* are two extreme right-wing parties: The German People's Party (DVU); and Republikaner.

THE CONSTITUTION

The official name of Germany is the Federal Republic of Germany (FRG). Its legal system is based on the *Grundgesetz* (Basic Law) of 1949. On 3 October 1990 the five states (*Länder*) of the former German Democratic Republic (GDR), or East Germany, acceded to the FRG.

Map 1   *The* Länder *of Germany*

The 16 *Länder* and their state capitals are listed below in alphabetical order; German translations are given in brackets where applicable.

- Baden Württemberg   Stuttgart
- Bavaria (Bayern)   Munich (München)
- Berlin   Berlin
- Brandenburg   Potsdam*
- Bremen   Bremen
- Hamburg   Hamburg
- Hesse (Hessen)   Wiesbaden
- Lower Saxony (Niedersachsen)   Hanover
- Mecklenburg-Western Pomerania
  (Mecklenburg-Vorpommern)   Schwerin*
- North Rhine/Westphalia
  (Nordrhein Westfalen)   Düsseldorf
- Rhineland-Palatinate (Rheinlandpfalz)   Mainz
- Saarland   Saarbrücken
- Saxony (Sachsen)   Dresden*
- Saxony-Anhalt (Sachsen-Anhalt)   Magdeburg*
- Schleswig-Holstein   Kiel
- Thuringia (Thüringen)   Erfurt*

(*Formerly comprising the GDR, together with East Berlin.)

ADAPTING TO THE NEW POLITICAL LANDSCAPE

The outcome of the 1998 national elections, in terms of percentage of the vote registered and seats held by the parties in the *Bundestag* before and after the election, is as shown in Table 1.1.

Table 1.1 *Percentage of registered vote and seats held, 1998*

	% vote	Seats After election	Before election
SPD	40.9	291	252
CDU/CSU	35.1	245	294
Green Party	6.7	47	49
FDP	6.2	44	47
PDS	5.1	35	30
Others	6.0	nil	nil

The member parties in the new government have been affected both by the experience of office and by extraneous events that were not predicted at the time when the 'Red–Green' coalition took power.

Chancellor Schröder gained office as the champion of the traditional SPD policies of social justice, not dissimilar from the raft of policies on which Tony Blair's New Labour Party had been elected to govern Britain 18 months earlier, in May 1997. Specific planks of the SPD policy platform were: corporate tax restructuring to create jobs by reducing the tax burden on small and medium-sized businesses (SMEs); levies on energy to raise funds that could be redeployed to support pension contributions; and plans for personal tax reform to assist the lower paid.

Although the SPD and Green parties had shared power previously at town and *Länder* levels, coalition at national level was a new experience, demanding the inclusion of environmental policies to satisfy the junior partner in government, of which a commitment to close Germany's power stations was the most controversial.

The new chancellor was thrust into the limelight of the international political stage by Germany's rotation presidency of the EU for the first six months of 1999. Initially, Mr Schröder put forward extensive proposals to reform the EU's social, regional and farm policies to prepare for the inclusion of new democracies from the Communist bloc of eastern Europe early next century; the progress of the ensuing debate is covered in Chapter 3. Other topics that have occupied the EU Council of Ministers during the German presidency have been the resignation under pressure of the entire team of EU commissioners and the accompanying issue of Commission accountability, the appointment of a new Commission President and EC budget funding.

However, all other EU issues and non-economic domestic priorities have been overshadowed by the war in Kosovo. The government's steadfast decision to commit German combat troops in support of NATO has been applauded by Germany's foreign partners but has caused serious splits in opinion within the SDP and even more so within the Green Party. The SDP conference in April, which should have been a celebration of Mr Schröder's appointment as party chairman, was dominated by a special debate on Kosovo. While the Kosovan issue has been divisive for the SDP, the fall-out has been mitigated to some degree by the healing effect of withdrawal from Mr Lafontaine's more inflammatory economic policies and his opposition to European Central Bank (ECB) monetary policy.

The effects of the government's military commitment to NATO have been far more divisive for the Green Party than for the SPD and especially testing for its leader and Germany's Foreign Minister, Joschka Fischer. At the party's special conference in May Mr Fischer and his supporters gained a reluctant endorsement for the German policy on Kosovo as the lesser of two evils, after some aggressive interjections by the less pragmatic members. While the party, which appreciated Mr Fischer's tireless efforts for a diplomatic solution, achieved a stabilising outcome at some cost to principles, acceptance by voters is less certain. The Green Party registered a sharp drop in support in the first *Land* elections in Hesse in February 1999, and in the Bremen elections four months later their vote slumped by four per cent to nine per cent.

The Green Party has also suffered set-backs on other policies that it has contributed to the government agenda. The nuclear industry has relaxed in the face of threats to shut down the country's 19 reactors, made by the incoming government as a key environmental improvement issue. In place of a rapid shut-down programme the industry now expects that a few reactors may be taken out of service over the next five years and the remainder phased out over a 20-year period.

Another high priority on the Green's policy agenda was the revision of Germany's citizenship laws, which are based on 1913 legislation and which determine German nationality by bloodline rather than place of birth and residence. This seems manifestly unjust to more than half of the 7.3 million foreigners who have lived in Germany for more than 10 years, principally the Turkish and other *Gastarbeiter* (guest workers) and their families. The original scheme agreed between the SPD and the Greens was to cut the length of residency before citizenship could be granted and to allow dual nationality, whereby foreigners could both gain a German passport and retain their original one. In the face of fierce criticism from the CDU and the CSU the government struck a deal with the FDP that enabled legislation to be passed on an 'option model', which allows children of foreigners generally to hold both German and their parents' nationality up to the age of 18, when one parent has lived in Germany for at least eight years. At 18, a further five-year period is allowed in which to decide which single nationality is to be adopted. This compromise falls short of the coalition's aspirations, but is undoubtedly historic. In his acceptance of office speech President Rau acknowledged its significance when he declared that he intended to be president 'of all the Germans'.

If the first eight months in office have been a tough and maturing experience for the two coalition parties, the same is certainly true for the CDU/CSU combine in opposition. Both parties, the CSU under the leadership of Edmund Stoiber and the CDU under Wolfgang Schauble, have maintained impressive unity with an agreed joint platform for the European elections. The CSU position in Bavaria appears rock solid, with a 53 per cent share of the votes in the 1998 national elections. Mr Stoiber has served as president of Bavaria since 1993; he is sceptical towards Brussels centralisation and European integration, a champion of future regional government across the continent, and professes a preoccupation with Bavaria that excludes him from federal government aspirations. While few believe that Mr Stoiber is not a potential candidate for the chancellorship, the precedent of Franz-Josef Strauss's defeat in the 1980 elections suggests to many Germans that the country is highly unlikely to elect a right-wing Bavarian politician as chancellor.

By contrast, although conceptually a more likely future coalition government leader, Mr Schauble has no regional power base. However, he has been successful so far in keeping opposition forces united and avoiding the rapid decline into internal warfare that has afflicted the British Conservative Party after its similarly disastrous defeat in 1997. As the next national elections approach, Mr Stroiber's and Mr Schauble's political interests are certain to diverge. For the time being they march hand in hand.

Despite its deep-rooted economic problems Germany approaches the millennium after another decade of solid achievement. The magnificent dome of the restored Reichstag in Berlin, to which the German parliament moves this summer after its 50-year sojourn in Bonn, mirrors Germany's new self-assurance in its relationships with its partners, neighbours and allies on the global political scene.

2

Another Quiet Revolution: Eastern Germany as a Reform Model for the Nation

Dr Hans Christoph von Rohr,
The New German Länder Industrial
Investment Council (IIC), Berlin

If Germany is going to maintain its world-renowned competitiveness, it must accomplish a number of tasks. There is no doubt that the products from the world's third largest economy remain excellent: the German export machine is in its highest gear ever, and quality is never an issue with something 'Made in Germany'.

The challenge then, is one of cost and flexibility – the foremost concerns of potential foreign investors when examining possible locations. Yet the preconceptions of a high-cost, inflexible Germany are being chipped away, and much of the credit can go to the new states (or *Länder*) of eastern Germany. This region has evolved, through a combination of necessity and creativity, into a national incubator for change. The positive effects are spreading throughout the country.

This trend is logical; eastern Germans are heavily predisposed to adaptation and innovation. They have already weathered a storm of social and economic change since the Berlin Wall suddenly crumbled in 1989. The 16 million citizens of the new federal states are proving they can successfully compete under the free market conditions they eagerly embraced nine years ago.

The conditions were at their worst right after the fall of the Wall. Within a year of reunification economic output contracted 30 per cent, and over three million people lost their manufacturing jobs. Eastern Germany had been one of the primary manufacturing powers of the Communist bloc, producing everything from autos to chemicals to computers. But the opening of the Wall caused the collapse of the principal export markets of the eastern bloc. At the same time, on an unprecedented scale, 14,000 formerly state-owned firms were privatised by the *Treuhandanstalt*, while another 4000 companies were liquidated within four years.

There were other problems to overcome as well. The environment was in a terrible condition, due in large part to air and water pollution from the former East Germany's industrial output. The cities had been neglected, with the lack of necessary infrastructure and maintenance work on roads or even apartment houses. Items such as a telephone or a car were luxury goods. Families shared phone lines, people waited decades to receive their Trabant autos, and the whole society lived under the watchful eye of a *Stasi* network of secret informers that numbered in the millions.

Those whirlwind, tumultuous days of change are over, and eastern Germany has bounced back through a combination of generous financial support from western Germany, vast amounts of investment and, most importantly, the talents and character of the region's people. Since 1991 GDP has expanded by more than 45 per cent, over half a million new firms have been successfully founded, and over US$137 billion have been invested in roads, railways, canals, schools, housing, industrial parks, environmental clean-ups, the technical retraining of 700,000 people, and what is now the world's finest telecom system. Current visitors to the area who saw what it was like a decade ago are often shocked at the speed and breadth of the transformation. An area the size of New York state has been catapulted into the 21st century.

Perhaps more important than the massive public funds are the US$685 billion already privately invested by thousands of German firms as well as nearly 2000 foreign enterprises. The names don't just include mainstays like Coca-Cola and McDonald's. Rather, many of the world's leading electronic, manufacturing, chemical and service companies have banked on eastern Germany. Sony Europe is building a massive new headquarters at Berlin's Potsdamer Platz. Siemens, Motorola and AMD are making semiconductors at new factories in Dresden. Ribozyme and other cutting-edge biotech firms are clustering in eastern research and development centres. Call centres are taking advantage of the low-cost, multilingual workforce and rock-bottom real estate prices. Auto giants like General Motors and Toyota are building parts facilities, and GM's Opel plant in Eisenach (Thuringia) is rated as the company's most productive operation in Europe.

With such investment, running at twice the per capita rate as that of western Germany (and 50 times the per capita private investment rate for neighbouring Poland), overall productivity has more than doubled since 1991. Manufacturing productivity has jumped 260 per cent and now averages 90 per cent of western levels. Combining state-of-the-art technology with skilled, eager eastern German workers has, in many cases, led to even higher productivity levels than those found in western counterparts.

Market

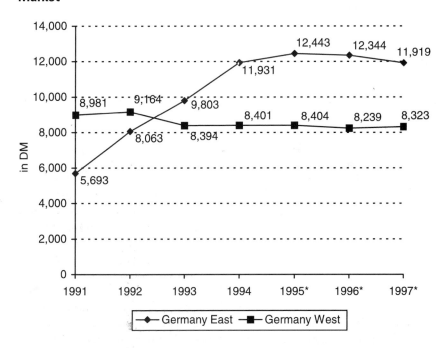

Since 1994 investment per capita in eastern Germany has averaged 46% higher than in western Germany. The private sector accounts for 83% of the DM1.3 trillion invested since 1991 in the new German states.

Figure 2.1   *Investments per capita – a Germany East/West comparison*

*estimated
Source: Ifo Institute; Federal Statistics Office

In addition to top corporations, eastern Germany has benefited from a new spirit of business creativity among small and medium-sized firms, especially in the booming IT sector. Top software company Intershop Communications, which sells e-commerce packages to businesses, was founded in Erfurt. Germany's No. 1 multimedia agency, Pixelpark, is in Berlin, and the fast-growing satellite communications firm Deutsche PhoneSat is led by former eastern Germans taking advantage of their old eastern European contacts.

The efforts, sacrifice and flexibility demonstrated by eastern Germans are the key factors for success. Eastern Germans defy the stereotype that many outsiders, especially Anglo-Saxons, tend to have of the German labour market: workers who turn out high-quality products but at high cost; strong unions that prevent flexible workforce designs; and workers who are disciplined but lack a creative edge. This caricature is simply not relevant in the new states. There, one can find a highly skilled, disciplined and innovative labour force, accustomed to change and fully open to new ideas, methods and solutions.

One unfortunate remnant from the tumultuous early 1990s is a persistent, double-digit level of unemployment, especially among women, who formed a large percentage of the former East German workforce. The pressure created by this situation is a primary reason why the eastern Germans have pioneered new paths of labour flexibility and innovation. They did so out of simple necessity. Ironically, they have adapted to the competitive conditions of the global marketplace perhaps faster than their comfortable counterparts in western Germany.

Many Westerners hear of the high unemployment and automatically think it is because the people have no skills. That assumption could not be more false – in perhaps the only good legacy left over from the Communist system, the people were extremely well educated. Eastern Germany has more holders of both advanced and medium-level degrees than western Germany, The Netherlands, France and the UK. Thus, with only minor training, investing companies have made use of the deep pool of available labour to pick the best employees possible. Many manufacturers have hired such high-quality workers to perform multi-tasking, thus reducing employee headcount and expenses.

Adapting to labour conditions that build profitable companies and job security is proving easier than coping with the demise of the socialist state. Union membership in the new states has dropped 50 per cent in the last five years, due largely to easterners' frustration at the high wage demands and other hindrances the western-based unions have

Workforce

▶ Types of collective bargaining agreements (%, 1997)

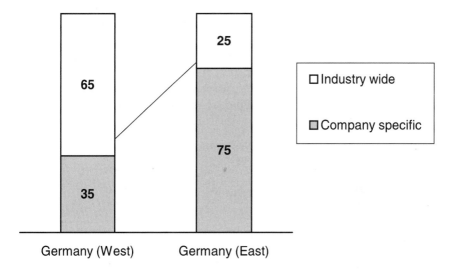

In contrast to western Germany, the vast majority of eastern German companies negotiate their salaries and working conditions individually, adapting to specific market conditions. This offers room for significant flexibility and, at the same time, reduced labour costs.

Figure 2.2 *Flexible and productive working practices*

Source: McKinsey, DIW

placed on the creation of new jobs. More than 75 per cent of all firms in eastern Germany now negotiate company-specific (or 'shop-level') wage agreements, rejecting the industry-wide deals that make up 75 per cent of all business in western Germany.

Consequently, workers in the east of Germany cost up to 45 per cent less while putting in up to 25 per cent more hours than in the west of Germany. They work longer weeks and readily accept night shifts, overtime, seasonal, holiday and weekend work at lower costs. Absenteeism and turnover rates are also lower. They take fewer holidays and sick days and forgo Christmas bonuses and 13th-month salaries. Moreover, bureaucracies in the region have been streamlined and permitting processes accelerated; and the new German state governments are leading the fight for tax reform.

Such major developments have not gone unnoticed. In recent months articles in both *The Economist* and *Wall Street Journal Europe* have praised the region as a model for Germany's new way in the global marketplace. Many Western CEOs now active in eastern Germany liken the situation to the former West Germany in the 1950s. Back then, it was clear that hard work and sound investment were laying the groundwork for unprecedented growth in the coming years. It is not uncommon to read similar accounts regarding the eastern states these days, whereby business leaders speculate that, in a decade's time, the east will be the gleaming showpiece of Germany.

Table 2.1   *Average total hourly labour costs (£)*

Western Germany	**16.87**
Switzerland	15.11
Denmark	14.34
Belgium	14.08
Sweden	13.87
Austria	13.71
Finland	13.70
Netherlands	12.89
Japan	12.31
Eastern Germany	**11.60**
France	11.28
USA	11.21
Italy	10.54
UK	10.07
Spain	8.80
Ireland	8.74
Greece	5.57
Portugal	3.89

Source: IW Cologne

The region of eastern Germany has seen a lot of change in the nine years since the Wall opened, but the people of the new German states have become accustomed to change. They have rediscovered a deep tradition of innovation and flexibility. The industrial revolution began in what are now the new federal states, based on the automotive, textile and machinery industries. The first German automobiles and aeroplanes were developed there, as well as the world's first computers and important advances in plastics and chemicals.

The sacrifices demanded by unification and a transition to a new market economy and social organisation have tempered the eastern Germans.

Now it makes sense that these same people are leading the way to important changes for the entire country – pointing the way to the kind of flexibility, the kind of sacrifice and the kind of entrepreneurial endeavour required for today's comparative framework. Yet eastern Germans have taken it upon themselves to make the most of the good things transferred from the West and to reject the bad. They are not waiting for change to be legislated; they are forging ahead on their own, leading a quiet revolution that is spreading throughout the country.

The dynamics of change in the new German states are already having an effect on the old German states. One could say that the second phase of reunification has officially begun. The first phase was marked by the transfers of know-how, capital and technology from westerners to easterners. Now the new flexible labour practices and regulatory systems of the easterners are being transferred to westerners. The second stage will be marked by the achievements in the new states – and how those achievements are also helping to elevate the competitiveness of the old states. Market forces will ensure that the process succeeds.

3
Eastern European Initiatives

Jonathan Reuvid

Germany's foreign policy towards the eastern and central European republics that were formerly part of the eastern bloc is necessarily articulated within the parameters of agreed EU policies and, in matters of defence and security, within the consensus of NATO policy. In both arenas Germany now plays a leading role. Within the forum of the 15, Germany carries an unchallengeable authority derived from its management of German reunification, being the only member state with practical experience of aligning and integrating a command economy with its attendant social and environmental deficiencies into a modern democtratic state governed by the highest international standards.

THE EXPANSION OF THE EUROPEAN UNION

In 1997 11 countries applied to begin negotiations with the EC to join the European Union. Of these, six were judged by the Commission to be ready to start negotiations in March 1998: the Czech Republic, Hungary, Estonia, Poland, Slovenia and Cyprus. The remaining five, all from central and eastern Europe – Bulgaria, Latvia, Lithuania, Romania and Slovakia – were not considered to be ready, although each of them will be subject to annual review.

All 10 candidates from central and eastern Europe have made rapid progress over the past decade; for each of the five candidate countries (and Cyprus), the Commission has focused on defining the priorities to satisfy accession criteria. Continuing pre-accession financial support will be available from the European Investment Bank (EIB) and from the restructured PHARE programme. It has been estimated that in the period to 2006 up to 21 billion ecus at constant 1997 prices may be made available through the various funding sources. Nevertheless, the upgrading of the environment, infrastructure and industry of each entry candidate demands much more than cash investment.

The criteria for accession were laid down at the Copenhagen Summit of June 1993. Candidates need to satisfy the EU on each of the following fundamental issues:

- the rule of law;
- the stability of institutions guaranteeing democracy;
- human rights and protection of minorities;
- a functioning market economy, sufficiently robust to manage competitive pressures within the EU;
- an ability to assume membership obligations, including the Economic and Monetary Union (EMU) and the EU's political aims.

The Commission and the Council's Enlargement Group represent the EU in continuous negotiation with each applicant that will define individual terms and conditions of accession. In principle, new members are obliged, upon accession, to adopt the *acquis communautaire* (body of law); in practice, some relaxation may be allowed in the form of transitional provisions.

PREPARATION FOR ACCESSION

There are problems for each of the five shortlisted central and eastern European applicants (and to a lesser extent Cyprus) in addressing each of the following areas:

- harmonisation of the local tax regime;
- the reform of social spending;
- improving the competitiveness of conditions for fair competition and of local companies:
- raising quality standards of products and services;
- export promotion;
- meeting EU standards of environmental protection.

Prior experience of entry negotiations causes Commission officials to conclude that highly detailed explanation of what the EU's *acquis communautaire* means is an essential preliminary. Applicants are required to enact more than 30,000 pieces of EC legislation by statute, and to install the mechanisms that will ensure that EC laws are enforced.

Nor are the problem areas entirely in the domain of the applicant countries. Reforms of the EU's budget, in particular structural and regional funding, and the Common Agricultural Policy (CAP) will have to be undertaken in advance of enlargement. Consensus among member states is proving difficult to achieve on both of these topics, as is agreement on tax harmonisation issues, a third topic demanding attention.

Under the German presidency of the EU in the first six months of 1999 progress has been made on the first two issues. However, it is doubtful whether the budget deal finally agreed in March 1999 will suffice. In particular, the proposed EU farm reforms, which are at the heart of the package, are widely regarded as inadequate and will probably have to be revised before the EU can accommodate its eastern neighbours.

The German proposal that national governments should pay a larger share of EU agricultural policies is sympathetic to the needs of entry candidates, but anathema to France.

At the second 1999 summit in June the European Council noted in its final statement 'that good progress has been made in discussions on the proposals for directives on the taxation of investment income. It welcomes the constructive discussions with third countries in Europe on more effective taxation of interest'. While the proposal to impose a withholding tax on investment income is considered as contrary to City of London interests, British officials are preparing a compromise to exclude institutional investors in the Eurobond market. In general, there is a basic division of opinion between those EU countries that favour tax harmonisation so that governments can maintain high levels of taxation to fund high levels of spending, and those maintaining that competition ensures that the public sector expenditure is controlled. The taxation of savings, the tax treatment of interest and royalties and agreement on an energy tax directive are all tabled as topics for the next year-end summit.

THE PACE OF EU EXPANSION

Inevitably, the warfare in the former Yugoslavia, first Croatia and then Kosovo, has had a negative effect on the acceptance of new candidates for entry to the EU. The financial burden on the EU of contributing to the economic reconstruction of south-eastern Europe will be heavy.

For Germany the economic disorders of Russia are also proving an exceptionally painful experience; reduced exports to Russia have seriously affected Germany's balance of trade. Other EU member states were less vulnerable.

In addition to the internal economic issues mentioned above, the EU has become increasingly concerned by unemployment, a topic that was high on the agenda again at the June 1999 summit. A European employment pact was crafted at the summit with sustainable reductions in unemployment as its objective. The agreement is based on providing a comprehensive pan-European approach to jobs, by deploying in concert all the EU's employment policy measures. However, the original proposals have been diluted so much that the overall impact may be slight. Member states will want to master the endemic problems of unemployment before moving on to an enlarged EU in which the original 15 may be exporting employment.

Processing time for the six applications in hand is uncertain, although the target date for EU entry is January 2003. As at the end of May 1999, seven months after the launch of substantive talks on entry, each of the European applicants had completed preliminary 'screenings' on seven or eight of the 37 chapters for discussion, against 10 completed in the case of Cyprus. However, when announcing the invitations to apply, the previous Foreign Affairs Commisioner commented: 'Our recommendation to open negotiations with [the] six has to do with our educated guess, through analysis, that these countries may fulfil all the requirements in the medium term'. Nobody has ever defined how long that 'medium-term' may be.

SOCIO-POLITICAL IMPLICATIONS

A report published in November 1998, *British and European Social Attitudes* (15th report, Ashdown Publishing), studied attitudes in Bulgaria, the Czech Republic, Hungary, Poland and Slovenia and concluded that the enlargement of the EU to include former Communist countries to the east is likely to enhance more traditional and conservative public opinion.

In the candidate countries for entry the electorates are more left wing and egalitarian on economic issues, more 'God-fearing' in countries where the Orthodox and Catholic churches are predominant, less 'permissive' about sexual mores and less 'progressive' on the role of women in society. However, the influence of the Communist heritage is judged to be slight. 'In most respects, the post-Communist countries differ just as much among themselves as do current EU states', the study concludes.

The two factors likely to shift attitudes further towards the EU norm are the currently high rates of economic growth in most of the eastern European applicant countries and generational change. Among existing EU member states there is no relationship between age and attitudes to economic policy except in The Netherlands, where the young are more left wing. By contrast, in the former Communist countries the young are significantly more right wing than the average population, reflecting the anti-Communist backlash and their diminished exposure to the ideology. In any case, the net effect on the EU socio-political profile will not be significant; aside from Poland, the candidate countries are relatively small. However, the irony remains that at a time when socialist parties are in the ascendant in western Europe influence from the east is to the right. Perhaps, at the time of entry of the next six members, political pendulums will have started to reverse their swings.

Economic Analysis

4

Economic Outlook within the Euro–zone

Jonathan Reuvid

THE EFFECT OF THE EURO

The fall in the exchange rate of the euro against the US dollar and, to a lesser extent, the pound sterling, during the first six months of its life, has caused some consternation within the Euro-zone. However, six months earlier the opposite concerns were expressed when continuing cuts in US interest rates were expected to boost the euro rate and cut growth. By the end of May 1999 leaders of the Euro-11 were engaged in an intense campaign to stem the slide of the euro towards parity with the dollar. Wisely, the European Central Bank (ECB) continued to defend the euro with words rather than actions, as it fell to a new low of US$1.030 on the eve of the June summit of European leaders – more than 12 per cent below its high of US$1.1877 on 4 January 1999. Wim Duisenberg, the ECB President, maintained a relaxed stance on the euro's low exchange rate, noting that differences in the US and European economic cycles would diminish over the 18 months to the end of 2000 and that the euro's effective exchange rate was broadly the same as that of its constituent national currencies in the summer of 1997 and spring of 1998. 'In the longer run,' he claimed, 'I see more factors pointing towards an appreciation of the euro than I can see pointing to a depreciation.'

Although the euro's fall may be bad for morale among the Euro-11, depreciation is providing some relief for exporters and for the currently weaker economies within the Euro-zone, notably Italy and Germany which has, hopefully, avoided a tumble into recession. During April 1999 import volumes of goods from outside the European Union fell 9 per cent, including trade in oil and more erratic items such as aircraft and jewels, compared to a month over month increase of 2.2 per cent in March.

In Germany, although a poll at the end of May found that 75 per cent of Germans believed that the euro's weakness was harming Germany's economic prospects, the evidence coming through on the performance during the first quarter of 1999 told a different story. A month-on-month increase of 3.3 per cent in manufacturing orders during April, in contrast to a decline of 0.7 per cent in March, implied that the economy might perform better in the second quarter of 1999 than the German government's 1.5 per cent prediction for the year.

GERMANY'S RECENT ECONOMIC PERFORMANCE

The 1997–98 economic turmoil in Asia and Eastern and Central Europe, especially Russia, took a heavier toll on the German economy than on other members of the EU, but the structural weaknesses of the economy itself, discussed below, have been the major factor in its inability to shake off a sluggish performance.

The headline economic data for Germany alone are summarised in Table 4.1.

Over the 12 months up to March 1999, Germany's nominal GDP grew by only one to two per cent within a rigid macro-economic policy. Under the single monetary policy, it is not possible to lower interest rates (the

Table 4.1   *The German economy*

	1995	1996	1997	1998	1998 Qtr 2 %	Qtr 3 %	Qtr 4 %	1999 Qtr 1 %
	Index: 1985: 100							
Retail sales (vol.)	118.4	117.2	115.8	115.7	−1.9	1.7	1.1	2.4
Industrial Prod.	115.4	114.9	118.1	122.7	3.9	3.7	0.6	−1.5
Unemployment (%)	9.3	10.8	11.7	10.7	11.0	10.8	10.7	10.5
Consumer prices	127.4	129.3	131.5	132.8	1.4	0.7	0.4	0.3
Producer prices	107.5	107.1	108.2	107.8	0.1	−0.7	−1.7	
Earnings	159.4	163.3	165.5	168.2	1.7	1.8	1.8	
Unit labour costs	110.8	109.7	103.1		−3.4	−2.6	0.5	

Source: The Financial Times, London

obvious remedy) so a more relaxed fiscal policy is the logical alternative. However, Euro-zone ground rules under the 'growth and stability pact' demand that member governments keep their budget deficits down, so this route is also blocked. Indeed, compliance might even cause the German government to cut public spending which is inappropriate for an economy so close to recession. Having permitted Italy to raise its budget deficit for 1999 from 2 per cent to 2.4 per cent of GDP, the EU finance ministers will be reluctant to permit Germany, the Euro-zone's biggest economy, to widen the breach further.

Before commenting on the structural issues in relation to the economy, and employment in particular, it is important to recognise the significance of the series of shockwaves that have impacted the German economy within the past decade. Of these, the most significant and longlasting was, inevitably, the unification of East and West Germany in 1990. The early, tax–driven investment from the West produced poor returns or, sometimes, sank without trace.The level of subsidy, at approximately 5 per cent of overall German GDP, has hardly fallen since 1990. More importantly, generous pay rises to the less productive easterners in the early days following unification added to Germany's high wage cost problem. Sharp appreciations in the deutschmark damaged exports further.

The second shockwave was from the economic crisis in emerging markets. Germany exports almost 30 per cent of its GDP, far more than any other major European economy, of which about a quarter is to emerging markets. Some exports, such as aluminium and chemicals, were already affected adversely by global over-capacity before the Asian crisis first hit Thailand in mid-1997. Basic producer and capital goods, accounting for approximately 80 per cent of Germany's exports, were hit particularly hard. Also, the disintegration of the Russian economy has had a similarly damaging effect on German exports.

The run-up period to monetary union was also unhelpful to Germany. While interest rates in other currencies fell in order to converge with the German level, their economies were boosted, thereby increasing the gap between Germany's performance and their own. At the same time the slowdown in the UK economy, one of Germany's biggest export markets, added to the erosion.

The final shockwave was the five month period in office of Finance Minister, Oskar Lafontaine, which confused German business, infuriated the ECB and dampened business confidence. The determination to boost growth by stimulating demand was understood, but Mr Lafontaine's calls for above-inflationary wage increases caused major concern among manufacturers struggling to maintain international competitiveness, and potentially dampened or delayed investment. Although his plans to reform corporate taxation were welcome, the pattern of legislation to curb tax breaks in advance of measures to lower overall corporate taxes was, in effect, confiscatory.

THE GOVERNMENT'S TASK

The new Finance Minister, Hans Eichel, has repaired much of the damage to confidence with his more cautious, methodical and open-minded approach, but the tasks which he and Gerhard Schröder face are formidable. First and foremost among the coalition government's objectives is the reduction of unemployment which remains stubbornly high, above four million, representing about 10.5 per cent of the workforce. In spite of this unacceptably high unemployment total, following recent pay awards in excess of 3 per cent and tax increases on energy, consumer prices are expected to climb by 1.5 per cent in 2000, more than double the 0.7 per cent rate forecast for 1999. So far, Mr Schröder has failed to talk Germany's EU partners into a pact on jobs with any substantive content.

EU-wide unemployment targets were found to be unacceptable to a majority of member-governments at the June meeting of Ministers, and French pleas for a formal EU growth target to promote jobs were rejected, even by Mr Schröder. Instead a 'macro-economic dialogue' has been agreed, involving employers and unions, in which social partners will exchange ideas twice a year with governments and ECB representatives. While it is intended that this will promote growth and employment 'while safeguarding price stability' it does not impress as an effective mechanism.

The almost geometric progression of the government deficit is a major cause for concern. From about DM314 billion in 1982 it had grown to DM600 billion by 1990 at the outset of reunification, and had mushroomed to DM1,500 billion by 1998. At DM82 billion, interest costs are now the second biggest item of government expenditure, after social security at 22 per cent, compared with 12 per cent in 1982. This poses the problem, with which the government is grappling, of how to restructure taxes without further increasing the deficit and its attendant interest cost.

The tax reform issue is certainly the most complicated facing the government. The fear remains that the Social Democrat dominated government intends to redistribute income at the expense of big business, although Mr Eichel has pledged to cut corporate tax rates, which run as high as 60 per cent. However, Mr Schröder has stressed the need to reform the welfare state, which was echoed in the joint agenda published by the German and British governments in June 1999, which declares that 'public expenditure as a proportion of national income has more or less reached the limits of acceptability'.

The tax and budget measures approved on 23 June 1999 have imposed cuts of DM30 billion in the year 2000 budget, and slashed the basic corporate tax rate from 40 per cent to 25 per cent. These measures are viewed as an important first step.

Two recent Constitutional Court rulings have proved unhelpful to the government's declared policy of lowering the tax burden. In May the Court ruled against a cut in pensions for the Elites of the former GDR which will add approximately DM600 billion to the annual bill; a decision to improve compensation payments to political prisoners and victims of discrimination in the GDR will add a similar amount. Likewise, a ruling of the Court requiring the tax treatment of child care allowances to be redrawn will also have a multi-billion deutschmark impact.

The large number of privately owned companies in Germany adds to the complications of corporate tax reform, because clear distinctions have to be drawn between company and private income. Eichel insists that the issues of corporate and individual tax reform have to be tackled together in the context of next year's budget and the medium-term budgetary demands to 2003. Also at issue are the massive state subsidies to industry, running at about DM120 billion annually, and areas such as social security, which are both eligible for pruning. The latter will be particularly unpalatable to the SPD rank and file; however, social security costs represent an effective tax rate of 42.5 per cent on employed labour and are a deterrent to the hiring of new staff. In the domain of social security costs, there is also the welfare time bomb arising from an increasing population of pensioners and the declining workforce, to which the only solution will be the encouragement of private pensions and healthcare contributions to offset benefit cuts.

THE GERMAN ECONOMY IN ITS EURO-CONTEXT

The fortunes of the German economy are inextricably tied to those of the Euro-11, and only slightly less to those of its five other EU partners. Equally, the fifteen other member countries of the EU are affected directly by the performance of the German economy. Tables 4.2 and 4.3

Table 4.2   *Output, demand and jobs*

| | GDP | | | | Industrial prod | | Retail sales (vol.) 1 yr | Unemployment % | |
	3 mths	1 yr	1999	2000	3 mths	1 yr		6/98	6/99
Austria	n/a	2.1	2.0	2.5	n/a	2.6	2.3	4.5	4.4
Belgium	−1.2	1.6	1.9	2.4	n/a	−3.2	7.6	11.0	11.9
Britain	−0.4	0.6	0.8	2.3	−1.0	−1.6	1.6	6.2	6.5
Denmark	−0.3	2.7	1.6	2.2	n/a	9.8	−5.8	5.9	6.9
France	1.2	2.1	2.2	2.6	−3.5	−0.2	6.6	11.4	11.9
Germany	1.8	0.7	1.4	2.4	−5.2	−1.3	6.8	10.5	11.2
Italy	−1.1	0.9	1.3	2.2	0.4	1.2	−0.1	12.0	12.0
Netherlands	2.4	3.0	2.4	2.6	3.9	0.3	2.5	3.4	4.5
Spain	3.0	3.6	3.3	3.4	−0.4	2.0	n/a	17.4	19.2
Sweden	5.7	3.2	2.3	2.7	−2.6	1.7	6.3	5.3	6.6
Euro-11	0.8	2.3	2.1	2.6	−0.5	−0.1	1.5	10.4	11.3

Source: The Economist, 12 June 1999

Table 4.3   *Prices and wages (% change at annual rate)*

| | Consumer prices | | (CP) forecast | | Producer prices | | Wages/earnings | |
	3 mths	1 year	1999	2000	3 mths	1 year	3 mths	1 year
Austria	0.8	0.3	0.9	1.4	3.8	−0.6	n/a	n/a
Belgium	2.7	0.8	1.2	1.5	−5.1	−3.2	1.1	2.5
Britain	0.7	1.6	2.0	2.3	3.4	1.0	6.8	4.8
Denmark	4.3	2.4	2.2	2.2	0.9	−1.4	3.7	4.5
France	1.9	0.4	0.7	1.1	−1.9	−2.6	1.8	2.0
Germany	1.7	0.4	0.7	1.3	1.9	−3.1	n/a	2.7
Italy	4.1	1.5	1.5	1.8	−1.6	−1.6	0.6	1.6
Netherlands	4.5	2.3	2.2	2.2	−0.4	−2.3	2.3	2.8
Spain	2.9	2.4	2.2	2.3	1.5	−0.8	2.3	1.9
Sweden	n/a	−0.1	0.4	1.0	−4.8	−1.8	1.4	1.6
Euro-11	2.1	1.1	1.2	1.5	−2.6	−2.3	n/a	2.1

Source: The Economist, 12 June 1999

compare current performance of EU members in terms of output, demand and jobs, and in terms of prices and wages respectively.

In terms of industrial production and GDP growth Germany is under-performing with regard to the Euro-zone average. Retail sales growth is considerably above average, and unemployment, although significantly higher than in Britain, Denmark, The Netherlands and Sweden, is in line with the Euro-zone composite total.

While remaining lower than in Britain, Denmark, The Netherlands and Spain, consumer price inflation is currently, and is expected to continue, below the Euro-zone average. Annual wage inflation is above the average and other EU partners except for Britain, Denmark and The Netherlands.

SIGNS OF ENCOURAGEMENT

Glimpses of a silver lining among Germany's economic storm clouds have emerged recently. There are signs of a new flexibility in collective wage-bargaining. Although IG Metall's 3 million members achieved an inflationary 3.5 per cent pay rise in their 'end to modesty' bargaining this time round, about 10 per cent of western Germany's workforce has been taken out of the traditional collective bargaining arrangements, compared to more than 50 per cent in the eastern Länder. Moreover, while in April the Ifo index, regarded as a reliable indicator of economic trends, fell to 89.7, from 90.2 in March, suggesting that the negative GDP growth of the final quarter of 1998 might be repeated, first quarter GDP growth of 0.4 per cent quarter-on-quarter (1.8 per cent annual rate) was better than expected and signalled that formal recession had been avoided. At the same time, business confidence in terms of sales expectations has bounced back almost to 1998 levels. Hopefully, 1999 will see the economy on the move forward again.

5

Competitiveness

Jonathan Reuvid

Following the formation of the Economic & Monetary Union (EMU), the competitiveness of Germany's economy now has to be viewed in relation to its Euro-zone partners, as well as the larger grouping of EU members and, externally, against the other developed countries with which Germany competes in foreign trade and inward investment.

In the first edition of *Doing Business with Germany* we focused on financial stability and convergence to EMU criteria, in addition to foreign trade, inward investment, living standards and overall economic performance as key indicators of competitiveness. Today, with the management of the Euro-11's monetary policy transferred to the ECB, the first two of these yardsticks have been subsumed and evaluations of an individual country's competitiveness are, in part, judgments about the Euro-zone itself within the global economy.

FOREIGN TRADE

In Table 5.1 the latest 12 months trade balance and current account balances are compared for each of the larger EU members, for the Euro-11 countries and for the major external economies with which Germany and the EU trade. In the case of the developed economies, current account balances are also expressed as percentages of forecast 1999 GDP.

In terms of trade balances Germany's standing among the developed economies is strong, accounting for 83 per cent of the aggregate positive trade balance of the Euro-zone. Only Japan achieved a stronger trade balance in the last 12 recorded months and the Euro-11 position is in

Table 5.1 *External trade balances (US$ billion)*

	Trade balance	Current account		% 1999 GDP
Germany	76.4	−4.9	(Apr)	−0.5
Britain	−38.9	2.5	(Q4)	−0.9
Italy	27.4	28.0	(Feb)	2.2
Spain	−25.7	3.3	(Mar)	−0.6
Euro-11	91.6	75.0	(Q4)	1.2
Australia	−7.0	−18.7	(Q1)	−5.5
Canada	15.2	−12.4	(Q4)	−1.6
Japan	125.7	118.8	(Mar)	3.4
United States	−267.8	−233.4	(Q4)	−3.3
Asia				
China	33.6	28.4	(1998)	
Hong Kong	−6.7	0.5	(1998)	
India	−7.7	−7.1	(Q4)	
Indonesia	21.2	3.0	(Q3)	
Malaysia	17.6	9.4	(1998)	
Phillipines	1.6	1.3	(Mar)	
Singapore	8.1	17.6	(Q4)	
South Korea	32.3	34.5	(Apr)	
Taiwan	10.7	5.7	(Q1)	
Thailand	10.9	14.2	(Q4)	
Latin America				
Argentina	−3.6	−14.7	(Q4)	
Brazil	−4.9	−34.2	(Q1)	
Chile	−1.0	−4.5	(Q4)	
Colombia	−1.7	−5.8	(1998)	
Mexico	−7.1	−15.8	(Q4)	
Venezuela	3.7	−0.5	(Q3)	
Others				
Egypt	−12.3	−2.6	(Q4)	
Greece	−17.4	−3.6	(Dec)	
Israel	−6.6	−2.3	(Q4)	
South Africa	1.4	−2.3	(Q4)	
Turkey	−16.0	2.7	(Dec)	
Czech Republic	−2.3	−1.0	(Q4)	
Hungary	−2.3	−2.5	(Mar)	
Poland	−13.6	−7.2	(Apr)	
Russia	19.2	2.4	(Q4)	

Source: The Economist, 12 June 1999

marked contrast to the heavy trade imbalance of the United States. On current account, Germany is presently running in deficit in contrast to the Euro-11 and its major EU trade partners but still compares favourably with the US, Canada and Australia. The outlook for trade with North America remains positive in the short-term until such time as the dollar exchange rate against the euro strengthens. The Euro-zone's trade surplus slipped in March to €6.3 billion against €7.5 billion in March 1998 but still contrasted sharply with the US trade deficit of US$19.7 billion in March 1999.

The Asian tiger economies are now showing current account surpluses, reflecting their economic recoveries and China, too, continues to achieve both a healthy trade balance and a current account surplus in spite of the current domestic economy depression. Only India's foreign trade remains in deficit. With the Asian recovery, prospects for increasing exports from the EU are now brighter and the relative weakness of the euro is helpful, particularly to Germany and Italy.

The Latin American economies continue to run trade deficits, and prospects for increased exports to Argentina, Brazil and Mexico for the EU and Germany are correspondingly weak. As for the rest of Europe, trade prospects are hardly buoyant, including Russia, where sharply reduced incomes have helped to restore healthier trade balances. However, Russia's foreign currency reserves at US$7.1 billion remain low and this will continue to have a dampening effect, particularly for Germany, which is Russia's biggest trade creditor.

INVESTMENT

For Germany, inward investment is fast becoming of less relevance to global competition than the restructuring which is taking place throughout the Euro-zone in order to gear-up industry for global competition, as well as trade opportunities, throughout the Euro-zone.

Some of the most conservative German companies have changed strategies in order to address the growth of new technologies and service industries, and are adopting more international practices including international accounting standards, listings on foreign stock exchanges and preparations to return money to shareholders through share buybacks. The process of change includes reductions in rigid working practices, following the example of the eastern federal states (Länder) where high unemployment has caused workers in jobs to accept change more readily. Flexible shifts and work patterns geared to production needs have raised productivity, particularly in the automotive and general engineering sectors.

As noted in Chapter 4, German business has yet to benefit from taxation and social security reforms foreshadowed by the SDP-led coalition government. However, this has not deterred industry from embarking on restructuring programmes, many of which have involved cross-border mergers. Among the most spectacular M&A activities was the DaimlerChrysler merger and the resultant pledge by the US-German auto group to launch a mass-market car in Europe in the year 2002 with annual sales targeted at 100,000 units. No less stimulating, in terms of investment response, was Volkswagen's increase in its author-ised capital of 40 per cent where further acquisitions are anticipated to supplement the economies of scale achieved through the successful integration of Audi, Seat and Skoda.

In the electrical and electronic engineering sector, Siemens, having sold about one-seventh of its businesses with sales of approximately DM17 billion, is forecasting double digit growth in sales and earnings in 1999 with three of its four loss-making divisions breaking even within 12 months. The transfer from general engineering to service industries is exemplified by Preussag which sold its heavy industy interests in coal and steel and, after buying the multi-modal transport group Hapag Lloyd and purchasing a controlling interest in Thomas Cook (the UK travel and financial services group) reported record profits of DM539 million for its last financial year.

Mannesman, the Düsseldorf based group, has switched from steel tubes to telecoms, where it is ranked second after Deutsche Telekom. It has launched a drive into internet commerce and new media services, and developed international aspirations through its agreements to purchase Olivetti's stakes in Omnitel and Infostrada, the Italian mobile and fixed line operations. Also in telecommunications, the proposed merger between Deutsche Telekom and France Telecom, involving cross-shareholdings, generated extreme opposition. In the aftermath, whereas Deutsche Telekom remains committed to expansion abroad, Italy seems a less likely target following the successful Olivetti bid for Telecom Italia.

There have been problems, too, in cross-border M&As, reflecting national sensitivities and the difficulty of agreeing the relative worth of companies based in different countries. The plan to create Europe's largest steel group failed after Salzgitter of Germany was unable to accept complete incorporation in Arbed of Luxembourg.

Likewise, the merger of the chemical group Hoechst with Rhône Poulenc of France sailed into stormy waters, because the French company found unacceptable terms that would have caused Hoechst to emerge with more than 50 per cent of the new group, Aventis.

In the financial sector, Germany's commercial banks are expected to show a major profit recovery in their 1999 trading. Although the banking industry remains the most fragmented in Europe with little evidence of domestic consolidation, the major commerical banks continue to scour the rest of Europe and the US for investment opportunities, particularly in investment banking. Leader of the pack is Deutsche Bank, which having taken over Morgan Grenfell, the UK investment bank, ten years ago in 1989, embarked on an extensive shopping spree in Europe last year. It acquired holdings in banks in Greece, Italy and Poland and the Belgian business of Credit Lyonnais and set out to develop wealthy client business in France. In the autumn of 1998, Deutsche Bank took over Bankers Trust for US$10.1 billion, the eighth largest US bank. The investment is a test case for the global expansion of German banking and success will be a necessary condition for Deutsche Bank's acceptance as a major player on Wall Street.

INFLATION AND UNIT LABOUR COSTS

Rates of consumer price inflation (CPI), producer price inflation (PPI) and unit labour costs have been coming down in Germany since the second quarter of 1999, mainly as a result of improved productivity and a period of restraint in wage increases over the 1997/8 period. Indeed, Germany's performance in respect of all three indicators compares favourably with those of its principal worldwide competitors, as Table 5.2 demonstrates.

Lack of labour cost competitiveness has been one of the main criticisms of German industrial performance. The launch of the euro has helped to highlight the wide differences in per capita labour costs across the EU, with substantial differences at the extremes. For example, average labour costs in Belgium are nearly four times higher than they are in Portugal, and total benefit costs add between 15 and 50 per cent to the cost of pay alone. On average EU labour costs are about 8 per cent higher than in the US, a differential that may be a significant deterrent to US investment in Europe.

However, unit labour cost is more significant than per capita costs in that it reflects the effects of comparative productivity gains. As Table 5.2 shows, the rate of increase in German unit labour costs was less than all its major international competitors in the second and third quarters of 1998 and less than all but the US in the fourth quarter. Against its major EU partners together with Japan, Germany's labour is becoming more competitive; government reform of social security financing may accelerate the process.

Table 5.2 *Prices and unit labour costs (Index: 1985: 100)*

	Germany	France	UK	Japan	USA
Consumer Prices					
1998 2nd Qtr	1.4	0.9	4.0	0.6	1.6
3rd Qtr	0.7	0.5	3.3	−0.1	1.6
4th Qtr	0.4	0.2	3.0	0.7	1.6
1999 1st Qtr	0.2	0.3	2.2	−0.2	1.7
Producer Prices					
1998 2nd Qtr	0.1	−0.3	1.0	−1.9	−0.8
3rd Qtr	−0.7	−1.3	0.5	−1.9	−0.6
4th Qtr	−1.7	−2.3	0.0	−2.0	−0.4
1999 1st Qtr	−2.3	−2.9	0.2	−2.1	0.7
Unit Labour Costs					
1998 2nd Qtr	−3.3	3.1	4.1	7.6	0.5
3rd Qtr	−2.4	2.5	3.8	7.7	0.9
4th Qtr	1.2	2.5	2.5	5.0	−0.7
1999 1st Qtr			1.3		−1.2

Source: Financial Times, 15 June 1999

While consumer price inflation remains low, German producer prices are declining more than those of its major competitors, except for France. Economic and monetary stability is not in question. If the economy is now growing again, as early movements in key indicators suggest, Germany's prospects for increasing international competitiveness appear sound.

6

Trends and Developments in German-British Business Relations

Ulrich Hoppe, German-British Chamber of Industry & Commerce, London

German-British business relations have always been strong, but over the last two decades we have seen a remarkable growth in bilateral trade and investment. In 1980, Britain exported goods to Germany totalling only DM23 billion; and Germany exported goods to Britain with the same value. But since the mid-1980s, when the restructuring of the British economy was in full swing and the shift of Britain's pattern of trade from the Commonwealth countries to the member states of the European Union gained even more pace, British exports to Germany began to rise substantially, reaching DM37 billion in 1990. German exports increased even more and amounted to DM55 billion by the same year. During the 1990s this trend continued and, with the recent appreciation of sterling, we saw a further increase in the value of exports from Germany to Britain, to over DM75 billion in 1998. Looking at the bilateral trade figures in relative terms, the UK is Germany's third largest export market, whereas Germany is currently one of Britain's largest export markets, rivalled in the past only by the United States.

Since the mid-1980s we have also seen a tremendous growth of German investment in the UK, which now stands at a total of DM55 billion. More than 1700 German companies have invested in the UK, contributing substantially to British GDP. German companies that have invested in the UK come from all sectors of the economy, ranging from financial services to manufacturing industries. The large number of German blue-chip companies operating in the UK proves that Britain has become a very attractive location to do business in and from. Britain is also an attractive location for small and medium-sized German companies because a high proportion of them use it as a first step in their inter-nationalisation strategy. Looking at British investment in Germany, the increase has been much slower over the past two decades. More than 600 British companies with a total investment of DM19 billion operate in Germany. The sectoral distribution of British investment in Germany is roughly similar to that of German investment in Britain, only with the service sector playing a slightly stronger role.

The positive development of German-British business relations can be summarised by two trends. First, that Germany has had a rising trade surplus with the UK, underlying its traditional strength as one of the world's major exporters. Second, that Britain's growing surplus with Germany in terms of bilateral investment underlies the UK's attractive-ness as an inward investment location.

The strong growth of German investment in Britain is based on the fact that German companies have become increasingly outward looking during the 1980s. As the German trade surplus grew substantially in the 1980s, some of that money was channelled back into the world economy by foreign direct investment. From the end of the Second World War up to the 1980s most foreign investment was generally driven by servicing local markets from a local production unit. This was partly due to the distance of some foreign markets, which made it more efficient to produce there, or due to protectionist measures that forced companies to produce locally in order to avoid high tariffs or other trade barriers that made exports to some markets prohibitively expensive. With the conclusion of the Uruguay round of GATT (General Agreement on Tariffs and Trade – now WTO or World Trade Organisation) and the general decline in real terms of transport costs, other reasons for investing abroad came to the fore. Today, we can see two major world-wide trends in foreign investment. The first is that an ever-increasing share of foreign investment is driven by the search for excellence in certain areas. This means that companies invest abroad not only to produce locally but also to carry out research internationally, if a foreign location is a major research centre in that particular field of the company's activity. This first trend can be seen in research-oriented industries like pharma-ceuticals, chemicals and in the IT sector. The second trend of producing locally is no longer driven by protectionist measures, at least not to the same extent as in the past. Today, a major reason for producing at a foreign location is often a marketing one, because for a large number of products, especially consumer goods, the market has changed from a seller's to a buyer's one. Physical proximity to meet customers' demands for individual specifications has become ever more important. The well-used phrase 'think global, act local' is a result of this development as successful multinational companies had to implement product and/or marketing differentiations to meet the local variations in demand.

In the financial services sector, which is especially important to the UK in terms of employment and with regard to the balance of trade in goods in services, we can see a similar trend. The large number of foreign banks operating in the City proves that, despite Britain not taking part in the euro, London has kept its place as the major financial centre in Europe. Of course there is the famous joint venture with the Frankfurt Stock Exchange, but as more people work in the financial services sector in London than Frankfurt has inhabitants, London will keep its position as a centre of excellence in this area. With the vast resources in terms of research and management expertise in the financial services sector, it will also attract new investment in the future. With today's communication links, it is no longer of prime importance where the transaction is physically and legally carried out. In terms of employment and income, it is important where the actual service is provided. Whether the transaction is settled on a computer system in Frankfurt or in London does not really matter; far more important is where the high value adding advice was delivered and, up to now and for the foreseeable future, London has an unrivalled position in Europe.

As most continental European countries still run a pay-as-you-go pension system, which in the future will not be able to provide benefits on the same level as in the past, we will see a growth in privately run pension funds. This development will sooner or later also take place in Germany, even if the present Social Democratic-led government is probably more in favour of a public pension system. Out of bare financial restrictions, existing and future generations will have to save more for their retirement than in the past. This development means that more savings will enter the German capital market, forcing German public limited liability companies to focus more strongly on the return on equity. Otherwise the increasing global integration of capital markets will result in a shift of these savings to foreign capital markets that offer a higher return. The euro will also widen the horizon of German investors as the currency risk of investing in companies from other 'Euroland' countries is now eliminated. With more pressure from shareholders German companies will become even more outward looking, in order to find the investment opportunities that will maximise the return to their shareholders. Cross-border take-overs and mergers like the one between Daimler and Chrysler or Hoechst and Rhône-Poulenc will probably be seen more often in order to capitalise on potential synergies. The acquisition of German Parcel by the Post Office is one example from the British-German perspective. We will also see a clearer focus of foreign direct investment as companies will concentrate more on their core areas and shed activities that they no longer perceive as such.

The expected future international harmonisation of accounting rules will also lead to a more global outlook by investors, as annual reports and reporting patterns will become comparable on an international basis. In Germany, the discussion sometimes focuses unduly on differences in the treatment of individual items rather than on disclosure of information. Disclosure issues are far more important because, as long as differences are properly disclosed, they become irrelevant when an investor can make an informed decision based on a benchmarking procedure against other possible investment opportunities. It is generally agreed that in the long run the industrialised economies will move towards the Anglo-Saxon concept of accounting, which will, from a technical point of view, also make it easier for small and medium-sized British companies to invest in Germany.

The general trend towards privatisation over the last two decades has also helped to make companies more global. Large shares in former state-owned companies were sold and, in order to get the best price possible, governments did not object too often to large stakes in the newly privatised industries being owned by foreigners. If a company is partly or fully owned by foreigners, it generally tends to become more outward looking, especially in order to produce the highest return on equity (at a given level of risk) for their shareholders.

Some of the foreign investment in Britain in the 1980s and 1990s from outside the European Union was carried out because of protectionist fears. But, as the EU did not become a 'fortress Europe', the motivation for this type of investment has been substantially reduced and Britain will have to capitalise on its other advantages to attract inward investment.

With the introduction of the euro a new period of stronger European integration is expected, especially within the participating countries' economies. Euroland locations might gain in attractiveness over other locations in the EU for market-driven foreign direct investment. If markets are becoming ever more similar in Euroland due to price transparency, further harmonisation of regulations and, even more importantly, a possible growing similarity in consumer tastes, one of the reasons for market-driven foreign direct investment (the proximity to the market) will be a strong factor for the Euroland countries. This will be especially true for the central locations in Euroland as they will capitalise on their location advantage over the next few years. Some of these regions have already reacted to this development, which can be seen from the cross-border co-operation of regions in the Benelux countries, Germany, France and northern Italy. This expected development could put Britain as a location for market-driven investment at a disadvantage if it does not join the euro over the next few years.

In Germany, with its well-known and competitive medium-sized and often family-owned companies, the *Mittelstand* demographic development (ie retirement of the owners) will lead to a large number of these companies being put up for sale. As the heirs will not always have a personal attachment to these companies they will look for the best possible price. This development will give foreign investors opportunities to acquire new customers in the largest market in Europe. An increase in foreign investment in German medium-sized companies is therefore expected over the next few years.

It is often said that Germany is not as attractive an investment location as in the past. The arguments of high labour costs and the high level of regulation are often quoted. It has to be borne in mind, however, that Germany is one of the world's major exporters and, despite all the negative publicity, continues to be so. With high productivity, quality of products and the advanced technology being used and produced, Germany has an advantage in certain areas over other locations. It is often forgotten that these strategic advantages also mean that Germany is only an attractive investment location for companies that are able to capitalise on these factors. Greenfield assembly-type investment can only be attracted into Germany with high costs to taxpayers in the form of subsidies etc. Therefore Germany will have to concentrate more on its true strategic location advantages in order to attract foreign investment.

To summarise, it can be argued that Britain often acts as a role model for Germany. If we look at the issues of privatisation and deregulation, we can see that developments have been pioneered in Europe by Britain and have subsequently moved to the continent to be embraced by nearly all governments in the European Union. On the other hand, Germany also acts as a role model for Britain, mainly in the areas of engineering, with the resulting effect of higher productivity in the manufacturing sector and in the area of vocational training, which enables companies to use sophisticated production technologies more broadly. But all these positive factors are often based on differences in mentality and culture, which in turn feed into different concepts of corporate governance. Britain and Germany will both be attractive business locations in the future, albeit for different reasons, which will be reflected in a varying distribution of incoming and outgoing investment.

Cultural Factors

LCT CONSULTANTS

7

Business Culture

Eric Lynn, LCT Consultants, Nuremberg

It takes time to do a thing well. (German proverb)

Recently Bill, a new recruit to the Manchester subsidiary of a German corporation, was sent on a five-day seminar to Hamburg. It was his first visit to Germany. On arrival at the seminar hotel, he met his German colleagues and was taken aback at their seriousness and the formality of the atmosphere. Although he found the work interesting, and despite the fact that they seemed to loosen up at the bar in the evening, he began to wonder whether he had made the right decision in joining the company.

It is 15 March and Tony receives an angry call from his Munich head-quarters asking for a set of quality reports that they claim they requested in November. On checking his files, Tony discovered the fax. It seems he had simply forgotten the deadline. 'No problem,' he said, 'I'll get them to you in the next couple of weeks.' He sensed that this made his German colleague even angrier.

These are two examples of misunderstanding due to differences in the way people work in Anglo-Saxon countries and in Germany. Differences are not a problem: not understanding why they exist, and how they affect business relationships, is.

Culture is simply the way things are done in any one particular place. The place may be Britain, the United States, western Germany, eastern Germany, or anywhere else. It may also be a sub-group within a society such as a corporation. It is important because it is the driving force behind the way people deal with others with challenges, problems, work – life. Understanding the influence of culture on international business is vital because, whatever the technology and whatever the benefits of a particular product, all business deals are made by people.

People behave differently for a variety of historical, political, sociological and psychological reasons. If we ignore these differences we cannot hope to understand what motivates and drives our business counterparts from abroad and we risk making very expensive mistakes as well as not achieving optimal results from those deals that we do pull off.

This chapter will look at the way Germans do business and consider how Germans tend to manage their dealings with business partners domestically and abroad. The most significant factors affecting German behaviour patterns and the driving forces behind these behaviours – values, society norms, historical factors – will be covered. You will gain an understanding of the reasons for German behaviour to enable you to interpret specific situations appropriately, as well as to modify your behaviour when dealing with German counterparts.

The business culture of Germany in the late 1990s is influenced by historical factors (eg the effects of the hyperinflation of the 1920s), political factors (eg the reunification of the country in 1990), sociological factors (eg the emphasis laid on specialisation in the education system) and psychological factors, which include not only these aspects but also the pressure from society to conform to accepted norms. Since late 1996 it has been more fundamentally influenced by a significant rise in unemployment, the rapid increase in the number of shareholders in the population (albeit from a very low base), the spread in the use of the Internet and e-mail as a medium for business communication and the increase in inherited wealth of the younger generation. Furthermore, it is guided by the people active throughout all levels of business life whose actions are motivated (whether positively or negatively) by the values that underlie society.

STEREOTYPES

Stereotypes exist about almost every ethnic or national group. Both Bill and Tony may have attributed some of these stereotypical behaviours to Germans: they are humourless, aggressive, distant, stubborn, unfriendly, sticklers for detail.

People who have been fortunate enough to get to know their German business partners well, and who have been able to consider why they behave as they do, will have realised that these stereotypes are anything but true.

Stereotypes and generalisations develop when one's own view of reality is imposed on a *foreign* (in this case German) situation. To a Briton or

American used to a working atmosphere where fun is combined with hard work, the German, for whom work is 'serious business', may appear to be humourless, if judged by *foreign* standards (in this case British or American).

Did the aggressiveness, personal distance or unfriendliness that Bill and Tony *perceived* really exist or did they misinterpret the signals? In his book *How Real is Real?*, Paul Watzlawick says: 'The most dangerous delusion of all is that there is only one reality.' He also says that 'our everyday, traditional ideas of reality are delusions which we spend substantial parts of our daily lives shoring up, even at the considerable risk of trying to force facts to fit our definition of reality instead of vice versa.' How many readers can honestly claim never to have been guilty of this kind of attitude?

Germans do tend to take longer to reach decisions. However, just because they favour analysing situations thoroughly rather than for example, the pragmatic short-term, solution-oriented approach preferred in Britain, can we really claim that they take *too long* to reach their decisions?

The best thing to do with stereotypes when doing business abroad is to forget them! Meet the challenge with an open mind and open eyes.

GERMAN VALUES AND BEHAVIOUR PATTERNS IN BUSINESS

Germany has one of the most successful and envied economies of the second half of the 20th century. Companies have achieved success by *hard work* and *efficiency*, both highly valued character traits. The *quality* of products is recognised throughout the world. Organisation is tight and *precise* (well-*ordered*); everybody knows his or her function. Decisions are made after careful, *thorough* and *precise* analysis. Risks are minimised; *security* is a lifeline. Time schedules are strictly adhered to: *punctual* delivery means on the day precisely! *Formality* is a necessary sign of respect. Business is *serious* business. These are the values that pervade society and are the foundation on which German managers build.

Forming successful business relationships with German companies does not entail taking all of these values on board, but recognising their importance to your business partner. It may also mean modifying your behaviour in the interests of achieving your business goals.

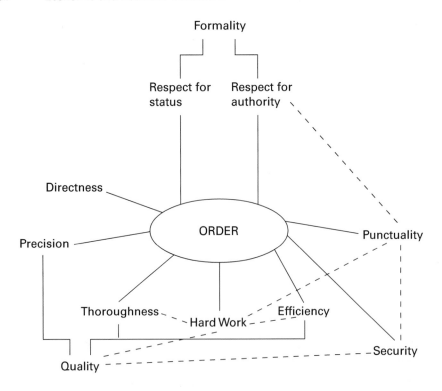

Figure 7.1   *The web of German values*

German business is male dominated. Although women account for about 40 per cent of the workforce, they are under-represented in management ranks. Specific sectors such as fashion and advertising are an exception. A woman in a position of responsibility may invoke surprise in her German (male) counterpart, which could lead to embarrassing situations whereby he assumes that she is a secretary or accompanying person. I even know of one business deal that broke down when a Canadian businesswoman felt so insulted that she got on the next plane home. You may ask yourself whose fault this was. The only realistic answer is that both parties were guilty of ethnocentricity and attribution (assigning their own norms to the behaviour of someone from another culture).

As most German managers you will meet will probably be male, they are referred to as male in this chapter. Please rest assured that this does not indicate any bias on the part of the author!

Managing people

Important qualities expected of a manager in Germany include the ability to assert himself, willingness to work hard, ability to lead, analytical ability and knowledge of the business area. A manager will usually have attained his position by rising through the ranks, having displayed these qualities. He will probably have at least one degree (65 per cent of German managers do) in which he specialised in engineering or business studies. He will initially have entered working life as a specialist and have proved his ability by producing quality solutions to specific problems, very often displaying the persuasive powers necessary to get himself noticed.

British (but not American) managers may be surprised to read that the ability to assert oneself is considered a quality. Both Britons and Americans may be surprised that analytical ability and knowledge of the business area are considered so important, having probably had a broader education that has prepared them for the world at large and endowed them with more general skills. They have learned to take the eagle's perspective, get the big picture, motivate others, take decisions and come up with and try out innovative ideas. They are supported by specialists who possess the necessary technical knowledge.

The roots of these differences are sociological and lie in the German education system. From an early age, children learn facts according to a structured plan. They learn, to think analytically and the importance of detailed knowledge. They are not trained to be innovative or question the status quo. They also learn that they have to speak up for themselves if they want to get noticed in class and get good grades: self-assertiveness. The system trains young people to realise the importance of personal success but does not train them to work together.

The German management press frequently speaks of the *Ellenbogengesellschaft* (the elbow society), in which advancement and success come with assertiveness. Hard work is considered a must and it is not uncommon for a leader to place a higher priority on his profession than on his family. This, however, cannot be generalised. The pressure to work hard and produce results is immense and this pressure will be passed down through the ranks.

Security is valued greatly in Germany. Not only do people need to feel financially secure, managers also need to feel secure in the knowledge that tasks they have delegated are carried out appropriately; they are responsible for the success of any project under their leadership. They tend to exercise a great deal of control over subordinates, demanding regular interim progress reports, but generally hand over responsibility for the approach taken to the task.

Until relatively recently motivational skills were not considered significant. Money and the satisfaction of carrying out a task successfully were considered sufficient motivation. Success is expected and praise is rare. Failure and mistakes, on the other hand, are not tolerated. They not only reflect on the person who made the mistake, they reflect on the manager responsible. Two responses are common: one is to criticise the culprit (possibly in front of colleagues), the other is to sweep the problem under the carpet, protect the culprit from outside influences by keeping him or her busy with tasks that will not be too challenging, thus protecting the reputation of the manager responsible. The realisation that undermotivated employees cost a company a great deal of money is resulting in an increasing emphasis on motivational skills in management training programmes.

In recent years the expectations of working people have been changing as they have become better off and more able to take advantage of a wide variety of leisure activities. This increase in personal wealth is partially due to a rise in income levels and partially due to an increasing number of people inheriting wealth from relatives who are now ageing. For many people in the younger generations (aged 20–45), life no longer revolves around work as it did during the 1950s, 1960s and 1970s. Having time to participate in leisure activities is becoming an increasing priority for them. They are demanding more from life than job security (which they are slowly beginning to realise no longer exists) and at work are demanding more responsibility and fulfilment. At the same time, the recent rapid rise in unemployment is resulting in a somewhat vain attempt by many employees to seek the kind of job security that existed until the late 1980s. This reflects the fundamental importance of security for German employees.

Authority

A German manager derives his authority from his position, which he will probably have attained having proved his professional competence, either technically or commercially. Whether or not he possesses the necessary people skills to motivate subordinates, he expects personal and professional respect to be shown *because* he is a manager. He has earned this respect with the promotion that has given him his position.

Respect for authority is a German value. Authority is automatic. This manifests itself in the way decisions are reached in meetings. Open discussion is accepted. Anyone can contribute as long as they have something to add to the theme under discussion – otherwise they are not expected to participate actively. The manager will weigh up the arguments, make his decision and delegate tasks. For him, there is no question but that his decisions will be implemented regardless of whether the person chosen to carry them out agrees. An employee will accept the decision and does not expect to participate in the decision-making process. Only senior people are in a position to question a manager's competence and decisions.

British and US managers in charge of German employees frequently express frustration at their subordinates' seeming inability to make decisions for themselves: they are simply not accustomed to doing so.

German managers responsible for joint groups containing British or American employees are sometimes overcome with disbelief and frustration when they find their decisions are not being carried out, failing to understand that, to Britons and Americans, respect for authority is not automatic. Furthermore, they may not realise that qualified British and American employees expect to share in the decision-making process before being asked to implement the results.

Decision making, problem solving and security

Risk avoidance and thorough analysis are the main concepts here. German managers tend to feel uncomfortable with situations over which they have no control (hence their control over decisions in meetings). As taking risks implies less than complete control, they attempt to control the risk by analysing all potential new projects thoroughly before making decisions. Why?

The reasons are historical, psychological and economic. Germans associate risk with the possibility of failure: something they have learned to avoid since their school days. Young people grow up in a system where mistakes are punished by negative grades and failure is punished by having to resit a school year. They learn to fear making mistakes. It is not uncommon, when presenting a new idea to Germans, to hear the response: 'What if it does not succeed?' They enter working life taking a low-risk strategy of avoiding undertakings that are not 'guaranteed' to achieve success. Before achieving their current status they will have learned how to balance risks and potential benefits conservatively.

This is done by objective analysis. Written documentation assists Germans in feeling more secure about unknown entities. A document is generally considered objective proof that thought has been given to the idea, which does not of course indicate that people will believe everything that is put on paper. Having read an analysis, they normally like to sit on the idea for a while and consider it in peace. Decisions take time, longer than in Britain and much longer than is standard in the United States. However, once Germans commit themselves, they do not generally turn back.

There are also significant historical and economic factors explaining the German aversion to risk taking. The rampant inflation of the 1920s, with its immediate economic and later disastrous political consequences, has taught Germans to be ultra-careful when investing, as well as to place faith in the status quo as long as it is serving them well. Having embarked on co-operation, they tend to remain loyal as long as they feel secure about the quality and conditions of the business relationship; which does not prevent them from attempting to renegotiate terms.

They like to seek long-term agreements that give them the security of being able to plan for the next few years. This has its roots in the structure of German industry, with family-owned, medium-sized companies that have grown over a period of decades by continuously reinvesting profits as the powerhouse. The relatively small number of incorporated companies are owned predominantly by the banks and other financial institutions. Their interest lies in perpetuating a system in which the company can continue to operate. Here again, surpluses are pumped back rather than distributed to shareholders. Contrast this with Britain and the United States, where the proportion of private shareholders, who expect results and dividends every year, is far higher. Planning periods therefore tend to be shorter.

The rapid increase in the number of private shareholders in recent years is slowly resulting in attitudinal changes among German managers. The concept of shareholder value has now entered the business person's vocabulary and returns on investment comparable with some leading Anglo-Saxon corporations are now being demanded by industrial leaders. While this rise in the number of people investing in shares indicates an increasing willingness to take risks and look for higher returns, risk aversion is still relatively strong among the same people in their corporate role as employees.

The German approach to problem solving is similar. If a unit ceases to work or a device under development is not functioning as expected, all components that might possibly be connected with the malfunctioning piece are analysed in detail until the cause is found. People can then feel secure in the knowledge that their solution is right. This is in stark contrast to the pragmatic 'get the unit working again as soon as possible' approach that tends to be favoured in Britain and the United States. It is hardly surprising that these differences result in countless, enormously expensive conflicts in US–German and British–German projects each year. A recent co-operation between German and US engineers developing a telecommunications chip was almost abandoned, not for technical reasons or because of challenges in meeting the tight delivery deadline, but because neither side could come to terms with the other's approach to solving the technical problems. The Americans would try to get over hiccups by finding a solution that worked, did not necessarily rule out future problems and did not get to the root of the original problem. The Germans would immediately stop further development until they had found and solved the cause of the problem. Both sides traded insults and allegations and both were convinced that theirs was the only approach – until they became aware that they were simply using different approaches that could be combined to good effect to produce a better solution.

This craving for security and 'objective' information displays itself in other ways. Employers and potential partners demand documents confirming one's qualifications, and therefore ability, to do the task. Just as it is inconceivable for a company to employ someone without having seen degree and diploma certificates, as well as testimonials from previous employers, a potential business partner will want to see documentation about a company and its products to help him feel more secure with a new, unknown and therefore risky undertaking.

The tightly woven social security net is highly valued throughout society, providing the necessary security for survival in old age or in case of misfortune. High quality is a must, as it guarantees reliability. This is not merely a matter of pride in producing a quality product, it is the security of knowing that it will function as and when needed. Safety standards and emission controls are extremely tough. Germans like to be secure in the knowledge that the risk of accidents is minimised and that the quality of their descendants' lives will not be compromised by environmental damage.

Presenting and negotiating

The key concepts are clear organisation, thorough analysis and serious, reputable argumentation. Thorough analysis includes a historical overview to add credence to your experience as well as detailed analysis of the path you have taken to reach your conclusions. The bottom line is important, but is only persuasive if the audience can see that it has been reached scientifically by carefully weighing up all possible alternatives. Presenters persuade by demonstrating their credibility through their *Fachkompetenz* (professional abilities) and proving their mastery of the complete situation. Presentations tend to be formal, which does not mean that there is no place for humour. However, the humour should be relevant to the theme and not laid on too thickly.

Although the relationship plays a significant role in negotiations, Germans tend to be more impressed with quality, reputability and reliability. Relatively little time is spent on small talk, the motto being 'let's get on with business'. Formality towards and a respectable distance from your counterpart are expected. This distance takes the form of recognition of his status (Herr Dr Peter Schmidt is to be addressed as Herr Dr Schmidt, not Herr Schmidt and certainly not Peter) and not appearing to push too hard for a close relationship (he has the authority to make a decision and will expect this to be explicitly recognised).

Teamwork

Unlike people in Anglo-Saxon countries, Germans do not learn to work together from an early age. The German concept of a team is more often than not a group of experts who work together on a specific task to reach a specific goal. Working together may imply adding their input following individual work on the topic of their expertise.

Only recently have they begun to take the Anglo-Saxon concept on board: working together, jointly coming up with creative solutions to new challenges. Although belonging to and having the security of a group is very important to Germans, at higher levels of management they tend to work alone.

Communication style

German verbal communication patterns are one of the greatest sources of confusion to others. In brief, they are very direct, short and to the point and can thus appear to be abrupt and demanding. The content of the message is more important than the means by which it is transmitted. The word *muß* (have to) is used much more frequently than in English. Germans whose command of English may be very good, but who lack an understanding of the undertones of communication styles with English-speaking people, tend to translate directly, producing English expressions using German communication patterns (see section below on language).

While Britons and Americans tend to value their independence and consider being asked rather than ordered to carry out a task as a sign of respect, Germans accept authority more readily and, although they may prefer to be asked, they will do something despite being ordered to. When faced with the German pattern of getting straight to the point, many non-Germans, and especially Britons who are accustomed to receiving instructions put in the form of a request, feel put upon and talked down to. Understatement will generally not be understood.

In German, the 'please' may be replaced by an acceptable friendly tone. They are also prone to forget it when speaking English.

The US anthropologist Edward T Hall uses the concept of high- and low-context cultures to explain these differences in style. In low-context cultures, people have a need for information to be transferred in great detail and very explicitly. High-context cultures, on the other hand, favour inference more than explicitness. Germany is a very low-context culture requiring explicit, to-the-point information. The United States is medium to low context, whereas Britain is medium to high context.

The widespread use of e-mail, especially for international intra-corporate communication and for day-to-day communication in international projects, is resulting in numerous conflicts, with many Britons and Americans complaining about the Germans' 'rudeness' and 'lack of respect' for their counterparts. While these complaints *may* appear justified if viewed only from the perspective of the receiver, the style of messages sent, in fact, needs to be viewed from the perspective of the sender (German), in addition to the context of international e-mail communication as a whole.

E-mail is a fast and easy-to-use communication medium. Consequently, it is frequently used quickly, without too much thought concerning the process. E-mail in itself is able to display almost no personal context between the parties communicating. It is therefore in itself direct. Added to the very direct German communication style, the result to the British, who value indirectness, and even Americans, who, although they too tend to value directness, also value a personal touch, may appear too hard hitting. The consequence tends to be unnecessary conflict. The solution is not to jump to conclusions about your German counterpart's intentions, but to recognise the directness as standard and to clarify his intentions by asking.

Make allowances for non-native speakers of the language. If faced with this seemingly abrupt communication style, it is useful to check back on what your counterpart really meant to say before making a value judgement.

Small talk plays a less significant role in building a business relationship than it does in the United States and is far less important than in Britain. It is normal to get down to business very soon after meeting a new prospect for the first time.

HIDDEN DIFFERENCES

Time

Punctuality is absolutely essential in business dealings with Germans. A 9 o'clock appointment means precisely 9 o'clock. To arrive late (without genuine extenuating circumstances, which are of course understood) is unacceptable. To arrive earlier than 8.58 might be interpreted as an infringement on your counterpart's time. This also applies to social appointments.

Business in Germany tends to be highly organised and regulated. Business people generally work under a great deal of pressure and organising their diaries helps them relieve this. It may be difficult to get an appointment at short notice, so it is advisable to plan ahead. It is also not unusual to arrange specific appointments for telephone calls. Germans like the security of knowing what will happen when, and prefer to plan their day in sequence, dealing with one thing at a time.

Punctuality is also considered an indication of reliability and reputability. Deadlines exist to be adhered to. Once fixed, they are only changed if circumstances make it impossible to meet them. Elaborate excuses for failing to meet a deadline only exacerbate the problem.

Language

This precision is also a feature of the language. It is structured and contains an abundance of rules stipulating sentence structure. This naturally mirrors German communication patterns.

Germans who speak English are also prone to succumb to a number of language pitfalls (known as false friends), which may lead to misunderstandings if both parties are unaware of them. Some of the most common are:

- *muß* (have to), which can give the impression that the speaker is giving orders;
- *Problem*, which literally means problem but is also used in place of theme, topic, issue, matter, due to the German habit of concentrating on possible difficulties;
- *aktuell* (current, up to date), which, if translated as 'actually', can give the impression that the speaker is stating his or her view of the real position very forcefully;
- *eventuell* (possibly), which, if translated as 'eventually', can give the impression that the speaker is trying to delay making a decision;

- *seriös* (reputable), which is often mistakenly translated as serious and may leave the impression that the speaker doubts your intentions.

Barriers

Germans are often perceived as distant and hard to get to know. They are not; it simply takes longer to get behind the barrier of the real person. They value their private sphere and draw a clear line between business and pleasure. They require time to come to terms with new people who enter their lives and will slowly search for ways of getting to know you. If they feel that a stranger is trying to get too close too quickly they feel threatened and may block. In their own time they open up and will begin to talk about their family and interests. First names and the familiar *Du* form will follow. Once you have been permitted to enter someone's life a deep, meaningful friendship, which is valued greatly, will follow. We can liken the German approach to building relationships to a pineapple – a relatively hard outer surface that takes a while to penetrate, but with a welcoming rich interior. The Anglo-Saxon approach is more akin to a peach – a soft, welcoming outer surface that goes relatively deep, but an extremely hard core that it is very rare for outsiders to penetrate.

Humour is often said to be out of place in German business. Nothing could be further from the truth. It is true that business is taken very seriously and that meetings tend to be formal, but this does not mean that people are humourless. They do not appreciate humour for its own sake and slapstick in business is out of place. However, a humorous remark that is relevant to the situation at hand is more likely to break down barriers than to create them. Outside the office, Germans like to laugh as much as anyone else.

Recognition of personal space is a matter of etiquette and status. In offices, doors are more often kept closed than open. This does not mean that nobody may enter, but generally expresses a preference for working undisturbed. It is expected that colleagues and visitors will knock before entering. Managers generally prefer visitors to enter via the secretary's office. The importance of a person in the hierarchy can often be recognised by the size and position of the office. The larger the office, the higher the rank. Corner offices and those on the top floor are generally reserved for those having the greatest amount of responsibility.

Status symbols

Germans take great pride in their achievements and are not ashamed to demonstrate their success. The most obvious status symbol is the car, which is frequently used to judge the degree of success a business partner is having. Mercedes, BMW and Audi are the three so-called noble brands driven most frequently by successful business people. If you wish to create a positive impression and you hold an appropriate position in your organisation, it might be advisable to hire one of these makes from the airport. If you are not a senior manager, get a car further down the range.

The size of one's house as well as the location are also indications of status. Not so obvious are vacation destinations. Many top managers, however, are content to spend their time off at a quiet location in Germany or one of the neighbouring countries.

CONCLUSION

With the increase in the volume of business globally and the improvement in communications technology, outside influences on German business practice are growing. The merging of the eastern and western German cultures, greater participation in international projects (with the resulting exposure to other successful ways of doing business), increasing competition from low-wage, high-technology countries abroad, the rising cost of maintaining the social security system and increasing demand for quality leisure time by employees are some of the significant changes that are slowly beginning to cause a shift in the mindset of German managers and employees. Cultures can be seen as paradigms – which shift.

Doing business in Germany is a challenge. Like all successful countries, Germans possess a firm conviction that their way of doing things is the best way. This by no means indicates that they are unwilling to accept alternatives or to try out new ideas. It does mean that you need to present very convincing and solid arguments in order to persuade them to change. To be successful (ie to obtain the optimum results from a business relationship with a German company), thorough preparation is essential. This includes research, preparation of documentation in a manner that will appeal to them and learning to communicate with them at their level. It means accepting their idiosyncratic behaviour and avoiding the trap of judging their procedures and standards on the basis of your own. Above all, it requires the will to succeed, and patience.

DIVERSOPHY®

diversiRISK™ –

Working temporarily with your company's joint-venture partner in Germany, you enjoy joking with your German colleagues, though they sometimes give you strange looks. Later, you feel that they are not involving you in important informal meetings. Work is serious business here. Germans do like to have fun, but it may take time for them to adapt to your style.

Think this over and share your thoughts before taking your next turn. Discard this card.

4 Points © 1999. GSI. All rights reserved. +31-20 52 41 439
info@diversophy.com www.diversophy.com **D083**

Q diversiCHOICE™

As a member of a predominantly German team with a German team leader, would you expect to play an active part in making decisions?

Yes or no?

3 Points © 1999. GSI. All rights reserved. +31-20 52 41 439
info@diversophy.com www.diversophy.com **D003**

A diversiCHOICE™

No, is most likely. While you can expect to be able to express your opinions openly, decisions are usually made by the team leader alone. Team members would expect the leader to take clear responsibility for overall decisions. Consensus decision making is rare.

If you chose the best answer, keep this card. If not, discard it.

3 Points © 1999. GSI. All rights reserved. +31-20 52 41 439
info@diversophy.com www.diversophy.com **D003**

DIVERSOPHY® is a philosophy and set of tools in the form of training games that support the acquisition of cultural competence among those who use it.

For further information please contact:
ericlynnlct@compuserve.com

Part Two

Business Practices and Development

8

Länder Profiles

(Statistical data edited by Jonathan Reuvid)

Federal state	Baden-Württemberg	Bayern	Berlin	Brandenburg	Bremen	Hamburg	Hessen
English translation	Baden-Württemberg	Bavaria	Berlin	Brandenburg	Bremen	Hamburg	Hesse
Area (sq km)	35,751	70,546	889	29,053	404	755	21,114
% of Germany	10.00	19.80	0.20	8.10	0.10	0.20	5.90
Capital	Stuttgart	Munich	Berlin	Potsdam	Bremen	Hamburg	Wiesbaden
Population ('000)	10,375	12,044	3459	2554	678	1706	6027
% of German population	12.60	14.60	4.30	3.10	0.80	2.10	7.30
Working population ('000)	4769	5701	1530	1115	277	786	2658
Unemployment rate (1995 average %)	8.70	8.70	17.30	18.90	16.80	13.00	10.40
% employed in							
agriculture, forestry and fisheries	2.58	5.70	0.52	5.02	2.53	1.02	1.87
manufacturing	41.08	36.64	23.14	33.18	31.77	24.05	31.49
trade & transport	19.96	22.40	22.94	22.24	27.44	28.50	24.42
other services	36.42	37.43	53.40	39.64	39.71	46.44	42.21
GDP total (DM billion)	523	615	156	74	40	143	353
GNP per capita (DM)	48,576	49,485	43,307	28,583	57,080	81,360	57,143

Federal state / English translation	Mecklenburg-Vorpommern / Mecklenburg-Western Pomerania	Niedersachsen / Lower Saxony	Nordrhein/Westfalen / North Rhine/Westphalia	Rheinland Pfalz / Rhineland Palatinate	Saarland / Saarland	Sachsen / Saxony	Sachsen-Anhalt / Sachsen-Anhalt	Schleswig-Holstein / Schleswig-Holstein	Thüringen / Thuringia
Area (sq km)	23,170	47,659	34,075	19,846	2,570	18,408	20,446	15,739	16,171
% of Germany	6.5	13.30	9.55	5.56	0.72	5.16	5.73	4.41	4.53
Capital	Schwerin	Hanover	Düsseldorf	Mainz	Saarbrücken	Dresden	Magdeburg	Kiel	Erfurt
Population ('000)	1817	7815	17,948	4001	1084	4646	2724	2742	2491
% of German population	2.30	9.30	21.72	4.82	1.32	5.66	3.36	3.31	3.07
Working population ('000)	777	3368	7392	1710	414	1921	1105	1230	1082
Unemployment rate (1995 average %)	20.30	12.90	12.20	10.30	13.60	18.40	21.70	11.20	19.10
% employed in agriculture, forestry and fisheries	6.43	4.33	1.92	3.16	1.21	2.97	4.34	3.09	3.60
manufacturing	29.47	32.27	35.35	36.55	30.92	37.12	33.94	25.93	34.47
trade & transport	23.04	23.96	23.17	21.75	24.40	22.23	22.08	27.24	21.26
other services	41.06	40.97	39.57	39.57	43.24	37.77	39.64	43.74	40.67
GDP total (DM billion)	49	316	799	157	45	123	70	112	65
GNP per capita (DM)	26,637	39,015	43,481	37,666	39,760	26,173	25,404	39,606	25,853
Foreign direct investment 1994 (DM million)	0.90	14.90	66.50	5.70	2.80	0.90	1.40	3.30	0.80

9

The Structure of Industry

Prof Dr Peter Oberender, University of Bayreuth[1]

In Germany more employees work in the industrial sector than in other countries. This is mainly due to the high percentage of exports in German industry. Even though there has been a reduction in recent years, 24.1 per cent of total employment is still in industry, creating 33.1 per cent of the total gross value added. The share of employment in industry in the old *Länder* (former West Germany) is rather higher than it is in the new *Länder* (former East Germany).

In international comparisons the industrial competitiveness of Germany shows some weaknesses. Yet with an export quota of around 32 per cent in 1997 Germany must face this challenge. Taxation of businesses has reached a high level. There are severe legal restrictions to promote ecologically sound production, licence requirements are strict and licensing takes a long time for some industrial sites. Moreover, costs per working hour are the highest worldwide. An important factor in rising costs per working hour is constituted by the additional personnel costs, which in 1997 amounted to 80.1 per cent of the total cost per working hour. The greatest share of these additional personnel costs is taken up by insurance contributions to the German statutory social security scheme that have to be paid by employers.

[1] I would like to thank Mr Matthias Sander for his qualified research assistance and my assistant Dipl. Volkswirtin Birgit Wezel who kindly agreed to translate this paper into English.

In Germany the statutory social security scheme is organised with social insurance on a pay-as-you-earn basis, in contrast to an insurance on a fully funded basis. This means that today's employees and employers pay into an insurance fund. The money that is collected is not used to build up a stock of capital but is paid out immediately for old-age pensions, unemployment benefits, health care and old-age care.

Because of the disadvantageous demographic development, increasing insurance contributions are to be expected in the future. With increasing insurance contributions, the burden on employers will also grow because they have to pay parts of the contributions for their employees.

Yet Germany as an industrial location also has important competitive advantages, eg a good infrastructure, highly qualified employees, a large investment in research and development, political stability, few strikes and high technological standards. Together these are factors that ensure high productivity and a high quality of products.

Overall one may say that the importance of industry for the German economy will remain great in the future, even if there will be a slight decline.

TYPES OF ENTERPRISES AND CAPITAL STRUCTURE

Three main categories of enterprises can be found in German industry: sole proprietors, partnerships and corporate enterprises.

With a sole proprietor only the owner has the legal right of management. The owner alone is liable for the company's liabilities, for business and private capital. The creation of additional business capital is limited by the owner's personal assets. About 74 per cent of all industrial companies are sole proprietors, employing 16 per cent of all industrial employees.

Partnerships are *Offene Handelsgesellschaften* (OHG: general commercial partnerships with an unrestricted liability of its partners for debts), *Kommanditgesellschaften* (KG: limited commercial partnerships) of GmbH & Co KG which is a limited partnership (KG) formed with a limited liability company (GmbH, *Gesellschaft mit beschränkter Haftung*) as general partner and the members of the GmbH, their families or outsiders as limited partners.

An OHG has at least two partners. All partners have unlimited liability for the partnership's debt. Management can be delegated or would otherwise be the joint responsibility of the owners.

A KG has one partner who is liable with all his or her private and business property (unlimited partner) and at least one partner who is only liable up to his or her share in the company but not with private property (limited partner). Only the unlimited partner is by law entitled to top management. Four per cent of all German industrial enterprises are KGs or OHGs employing 8 per cent of the total workforce. On average, each such enterprise has 49 employees.

A GmbH & Co KG is a typically German form of enterprise. The characteristic feature of this type of enterprise is that in the end all partners are limited partners only. Five per cent of all enterprises are GmbH & Co KGs, encompassing 18 per cent of total industrial employment.

There are also three types of limited liability companies: GmbHs *(Gesellschaft mit beschränkter Haftung:* limited liability company, roughly comparable with a UK limited company), KGaA *(Kommandit-gesellschaft auf Aktien:* commercial partnership limited by shares; no UK equivalent) and AGs *(Aktiengesellschaften:* joint-stock companies).

In the GmbH top management is in the hands of a manager who is appointed by the partners. The liability of the partners is restricted to their interest in the company. Sixteen per cent of all companies are GmbHs, comprising 34 per cent of total employment. On average GmbHs have 54 employees. During recent years more and more general partnerships have been transformed into limited liability companies.

For the AG top management is in the hands of the executive board, the board of directors and the general meeting of shareholders. Financing capabilities are exceptionally good for this type of enterprise. On the one hand creditability is high because of the distinct protection of creditors; on the other hand the possibility of raising new capital by issuing additional shares is good as well. Additionally, there is a high level of protection for shareholders.

Only 0.2 per cent of all enterprises are AGs and KGaAs. On average they employ 3000 people, 24 per cent of total industrial employment.

In comparison to other highly industrialised economies, in Germany joint-stock companies are of minor relevance only. In 1994 a special law, the *Finanzmarktförderungsgesetz* (a law to help develop financial markets), was passed to make the founding of a joint-stock company more attractive and to encourage the transformation of existing enterprises into joint-stock companies. This law introduced legal simplifications, especially for small joint-stock companies.

While in an average German enterprise only 18 per cent of the total capital is equity capital, the share in industrial enterprises is 23 per cent. Taking methodological differences into account one finds that in comparison to other European enterprises German industry does not have a significantly lower share of ownership capital, even though empirical research has quite often emphasised the opposite. The 77 per cent share of loan capital consists of 43 per cent short-term liabilities, 14 per cent long-term liabilities and 20 per cent reserves (among which 8.9 per cent are pension fund reserves).

In industrial sectors the share of equity differs greatly. In the chemical industry it reaches 38.4 per cent, in electrical engineering 24.3 per cent, while it only amounts to 21.4 per cent in textile and 11.3 in wood-based industries.

COMPARISON OF INDUSTRIAL SECTORS

Motor vehicle construction

In 1996 motor vehicle construction, with a turnover of DM353.5 billion, was the most important German industrial sector (76.4 per cent of total industrial turnover).

After a decline in employment at the beginning of the 1990s the sector is growing again, with 849,300 employees in 1996, 13.8 per cent of all employment in the industrial sector. The export quota of 51.7 per cent is extraordinarily high. Thanks to extensive rationalisation profits have improved again recently after their drastic decline during the 1993 recession. In Germany the motor vehicle construction sector is highly concentrated. Half of the total employment in this sector is with the three leading companies: Mercedes-Benz, Volkswagen and BMW. For the years to come it can be expected that motor vehicle construction will continue to grow.

Mechanical engineering

In 1996 the turnover of mechanical engineering reached DM267.9 billion, which accounts for 12.4 per cent of the total industrial turnover. The number of employees has declined during recent years to a total of 981,600 (or 15.9 per cent of total employment in industry). Because of its high export quota (46.7 per cent) this sector is strongly affected by international competition, the unfavourable exchange rate of the deutschmark and high German production costs. The sector comprises 14.5 per cent of all the enterprises in industry and is, with its 152 employees per enterprise, a typical sector of medium-sized enterprises. In the medium term prospects for growth are about average, therefore the engineering sector will remain of great importance for German industry in the future.

Electrical engineering

Electrical engineering and the manufacture of office machines were responsible for 13.9 per cent of total industrial employment, which amounts to 856,500 employees, generating a total turnover of DM254.5 billion (11.8 per cent of total turnover). This sector is also highly dependent on exports, with an export ratio of 39.2 per cent. In 1996 the enterprises in this sector reached a profit–turnover ratio of 0.8 per cent (after tax) and a return on equity of 8.5 per cent.

Electrical engineering is also a highly concentrated sector (major companies being Siemens and Bosch). Additionally, there are numerous medium-sized businesses.

Prospects for growth in this sector are good, but enterprises face strong international competition.

Chemical industry

Total turnover in the chemical industry was DM230.2 billion (10.7 per cent of total industrial turnover). The sector employs 500,500 people, or 8.1 per cent of the total workforce. The export quota was 45.9 per cent. Profits and net creation of value were above average. The profit–turnover ratio was 4.6 per cent (after tax) in 1996.

The German chemical industry is also a highly concentrated sector, averaging 202 employees per enterprise. Dominant companies are BASF, Hoechst and Bayer. The industry's share of total industrial production will remain stable in the medium term.

Food-processing industries

With 502,700 employees (8.2 per cent) the food-processing industry has a total turnover of DM225.7 billion (10.5 per cent). The sector has an extremely low export ratio of only 11.7 per cent. Profits are average and the profit–turnover ratio was 1.9 per cent in 1996.

This industry is less concentrated, with an average of 104 employees per enterprise. Prospects for growth are below average, though the sector is somewhat cyclical.

Manufacturing of metal products

The manufacturing of metal products comprises steel and light metal engineering as well as the manufacturing of ironmongery, tinware and metalware. In 1996 there were 600,000 employees (13.5 per cent) working in this industry; turnover reached DM127,663 billion (10.7 per cent); the export quota was 10.7 per cent and profits were positive. In 1996 a profit–turnover ratio of 2.6 per cent was realised.

The sector mainly consists of medium-sized enterprises employing an average of 120 employees. Prospects for growth are average.

Paper manufacturing, publishing and printing industries

This sector realised a turnover of DM123.4 billion (5.7 per cent) with its 406,400 employees (6.6 per cent). The profit–turnover ratio was above average (2.3 per cent in 1996). The sector is dominated by medium-sized enterprises (on average 104 employees per enterprise) and prospects for growth are average.

Production and primary processing of metals

Metal production and metalworking comprise the iron and steel producing industry and non-ferrous metal production. The 299,000 employees in this sector (4.6 per cent) achieved a turnover of DM103.3 billion (5 per cent). Exports make up 35 per cent of the sector. Prospects for profits have been and will continue to be negative. Prospects of growth are also negative. The branch is highly concentrated (on average 260 employees per enterprise).

Rubber and plastics industries

This sector employs 342,800 employees (5.6 per cent) and achieves a turnover of DM89.8 billion (4.2 per cent). The profits of the mostly medium-sized businesses are good. In 1996 a profit–turnover ratio of 2.4 per cent was realised. On average there are 117 employees per enterprise. Future prospects are positive for the plastics industry. The rubber industry, on the other hand, expects a below-average growth rate.

Glass manufacturing, ceramics and manufacturing of stones and non-metallic mineral products

This sector has 257,200 employees (4.2 per cent) and had a total turnover of DM70.2 billion (3.3 per cent) in 1996. The profit–turnover ratio is relatively high, but only 8.4 per cent of all German industries are in this sector. Enterprises are smaller than in most sectors, employing only 69 employees on average. Prospects for growth are average.

Textile and clothing industries

This sector has a turnover of DM54.1 billion (1.5 per cent) with 219,900 employees (3.5 per cent). In 1996 the profit–turnover ratio was 0.5 per cent. Medium-sized enterprises are the characteristic feature of the sector with an average of 99 employees per enterprise. Prospects are negative because of strong competition from very cost-efficient competitors abroad, especially in the clothing industry.

Overall one may note the great importance of the motor vehicle industry, mechanical and electrical engineering and the chemical industries. These four branches alone make up 52 per cent of total industrial employment, accounting for 50 per cent of the total industrial turnover with a 60 per cent share of total industrial exports.

THE GOVERNMENT'S INFLUENCE ON INDUSTRIAL DEVELOPMENT

To ensure the efficiency of markets and to safeguard competitive market processes against the abuse of economic power, an anti-cartel and anti-trust law has been passed (*Gesetz gegen Wettbewerbsbeschränkungen*). The law first and foremost forbids cartels (though exceptions are possible, mainly on request). Furthermore, the law provides for the federal cartel office (*Kartellamt*) to implement measures to control businesses with major economic power in their specific markets.

The state also intervenes in the economic through regulations that interfere with businesses' contractual and economic freedom. In Germany industry complains about the growing bureaucracy, too many restrictions on environmental matters compared to foreign countries, many restrictions regarding production technologies and extremely lengthy licensing procedures. Furthermore, entrepreneurs face disadvantages because of far-reaching employee rights, high personnel costs (wages and social security contributions) and a high level of taxation. An intense discussion has arisen in Germany about the necessity for deregulation. Progress is still slow, especially because of the strong influence of pressure groups. However, netbased markets such as energy and telecommunication were opened for competition. State-owned or state-run enterprises are only of minor importance in the German economy. Under the chancellorship of Helmut Kohl governmental interests in such enterprises as Lufthansa, Volkswagen, VIAG, Veba and the *Industrieverwaltungsgesellschaft* have been reduced or sold off altogether.

A major part of governmental influence comprises subsidies. Subsidies occur as financial assistance or as tax reductions and tax exemptions. Subsidies' share of GDP is 5.7 per cent, of which one-fifth goes to manufacturing industries. In the former East Germany subsidies made up a quarter of domestic product.

Subsidies aim at the preservation of existing structures, a reduced pace of adjustment to new circumstances and supporting new branches that are expected to be of high potential for future economic development. These receive subsidies because they are thought to carry high risks and to cause extremely high costs that cannot be borne by private enterprises alone. Additionally, subsidies are supposed to increase incentives for investment, research and development, to help someone start in business and to revitalise disadvantaged regions.

There is a high concentration of subsidies in manufacturing industries. Sectors that gain specifically from these subsidies are the mining industry, shipbuilding industry, the very capital intensive tobacco and mineral oil industries, the iron and steel industries and the aircraft and aerospace industries, because of their high potential and promising future outlook. During recent years the share of subsidies used to support research and development has fallen dramatically. Subsidies therefore now have more of a conservational character, eg for specific industries, structures and regions.

Considerable influence on subsidies for the former East Germany was exercised by the *Treuhand* (the agency responsible for privatising East German industry). Its explicit aim was to safeguard employment, especially in industry, by granting subsidies. Subsidies were given in different forms: the assumption of losses and financial assistance for investment projects, loans to form equity capital and allowances by ensuring low prices when privatising companies. A major incentive for investment in the former East Germany came from new forms of tax relief, especially financial assistance for producers' durable equipment and extraordinary depreciation of up to 50 per cent of the total investment sum.

Chapter 15 will exemplify some possibilities of assistance for enterprises and those wishing to go into business.

NATIONAL PLAN FOR BUSINESS PROMOTION

There are special federal promotional measures for medium-sized businesses. First of all, general financial assistance is available, eg the

European Recovery Programme and the programmes of the German Reconstruction Loan Corporation *(Kreditanstalt für Wiederaufbau)*. Prerequisites for this assistance are investment in new businesses, the enlargement of existing businesses or job-creating investments. Loans are generally long term and are characterised by extremely low interest rates and redemption-free periods.

On behalf of the federal or the *Länder* governments, banks also give guarantees for loans. These loans are to be used to improve a company's competitiveness. Within the tax legislation, special forms of depreciation and depreciation on savings to help small and medium-sized enterprises are available.

Moreover, federal financial assistance is available for research and development, eg a programme for innovation by the Reconstruction Loan Corporation *(Kreditanstalt für Wiederaufbau)* or the programmes of the Ministry for Education, Science and Technology for specific projects in these fields.

The joint task force for improvement of the regional economic structure *(Gemeinschaftsaufgabe Verbesserung der regionalen Wirtschaftsstruktur)* gives, for example, regional investment grants to those companies investing in disadvantaged regions. Specifically for medium-sized enterprises there are programmes for the improvement of the environment, for encouraging advice on business and to support information and training.

In addition to special programmes for medium-sized enterprises there are programmes for those willing to start a new business. The federal government offers a programme to help create equity capital. There are also programmes from the European Bank for Reconstruction and the Deutsche Ausgleichsbank specifically for those starting a business. The third financial markets promotion law *(Finanzmarktförderungsgesetz)* of 1997 allows small and medium-sized businesses better access to capital markets and improves the opportunities for private venture capital.

Additionally, there are programmes by the European Commission for medium-sized enterprises. These programmes primarily offer loans from the European Investment Bank and financial assistance for venture capital.

The German *Länder* also offer assistance. Regional business promotion occurs in the form of reductions in business tax or by giving subsidies when offering property to set up businesses. In the case of investments in the former East German *Länder,* the federal government offers additional assistance, eg grant for investment, special forms of depreciation, assistance for innovation projects and job-creating programmes.

IMPORTANT INSTITUTIONS OF THE GERMAN SOCIAL AND ECONOMIC SYSTEM

A peculiarity of the German social and economic system is the existence of quasi-governmental institutions. Chambers of Commerce, Chambers of Handicraft and Chambers of Agriculture are corporations under public law *(Körperschaften des öffentlichen Rechts)*. They are institutions exercising sovereign powers, organised by direct self-administration. Their sovereign powers include, for example, arbitration in disputes between competitors, the offering of expert opinions and participation in the area of professional education. They influence economic policy by offering comments and giving advice and they inform their members about current issues in economic policy. The Chambers encompass all entrepreneurs due to compulsory membership.

Another set of quasi-governmental organisations are the associations of employers and the trade unions, both called *Sozialpartner* (social partners). Both are 'partners' in the labour market. They arrange agreements on working conditions, especially wages, working hours and additional voluntary social security for their members. Furthermore, they are representatives in the self-governing boards of the German statutory co-determination (employee participation: *Mitbestimmung*).

Another representative in internal employee participation is the local employee council *(Betriebsrat)*. An employee council can be elected in all enterprises having at least five employees. The council is elected by the employees of that enterprise. According to law, co-determination of the employees' council is possible in social matters (eg social institutions within the company, working hours), in personnel matters (eg hearings in the case of dismissals) and in economic matters (eg information and advice when internal changes in the company are being planned).

Apprentices face a dual system of training in Germany. This encompasses a period of theoretical training in school for two or three years while at the same time taking part in practical training within a company. The legal foundation for the training of apprentices is the *Berufsbildungsgesetz* (law on professional training) and the *Handwerksordnung*. German industry offers more than 100 different courses for apprentices. At the end of an apprenticeship the apprentice has to pass an examination and receives a diploma from the Chamber of Commerce, the Chamber of Handicraft or the Chamber of Agriculture, depending on the kind of apprenticeship completed.

REFERENCES

Bundesministerium für Wirtschaft, *Jahresbericht der Bundesregierung '96, '97.*

Bundesministerium für Wirtschaft, *Das ERP-Programm,* Bonn 1972–84.

Bundesministerium für Wirtschaft (ed.), *Wirtschaftliche Förderung in den neuen Bundesländern,* Bonn, 1991–4.

Bundeszentrale für Politische Bildung (ed.) (1991) *Informationen zur Politischen Bildung 175, Wirtschaft 2, Arbeitnehmer und Betrieb,* reprinted 1991, Bonn.

Deutsche Bundesbank (1994) *Monatsbericht Oktober 1994,* 46. Jahrgang, No. 10, Frankfurt am Main.

Hohe Subventionen in Ostdeutschland – Wenig Abbau in Westdeutschland, in Deutsches Institut für Wirtschaftsforschung, *Wochenbericht 1995,* 62. Jahrgang, pp. 106–117.

Lampert, H. (1980) *Volkswirtschaftliche Institutionen,* München,

Lampert, H, (1992) *Die Wirtschafts- und Sozialordnung in der Bundesrepublik Deutschland,* 11th edn, München.

Oberender, P. (ed.) (1984) *Marktstruktur und Wettbewerb in der Bundesrepublik Deutschland-Branchenstudien zur deutschen Volkswirtschaft,* München.

Oberender, P. (ed.) (1989) *Marktökonomie – Marktstruktur und Wettbewerb in ausgewählten Branchen der Bundesrepublik Deutschland,* Munchen.

Schierenbeck, H, (1998) *Grundzüge der Betriebswirtschaftslehre,* 13th edn, München.

Weiß, J-P. (1993) *Wirtschaftliche Entwicklung Deutschlands bis zum Jahr 2000,* Wiesbaden.

STATISTICS

Bundesministerium für Wirtschaft (ed.) *Leistung in Zahlen,* Bonn.

Deutsche Bundesbank, *Monatsberichte der Deutschen Bundesbank.*

Institut der deutschen Wirtschaft (1998) *Zahlen zur wirtschaftlichen Entwicklung der Bundesrepublik Deutschland 1998,* Köln.

Statistisches Bundesamt, *Fachserie 4, Produzierendes Gewerbe.*

Statistisches Bundesamt, *Statistische Jahrbücher der Bundesrepublik Deutschland,* Stuttgart/Mainz.

10

The *Mittelstand* on the Threshold of the 21st Century

Prof Dr Horst Albach, Wissenschaftszentrum, Berlin

When the first millennium came to an end a thousand years ago people did not believe they were on the threshold of the eleventh century. Rather, they believed that the biblical prophesy 'the Kingdom of God is nigh' would be fulfilled. Kaiser Otto III expected his Kingdom to perish; he believed that he was on threshold of God's kingdom.

Present day people – the believers and the profane – talk about the threshold to the 21st century or think that we should 'build bridges into the 21st century' knowing indeed that 1 January 2000 will be no different from 31 December 1999, except for the date.

Leaving aside meaningless talk of thresholds and bridges, we should ask ourselves which problems and prospects face the *Mittelstand* today, and what must be done to overcome the problems and make full use of the prospects.

THE SITUATION

The position of the *Mittelstand*

If these questions are to be answered, the starting-point must be known. SMEs are at the forefront of business but their position is very varied.

For example, about one third of SMEs in trade and industry are doing well, but another third are doing badly. The divide between successful and unsuccessful SMEs is growing wider and wider. The statistical average on which economic policy is mainly based is of no informative value.

In the retail trade the situation is even worse. The number of bankruptcies has risen dramatically in recent years; in 1994 there were 19,000, in 1995 22,000, with a rising trend for 1996.

The situation in the new *Länder* (federal states) is particularly threatening. During 1994, 119,000 businesses were deregistered and in 1995 this figure rose to 131,000. In the meantime, in the small and medium-scale sector of the economy, collective agreements are no longer worth the paper they are written on.

The overall economic situation

The overall economic situation is typified by high unemployment and stagnant growth. By the year 2000 the unemployment figure should have halved, but still large companies are making massive redundancies, and calling them: 'lean production, business reengineering, spin-off, farming out and opportune structural measures' and in the case of management-level dismissal, 'out-placement'.

The solution to the unemployment problem is therefore expected to come from the small and medium-scale sector of the economy. Birch's famous thesis, in which the employment miracle in the USA began with SMEs, was applied only too readily to Europe and Germany. However, such hopes of job generation – and also the shifting of responsibility – are built on sand. Those who do not earn enough are not suitable partners for 'work alliances'.

The sheer size of the problem makes it clear that incantation will not improve the economic situation. Assuming that one million unemployed people could really find jobs in existing SMEs by the year 2000, another million would have to find work in new enterprises. With the current figures on employment in newly registered and de-registered enterprises – because only the balance counts – this means that by the year 2000, 800,000 new enterprises must be founded in the old *Länder*, and 300,000 in the new *Länder*.

If one also adds the fact that in many SMEs employee turnover is inevitable and employment problems are getting greater rather than smaller, then every year until the year 2000, 300,000 people must be ready to take up the profession of entrepreneur. With some 600,000 companies being founded each year in Germany, this means an increase of 50 per cent in the number of essential business formations. That is a mighty task! In the coming years, for every fifty wage and salary earners, somebody must come along who is willing to deal not only with competitors, but also with trade unions, official bodies and the tax office.

DEVELOPMENT TENDENCIES

The institutional environment

Turning to the development tendencies and the problems and prospects which arise from them, here it is the development of the institutional environment that is significant for the small and medium-scale sector of the economy. Two development tendencies have to be distinguished:

The development of regional blocks of the economy

On 1 January 1999 European monetary union began. This denoted a single economic and currency union and heightened competition for SMEs in Germany; the competition of the system had to be added to the competition on the market. Discussions about a minimum wage during the creation process showed how ineffective the means were which tried to mitigate this competitive pressure.

However, for the small and medium-scale sector of the economy this is also a great opportunity. In this way, as earlier, many small and medium-sized businesses set up manufacturing operations in Ireland, so they can now take advantage of the local competition in Europe, and within interrelated production also manufacture in Portugal or northern Italy.

What is being done in Europe and the EU is also taking place in other areas of the world. Indeed, the term 'global market' is on everybody's lips but in fact three large economic areas are being formed in which industrial SMEs are represented with manufacturing facilities, and in which trade supplies its goods at favourable prices. For this purpose, it will be taken for granted that the former Soviet Union will belong entirely to the European economic region.

The development of new institutions

The development of large economic regions with competition between them and systems competition within renders proven institutions obsolete. This applies above all to the parties to pay deals. We note how

SMEs negotiate outside the protection of Employers' Federations in order to be able to better adapt working hours and pay to the situation in which they are operating; we note the loss of social consensus among the parties to pay deals; we note increasing conflict between trade union officials and Works Councils; we note the shrinkage in trade union membership; we note the dispute between the Federation of German Industry and the Federation of Employers' Associations. Those responsible, and people responsible in an official capacity, do not quarrel because they would rather not; they contest the strategic realignment of their organisations as well as legitimisation in a changed world.

It appears that the parties to pay deals are institutions of a 19th century world that no longer fit into that of the late 20th century. This statement, so it appears, also applies to a series of other institutions. What, however, is the world of the 21st century?

The technological environment

Information technology

It is a platitude to characterise information technology as a determining characteristic of the environment in which we live, and the 21st century as the 'information society'. Even 10 years ago this was not the case: in our living experience, the reconstruction of the new *Länder* did not make progress mainly because the telephone connections were missing. Today Deutsche Telekom is confronted with a totally unexpected mountain of applications for ISDN connections, and the number of mobile phones has increased to such an extent that we are now talking about 'electrosmog'.

'Briefcase' is a word of the past – today we talk about 'laptops'. Recently, during a conference in Chile, an American professor asked how many of the participants were connected to the internet. When 80 per cent raised their hands he stood aghast. In Germany, those who have no e-mail address on their personal visiting card count as helpless 'oldies'.

Many, even entrepreneurs, ask what we should do with this mass of information and whether we need it at all. The fact that there is a vast supply of it shows that there is demand. The fact that there is CNN, the World Wide Web and the internet is proof that the information is needed and used. What is more, it is to the benefit of those who use it.

It is therefore no longer a question of 'whether' but 'how' it is used. Also, while we still surf the internet by hand, in Singapore there are electronic search routines in use which 'browse' automatically for important information. It is a matter of efficient use of information and in this the Asians – above all the Japanese – are way ahead of Europeans. The universities, the large trading companies and JETRO (Japan External Trade Organisation) all specialise in collecting information systematically, processing it in a standardised way and converting it on the international markets into competitive advantages.

Modern communications technology makes totally tailor-made, personal marketing possible. Many observers even believe that in the 21st century one will no longer talk about markets, but only of individual customers. Thanks to information technology, and according to the thesis, the markets of the 21st century will be single households and individuals. That sounds more revolutionary than it is. Even today there are already personal sales and telephone sales. In future it will be even easier to convert this basic idea of personalised marketing into technology, if one can go to visual interactive sales talk all over the world via the internet.

Innovations

A second characteristic of the technical environment in the next century will be the importance that technical innovations and new services will assume in world-wide competition.

The fact that information is available all over the world has the effect that new products and services become known world-wide practically in real time. Thanks to smaller products and improved transport technology, they will also be rapidly available worldwide. Through the internet and proprietary networks new products can be offered and targeted at the company's customers. Those who create the channels and networks to customers, the channel providers, will also be decisive regarding the success of the innovations.

Competition in innovation will be of greater significance than price competition. Price competition will be limited to hold off potential competitors from wanting to gain customers from established companies. The established companies will try to keep their customers through innovations for their special needs. New suppliers must create new markets if they want to be successful.

THE TASKS

What follows now from the analysis of the situation and development tendencies for SMEs with regard to requirements and which requirements stem from the State's SME policy?

The tasks for enterprise

The tasks for business are therefore clear: they can be described as the three 'I's:

- innovation;
- information;
- integration.

Innovation

Improving innovation capacity means:

- developing new ideas for products and services;
- transforming ideas into new products and services;
- reducing the necessary time and costs for the above.

That is simply worth considering, but that is not sufficient. Obviously it is highly dangerous if it transpires afterwards that an idea was not new, which is more often the case. It is also highly dangerous if it takes so long to develop an idea into an innovation that a competitor with a similar idea and the relevant innovation is earlier on the market. Then the innovation is likely to fail. The innovation period can be shortened, while a company catches on to ideas from competitors and brings them on to the market copied and improved. Japanese companies are not afraid of this, neither are the better SMEs in Germany.

Information

Innovation without information is impossible. Information here means:

- knowledge of the state of technology;
- knowledge of customer wishes;
- knowledge of customer problems;
- knowledge of potential competitors.

Information also means not leaving this knowledge to chance. Every business should have its own 'CIA' – an environmental information system. Good businesses already regularly evaluate patent applications, keep in regular contact with technical schools and university institutes, systematically assess invitations to tender and job advertisements and maintain information networks with customers and competitors.

Integration

By integration, here above all we should understand the inclusion of suppliers and customers in the development of innovations. Today, 'customer proximity' is often cited as the decisive factor for SME success. 'Supplier proximity' however, is no less important. Customer proximity also means knowing customers' problems as if they were one's own. Only then can one succeed in offering the customer affordable solutions of the desired quality. Without suppliers' integration cost-effective innovations will not be achieved.

This task of integration is naturally not restricted to Germany. It embraces a world-wide network of suppliers and customers as well as certainly all manufacturing operations and branches of the organisation the world over.

Germany's task

Tom Peters said that excellent companies distinguished themselves by fighting over every customer, as if it were the last. This realisation has not yet penetrated Germany. Nevertheless, it will be part of the decisive acknowledgements and important tasks of Germany in the 21st century to fight for every entrepreneur, as if it were the last! International local competition will teach the State to take this task seriously if it does not already do so. The debate over the German economic position allows me to hope that the State recognises and resolves this problem before it is too late.

What does it mean then, to fight over every entrepreneur as if it were the last? It means the provision of four things:

- good sources of finance;
- good infrastructure;
- SME-friendly administrative departments;
- a competitive tax system.

Good sources of finance

That SMEs in Germany have good sources of finance would certainly be maintained only by those who consider the bank loan the yardstick for all things and internal auditing banks as the businessman's house doctor. It is not however, a healthy financial structure if the shareholders' interest is only 15 to 20 per cent.

Good sources of finance mean then a shareholders' interest of at least 35 per cent and, if possible, over 50 per cent. Only then does the banker run after the entrepreneur rather than the entrepreneur running after the banker. SMEs in Germany are nowhere near this situation.

What should be done? With the law on small limited companies, a first step in the right direction has been taken. Now it is worth creating special equity markets for SMEs under entrepreneurial management and State control, free from the influence of banks. It is possible that the new *Länder* will take the lead down this road. However, without supporting tax measures, even such a reform of the capital markets situation will not become a great success.

Good infrastructure

No less important than good sources of finance is sound infrastructure. When Nixdorf planned to build his computer factory in Paderborn, he insisted on the Regional Government building an airport in Ostwestfalen. Today, apparently the situation is different. The debate over the night flight ban in Cologne-Bonn and the debate about housekeeping in the Düsseldorf provincial Diet hardly gave reason to hope that the transport infrastructure would be expanded according to the needs of the 21st century.

However, it is not only the transport infrastructure that will be the determining factor for the SMEs to address the challenges of the future with success. Scientific infrastructure is also a part of good infrastructure conditions. A great deal has happened in Germany in recent decades in this respect. The founding of the Institute for SME Research at Trier University is an example that in recent years the knowledge infrastructure has been improved, also encompassing SMEs.

SME-friendly administrative departments

Sound infrastructure does not only consist of hard elements such as transport systems, communications networks, school and laboratories. It also involves the people in the administrative departments and authorities, the rules and regulations that are applied to the entrepreneurs – the so-called 'soft elements'.

With regard to these soft elements the economic area of Germany fares particularly badly. The 'climate of social openness in respect of new possibilities for future scope', as the former Federal Chancellor called these factors, is particularly bad in Germany compared to the USA and Japan and also even to Austria and England.

For example, what should an SME do, if a large company in a large Bavarian town has already been trying in vain for the past two years to convert an industrial plot of land into a mixed area and has had to present enormous quantities of documents to 32 offices? At present, this application is in the hands of the municipal environmental authority because a rare species of toad has made its habitat on the plot of land, which has been industrial fallow land for two years. The toad would have to abandon its home. This is not an isolated case. Plans for deepening the Stuttgart Railway Station were blocked because the track had become the habitat of irreplaceable fauna and flora. Examples are numerous.

In his book *How Germany Conquered the Future*, van Scherpenberg describes municipal administrative departments, municipal building offices, job centres and other municipal set-ups which, thanks to a basic fiscal reform, have transformed themselves into service provider companies for both SMEs and people. He calls this idea of the 21st century a vision, not Utopia. SMEs could overcome their problems more easily in the future if this vision became reality.

Competitive tax system

Only recently did the Prime Minister of a neighbouring country turn against the abolition of the net worth tax with the argument that the tax burden of German companies is not high when compared internationally. Tax bills generally are a problem and, with international comparisons in particular, a Prime Minister cannot be expected to understand such types of fiscal statistics. Neither will an attempt to explain these types of bills be made here.

First, the taxes paid by German industrial limited companies in accordance with their published Annual Accounts and the percentage of net income (the sum of net profit and taxes) were examined; then the lowest third of these companies, (ie the companies which had earned the least that year): among those in the 1960s only 7.1 per cent paid more than 80 per cent tax from their net income, compared to 42.4 per cent in the 1990s! The tax burden is therefore highest, precisely for those companies that are doing badly. The tax authorities have heightened the crisis instead of helping companies to overcome it. These companies account for about 12 per cent of all jobs. Thus the State endangers jobs with its tax policy instead of safeguarding them.

The Federal Government with its current tax package wants to remedy this nonsense. That is important. The problem is how to finance it. An increase in VAT would, theoretically, be correct and at least neutral with regard to employment policy. However, due to EU harmonisation, the VAT increase seems to be available no longer. The fact is, as could be deduced from the press, that in Bavaria there are discussions about taxing life insurance and in other places raising the inheritance tax. It is difficult to see how, on the one hand, the willingness of inheritors and leading members of staff to continue operating SMEs can be reinforced, while on the other hand, the millstone of yet higher inheritance taxes is put around their necks. These taxes can only be financed from the profits of the years following the succession. In Japan, in practice they do the opposite in order to facilitate the generation change which is now very appropriate by lowering inheritance tax rates.

CONCLUSION

In this chapter some of the problems which will arise for SMEs as a consequence of the integration of economic areas through information technology have been highlighted. Also indicated are the personalisation of markets, interaction with customers through new information technology and the significance of innovations and integration that results from this. The story and historical anecdote (see below) underline these problems, while at the same time showing that they are not new in principle, but have merely been placed in a changed political and technical environment.

A German SME that manufactures refined chemicals, sold to a Japanese tyre manufacturer a powder which was mixed with synthetic rubber in order to stabilise attrition at very varied temperatures. It was a dirty grey product of excellent quality. One day the Japanese purchaser requested that the German representative in Tokyo supply a pure white powder. The representative bit his lip and passed the request on to Germany. From there the answer promptly came as to whether he had gone mad. Tyres are black anyhow, therefore why should he want a pure white powder. He should kindly make that clear to the customer. The representative faxed back, 'Do you want the order or not?' It was an order of several million deutschmarks. Two months later he had the white powder and a satisfied customer.

A Chilean entrepreneur who had experienced a very similar story emphasised it with an anecdote: in the year 1000 the Ambassador of the Governor of Nagasaki travelled to the Chinese court in Beijing. The Emperor asked him to describe his country. He only had time however for two sentences. The Ambassador said:

- 'In my country a man is a good man if he fulfils his duty';
- 'In my country attention to detail is always expression of the meaning of the whole matter'.

If German SMEs take to heart both these sentences in their customer relations, they can cross the threshold confidently into the year 2000.

11

The Dual System of Vocational Education and Training*

Dr Hermann Schmidt, University of Duisburg and Dr Laszlo Alex, Federal Institute for Vocational Training (BIBB), Bonn

BACKGROUND

Vocational education and training (VET) in Germany continues the tradition of medieval guild training, as practised all over Europe. However, in contrast to other countries, this system of practical and theoretical learning was adapted for the purposes of industry in the nineteenth century. Systematic on-the-job training was provided in workshops and was complemented by general education and occupation-related theory in colleges. In the course of the twentieth century, practices across different industrial sectors were brought together into a modern vocational training system, and were codified in the 1969 Vocational Training Act *(Berufsbildungsgesetz)* and Education Acts for VET in the *Länder* (federal regions).

At present, companies train 1.6 million young people between the ages of 16 and 22 in more than 300 recognised training occupations. This means that two-thirds of the age cohort are covered by this form of transition between school and work, of whom 58 per cent are young men and 42 per cent are young women.[1]

*This article first appeared in the National Commission on Education's March 1995 bulletin.
[1] *In 1950 the equivalent figures were 75 and 25 per cent*

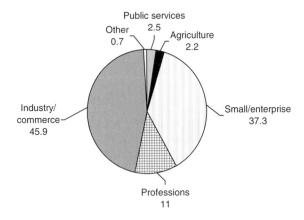

Figure 11.1 *Participation in training by sector (% of those aged 16–22, 1992)*

Figure 11.1 shows their national distribution across the half million accredited training companies, by occupational sector.

THE BASIC STRUCTURE OF GERMANY'S EDUCATION SYSTEM

There are 3.5 million pupils in primary schools in Germany. From there, pupils go on to a number of different types of secondary schools:

- *Hauptschule* (equivalent to a secondary modern school);
- *Gymnasium* (equivalent to a grammar school);
- *Realschule* (in between a secondary modern school and a grammar school);
- Comprehensive school;
- Special school.

The first three types each cater for around 1.5 million pupils.[2] Most of the 16 *Länder* have introduced comprehensive schools as an additional type of school, catering for 0.4 million pupils; 250,000 pupils attend special schools.

At the level of upper secondary education (after 15), the *Gymnasium* prepares young people for higher education and the Dual System prepares young people for work in particular occupations. It is 'dual' in the sense that it combines employer-provided training with part-time education at vocational schools *(Berufsschulen)*. In addition, a large

[2]*Source: BMBW, Basic and Structural Data 1993–4*

number of full-time vocational schools offer 1–3 year programmes which have three functions:

- preparing young people for higher education in a vocational sixth form (*Fachoberschule*);
- improving the chances of school leavers obtaining the most sought-after places in the Dual System;
- offering a broad foundation in areas such as technology or commerce, designed to facilitate the transition to work.

Participation trends in upper secondary education between 1975 and 1992 show increased percentages of the 16-19 age cohort through all of the various routes. In fact, adding up the figures for 1992 gives a total of 137 per cent, showing that many young people in Germany use more than one opportunity during these three years to improve their competencies, after leaving compulsory education and before taking up work. This is one of the explanations for the relatively low rate of unemployment among young people.

ACHIEVEMENT AND PROGRESSION

Over the last 30 years Germany has seen changing attitudes towards education, with important implications for the flow of learners through the education and training system.

While the typical craft-level trainee in the 1960s came from a *Hauptschule* (more than 80 per cent), such trainees are in the minority today (40 per cent). In the 1960s, fewer than 3 per cent of trainees had achieved the *Abitur*, mainly in some selected commercial training occupations (eg banking, insurance). Today 15 per cent of all trainees (over 200,000) start with the *Abitur* behind them, in technical, commercial, craft and agricultural occupations, and also in SMEs (small and medium-sized enterprises).

The growth in education and training in the Dual System has contributed to the overall trend of rising educational achievement. Today, about two-thirds of young people start their training in the Dual System, while just 15 years ago it was less than 50 per cent.

Roughly one-third of young people study at some point for the *Abitur* at a *Gymnasium Oberstufe*, and 6 per cent attend a *Fachoberschule* leading to a *Fachabitur* (equivalent to vocational 'A' levels). A further 10 per cent of an age cohort attends other full-time vocational schools for a year of vocational preparation (*Berufsvorbereitungsjahr*) or a year of full-time education and training in an occupational training field

(*Berufsgrundbildungsjahr*). These two programmes aim to help young people make a start in the Dual System or in work. It is worth noting that full-time vocational schools have *increased* in importance as a result of the growth of the Dual System. Moreover, increasing participation in education and training over the last 20 years has made attendance at consecutive programmes of advanced-level secondary education commonplace, for example two year full-time vocational schooling followed by training in the Dual System.

The growth in participation in education and training for each generation has brought about a considerable improvement in the structure of qualifications and competence among the working population. Those holding vocational or professional qualifications have grown from 65 per cent to over 80 per cent in the last 15 years. By 2010 this percentage is expected to be 90 per cent of the working population.

ASSUMPTIONS AND CHARACTERISTICS OF THE DUAL SYSTEM

The Dual System is founded on close links between public and private training organisations, between statutory provision and provision governed by collective agreements, and between public training policy and private training investment. Its most significant characteristics are as follows:

- participation of companies is voluntary;
- standards and content of three-year training are agreed by employers and trade unions and then legally codified;
- co-operation between employers and trade unions at various levels supports and renews the system;
- independence of the system is preserved through corporate bodies (chambers);
- the system is financed mainly by corporate training providers, with supplementary funding coming from government;
- the provision of further education includes both general and occupation-related theoretical study.

A number of factors, many of them specific to Germany, contribute to the notably positive response of young people to the Dual System.

The dual system is successful because:

1. A vocational qualification confers high standing in Germany, where it is recognised that the nation can succeed in international competition only with as competent a workforce as possible.

2. In the mid-1980s, employers and trade unions placed the ability to act independently at the centre of all training programmes. The aim was for all young trainees to be able to plan, carry out and manage their own work tasks.

3. Skilled blue- and white-collar workers and SME craftsmen enjoy a high status in society. Contributing factors are the attitude of the trade unions, which see themselves as a community of skilled workers, and the important role which SMEs play in the German economy. By the 1980s the prestige of the Dual System had increased to the point that a significant proportion of all *Abitur* holders participated in it.

4. VET is a primary political concern. Since the 1970s, the government has prepared an annual report about the state of VET, including any shortcomings which have appeared. An adequate supply of accredited training places has long been a concern of the prime minister, employer organisations, trade unions and the media.

5. The Dual System is not questioned by any major political party as the most suitable system of VET. Likewise, both employers and trade unions regard it as the stable basis of their VET policy relationship, whatever other differences of outlook they may have.

6. Two large research and development institutes, the Federal Institute for Vocational Training (*Bundesinstitut für Berufsbildung*) and the Institute for Labour Market and Occupational Research (*Institut für Arbeitsmarkt- und Berufsforschung*) offer a database and advice to employers, trade unions and the government. They provide a platform for joint planning and for the improvement and adaptation of vocational training.

7. A substantial infrastructure of 385 authorised institutions manage and regulate vocational training. Most of these are the professional chambers such as those of industry and commerce, of SMEs [*Handwerks-kammer*] and of medical practitioners and of lawyers. Membership of the chambers is a statutory obligation, and they accredit organisations for training, register all training contracts, assess trainers, and conduct intermediate and final tests with the aid of tripartite examination commissions (employers, trade unions and FE teachers).

8. When planning VET (eg duration, content and level of training occupations), the government acts on the consensus principle, by building on the agreement of employers and trade unions.

9. Employers and trade unions provide on-going renewal of the training content and the examination syllabus. They are supported in this task by the Federal Institute, which continually observes changes in work processes, conducts research and

collaborates with specialists of the 'social partners' in revising the training regulations.

10. Each year 34–40 training regulations (of the 370 occupations) are revised.[3] These are frameworks and do not prescribe methods or procedures, so can be implemented by the most modern means available to training providers.

THE *BERUFSSCHULEN* IN THE DUAL SYSTEM

The *Berufsschulen* (equivalent to FE colleges for initial vocational craft/ technician level education) work in tandem with companies in three-year programmes of VET for young people in the Dual System. They operate under the jurisdiction of the *Länder* and, with schools, are within the portfolio of their Minister of Education.

Teachers in *Berufsschulen* are civil servants of the *Land*. They have a university degree (eg in economics or engineering) and a teaching diploma in a vocational field. They teach on part-time or full-time courses in initial or further vocational education and are expected to keep in touch with problems of industrial practice on a continuous basis. Instructors, on the other hand, teach workplace practice in workshops or laboratories. They are qualified as technicians or *Meister* (qualified supervisors).

Given the wide range of their tasks, *Berufsschulen* have remarkable achievements to their credit, but they are often the target of criticism. For example, changes in companies' work organisation, technology and personnel practice take place at widely different rates, but *Berufsschulen* are expected to be at the forefront at all times. Their standards are frequently compared with those of leading-edge companies, despite the limited resources at their disposal. Meanwhile, many companies, especially those with out-of-date production methods, cannot see any need for *Berufsschulen* because they fail to appreciate the importance of underpinning theory.

The Education Ministers of the *Länder* oversee the development of syllabuses for the *Berufsschulen*. These are aligned with current training regulations, and with the actual training given in companies at the local level, subject to agreement between the *Berufsschule* teachers and trainers.

---

[3] *Of the 370 odd training occupations about 100 are hardly used, though are still nominally in force*

In most of the *Länder*, weekly release from the company is legally fixed at 12 hours. The task of *Berufsschulen* is to foster the personal development of young people by means of general education (mother tongue, early stages of foreign languages, politics, sport and religion) and through an understanding of the theoretical basis of the occupation. These requirements have grown considerably in the last 20 years. Moreover, during this period the *Berufsschulen* have catered for an increasingly broad variety of students, from those without a leaving certificate up to those with the *Abitur*. The curriculum of one group may take 3.5 years while that of another takes only 2 years, although, given good performance, training contracts between trainee and company may be shortened by six months. Finally, there also remains the obligation to teach those young people without training contracts, since young people are obliged to undertake vocational education until they have reached the age of 18.

Taking into consideration the exceptionally complex tasks of the *Berufsschulen* today, they achieve their technical and pedagogical aims to a high degree.

COSTS AND BENEFITS OF VOCATIONAL TRAINING

The costs of in-company training vary widely and depend on:

- trainee wages, which are negotiated through collective agreements and depend on occupation[4] (and represent 49 per cent of the gross cost of company training);
- the extent to which training is on the job or in a training workshop;
- the use of full-time professional trainers (about 40,000), part-time qualified trainers (about 700,000), as well as a large number of 'training-qualified' blue- and white-collar workers. The cost of training personnel is 39 per cent of total costs;
- costs of management, examinations, teaching and learning materials (12 per cent of total costs).

As a result, the gross costs per year vary, according to occupation, between DM5000 and DM50,000. The Federal Institute has estimated the 'average annual gross training cost' at DM30,000. However, trainees also contribute to production, which reduces this sum by an average of DM12,000. Hence, the average net annual cost per trainee is DM18,000. In many enterprises, particularly small ones, trainees can contribute a

---

[4]*In 1993 they varied between DM680 and DM1870 per month, with an average of DM1055;*
[5]*the trainee quota is the ratio of trainees to the total employed in the company.*

great deal to production, with the result that their output at least covers the cost of their training.

There are other benefits for companies which, while often recognised, are rarely measured in cash terms. For example, training companies save recruitment and personnel costs, reduce the risks of bad selection, and save induction and socialisation costs. It is therefore not surprising that many companies attribute great advantages to training and train more young people than they need, often considerably more than the 'trainee quota'.[5]

During the latest recession, many companies, particularly large ones, drastically reduced their training effort to save expenditure.[6] Politicians, employer organisations and trade unions started a campaign to increase further the number of available training places. This campaign is already having positive effects.

The amount of trainee wages is negotiated between the employers and trade unions for each sector of industry (for example, the engineering or chemical industries). The actual amount reflects the supply of and demand for young people in the different labour markets; it averages, for example, DM700 a month for hairdressers and DM1800 for brick-layers.

The development of key capabilities

Learning through working is the fundamental principle of vocational training. It offers the most favourable conditions for the development of so-called key capabilities. These capabilities are in great demand in all forms of work because of the uncertainties and the rate of change which are a characteristic of our era. Key capabilities include the ability to take responsibility for achievement of occupational tasks, the ability to work and communicate effectively with colleagues in teams, the ability to think in terms of systems, and to learn how to learn.

However, such key capabilities are an empty shell without occupation-related skills and theoretical knowledge. The dual education and training system in companies and colleges can link practical application and experience in the workplace with underpinning theory and reflection.

Time is a key factor in the development of key capabilities. This is one of the important reasons for the relatively long duration (three years) of the dual training system. It is significant that unemployment among

[6]*eg in engineering the trainee quota fell from 6.5 to 3.5 per cent*

Dual System 'graduates', especially in the younger age groups, is persistently below national average figures.

Environmental protection in vocational education and training

Since the early 1980s, VET objectives for environmental protection have become part and parcel of curricula in in-company training and further education. Right from the start, the principle was established that VET in all training occupations should be committed to environmental protection.

In the established training occupations, the following aims are pursued with varying intensity:

- awareness of environmental issues and development of an environmental conscience;
- environmentally conscious behaviour at the workplace, especially efficient use of resources, avoidance of waste, and recycling;
- environmental protection as an occupational competence, eg in chemical occupations.

Over the last 15 years, and in pursuit of these aims, a number of concepts and measures have been developed in initial and continuing training. They now play an important role in the final tests and examinations.

PUBLIC INVESTMENT IN VOCATIONAL TRAINING

In the Dual System, enterprises bear the costs of practical training while the *Länder* pay for the further education component. The federal government and *Land* governments subsidise, or sometimes pay in full, specific areas of special interest to the nation. Some examples are discussed below.

Research in vocational training at the Federal Institute for Vocational Training

In 1996 the cost of this work was DM50 million. It was completely financed by federal government.

Promotion of group training centres

Two-thirds of all trainees are in firms with fewer than 50 employees. The federal and *Länder* governments subsidise the training efforts of these companies through group training centres, usually managed by the chambers. In 1994, subsidies for building and equipment investment costs, as well as running costs, amounted to around DM700 million.

Innovation in vocational training

The Secretary of State for Education and Science offers incentive grants for innovative developments in in-company vocational training. These amounted to 75 per cent of the costs of pilot projects, around DM15 million, in 1996. They covered such areas as the development of new methods, adaptation to technological progress, and special needs training.

Supply deficiencies in the Dual System

The Dual System does not oblige employers to train. As a consequence, several factors affect the availability of training places:

1. Since employers bear the cost of training, the general economic situation is of particular importance.
2. The geographical distribution of 'training companies' results in regional differences.
3. What training is available depends on the structure of different industrial sectors, eg mechanical engineering, car manufacture and repair, building and construction.
4. The present lack of a sufficient number of medium-sized companies in former East Germany has created a special regional problem.

However, the Federal Constitutional Court, the highest German court, ruled in 1980 that the government is responsible for ensuring that sufficient training places are provided when companies cannot secure an adequate supply of training.

Lack of in-company training places in East Germany

The national training system is spreading into the new private company structures in former East Germany. In practical terms, this means building a new Dual System in East Germany. Public funds are being used to rent additional training facilities, engage training personnel and subsidise training places in companies. The Federal Labour Office (*Bundesanstalt für Arbeit*) finances around 15 per cent of the 280,000 training places in special training facilities at an approximate cost of DM900 million in 1996. Meanwhile, the new *Länder* encourage new enterprises to provide training by offering them special grants costing in excess of DM400 million.

The training of those with special needs

It is an agreed policy to train as many young people with special needs as possible in the Dual System. This is reflected in the fact that each year there are between 30,000 and 40,000 young people without a certificate of secondary education, or coming from special needs schools, who gain access to the Dual System. There is also special provision for both young people and adults so severely handicapped that they cannot be placed in ordinary employment. Initial and continuing training facilities have been put in place by the Secretary of State for Employment and Social Services in which such people with special needs (more than 90,000 in 1995) are trained and cared for. This is funded by the Federal Office for Labour to the extent of DM2500 million in 1995.

OUTLOOK

During the coming decades, an increase in the popularity of school leaving examinations, especially the *Abitur*, is likely, widening access to further and higher education.

A survey of secondary school pupils early in 1995 showed that the modest decline in demand for training places in the Dual System has come to an end or is reverting to slow growth. Therefore, we can anticipate a general increase in participation in learning activities, with further increases in the demand for educational provision in *Gymnasia*, vocational full-time schools and in the Dual System, at the expense of the *Hauptschulen*.

12

The Role of Trade Unions and Works Councils

Dr Wolfgang Lecher, Lecturer in Sociology, Economics and Philosophy, Tübingen and Frankfurt am Main

THE CORE OF THE GERMAN INDUSTRIAL RELATIONS SYSTEM: WORKS COUNCILS AND COLLECTIVE BARGAINING

Industrial relations in the Federal Republic of Germany are defined by the dual system of representation of interests embodied in 'collective bargaining freedom and participation'. (Possibly the best introduction in English to the German industrial relations system is given by Jacobi *et al.*, 1992.) In the German collective bargaining system, the institutions are separated into trade unions and works councils. There is a corresponding separation of trade union collective bargaining policy and works council policy on internal agreements; and there is a separation of the right to strike at the collective bargaining level, and peace in industrial relations at the works constitution level. In this structure of representation, collective bargaining freedom and (participatory) rights which are provided by law play the predominant role; a fact which clearly indicates the very high level of statutory regulation of industrial relations in Germany compared to the situation in many other countries. But these rights merely establish the basic outline. How industrial relations are organised in concrete terms depends on many different circumstances, such as the industrial relations climate between state, employers' associations and trade unions (which is determined by the political climate); on the state's informal moves to intervene in collective bargaining disputes; on the strengths and weaknesses of the contracting parties in collective bargaining; and on the varying impact of participation at workplace, plant, group, macroeconomic and, more recently, also European level (European works councils).

Collective bargaining freedom in Germany is determined by the only 'group right' in the German Constitution and safeguards what is known as coalition freedom, coalitions being trade unions and employers' associations. The actual collective bargaining policy pursued within the framework of the Constitution is not determined by the trade union or employer umbrella organisations but by the individual unions and the sectoral employers' associations. Legally, the state has no right to intervene in their collective bargaining freedom and there is thus, for example, no compulsory arbitration by the State in the event of a strike. This, however, does not preclude possibilities of bringing influence to bear indirectly through targeted information, media policy, public pressure by the government, etc.

As is the case in other countries, collective bargaining policy relates primarily to wages, working conditions and working time. These are negotiated by collective bargaining parties, and any government regulations have to come second. The trade unions are not subordinate to political parties; the principle of the non-partisan, united trade union precludes such indirect government or party influence on trade union policy and thus on collective bargaining policy such as occurs in countries with factional trade unions. On the contrary, the parties are assessed by the trade unions and gauged according to the extent to which they are geared to working people. This is done regularly in elections by means of what are termed trade union electoral touchstones. The trade unions are thus non-partisan but by no means non-political.

The right to strike is an important trade union instrument in the context of collective bargaining freedom and an important means of exerting pressure in order to achieve the conclusion of collective agreements; its employer counterpart is the lockout. This is where bargaining freedom becomes practical, although the trade unions take the view that the possibilities for lockouts in Germany, which, compared to other countries, are very extensive, violate equality of weapons. As a result, the fight against lockouts is a constant topic of debate in industrial relations in Germany.

Some figures will give a general idea of the dimension of collective bargaining (discussed in detail in Bispinck, 1993): there are currently some 35,000 collective agreements in effect in Germany covering

90 per cent of the labour force. The subjects of these agreements are wages and salaries, fringe benefits (holiday bonus, insurance contributions, employers' contributions to tax-deductible savings schemes, etc.), working time, qualification and further training; in other words, working conditions in the broadest sense of the term. The terms of the agreements and terms of notice are laid down in each specific agreement. Employers and unions are then committed to refraining from industrial action during those periods. Both sides must belong to associations which are authorised to bargain collectively. Where this is not the case, the collective agreement is void and its obligations are not liable to penalty by law. If a strike is to be called when the commitment to refrain from industrial action expires, a strike vote must be held by secret ballot and a vote must likewise be held on termination of the industrial action.

Improvement of the collective agreement on individual points may be, and indeed is, achieved in company agreements concluded between the works council and the management. This is one of the most important functions of works council participation and it thus constitutes one of the links between collective and company bargaining policy. One of the major objectives of the trade unions is thus to achieve a system of representation, ie a system where elected representatives (from trade unions as far as possible) carry out the function of participation, and thus can carry through their own ideas on economic and social policy as distinct from those of parties and the state. The struggle for participation in the narrower sense is thus always also a struggle to extend trade union rights. The current participatory institutions cover various levels, various forms and varying prospects of exerting influence (see Lecher and Naumann, 1991). These levels include:

- the workplace: efforts are being made to develop this level further, particularly since it has been becoming increasingly clear that the workplace level is gaining considerable significance as a result of the introduction of new technologies and new modes of work organisation in companies, and the provision of qualifications which this requires (further details below);
- the plant/company: the *Works Constitution Act* applies here, laying down the rights of works councils. The same applies in the case of the public services with their *Staff Representation Act* and staff committees;
- the undertaking: the statutory rules on supervisory board participation apply here for supervisory boards on which the parties have different ratios;
- and finally, the macroeconomic level: there are as yet no arrangements governing participation at this level. Regional co-ordination (in the context of European structural aids, for example), which

is becoming increasingly important, has been carried out to date without any appreciable trade union influence.

The various participation possibilities are as follows:

- systems of representation: these cover works councils and supervisory boards, where the same persons are sometimes members of both bodies;
- sectoral collective agreements, which, both qualitatively and quantitatively, have always been, and still are, the most important field of action in the German industrial relations system;
- informal corporate arrangements between the management and the works council on possibilities for participating in efforts to resolve company problems; these arrangements are not safeguarded by legislation and thus depend on the readiness of both parties to negotiate. They include, in particular, arrangements on the introduction of new technologies and the changes in the organisation of work which this necessitates. This is a possible field of action for the participation of works councils in decisions concerning the workplace, and for the prospective action of European works councils at group level.

And finally, participation rules have varying prospects of exerting influence, for example:

- the right of initiative and the right of veto, particularly in the context of the *Works Constitution Act* and, here again, on personnel issues and questions of working time. Works councils have a right of veto, for example, with regard to the approval of overtime;
- monitoring rights, which are granted to supervisory boards in particular. These rights have recently been a subject of debate, however, because trade union and/or company supervisory boards generally do not have the same level of information at their disposal as do providers of capital, and their rights can therefore only be exercised to a limited extent;
- the consultation rights, which works councils hold primarily in economic questions and which are exercised much more frequently;
- the information rights to which the works council and the supervisory board are entitled in economic and social issues. These also form the crucial field of action of the European works councils.

As regards the various levels, forms and prospects of influence, it can thus be concluded that statutory participation rights differ widely from relative strength on the one hand, so far as personnel and social measures are concerned, to relative weakness on the other, in the case of economic decisions.

TRADE UNIONS: STATE AND PERSPECTIVES

How has this industrial relations system with its two fundamental components of 'collective bargaining freedom' and 'participation' (and, above all, the combination of the two) – a fairly original system compared to those prevailing in other countries – stood the test of time in the past few years? At first sight, the German trade unions are quite impressive. Membership density is about 40 per cent and 35 per cent of the membership are organised in DGB (German TUC equivalent) affiliates. In absolute figures in 1995 9.35 million employees were organised in DGB unions. Compared to the drastic drop in membership figures in many other European countries and the situation in the United States and Japan, one can talk of relative stability as far as Germany is concerned. Membership structures, however, correspond less and less to employment structures. Whereas the proportion of white-collar employees has now increased to over 50 per cent of the total number of employed persons, now only 23 per cent of the members of DGB unions are white-collar workers. The proportion of women members is also 23 per cent, whereas almost 40 per cent of the total number of people in work are women. The trend is even less favourable when it comes to young workers; only 13 per cent of young workers are members of a trade union, and the number of young members has been on the decline for years in the majority of DGB affiliates. There is also a shift in the ratio of full-time employees to part-time employees, the unemployed and retired workers. These structural shifts are reflected not least in the growing financial difficulties experienced by the trade unions, whose membership as a whole is decreasing due to rising unemployment, part-time work and the disproportionately low percentage of highly skilled and thus well-paid workers.

If we attempt to summarise the trade union situation in comparison with the other EU countries, the following comments can be made:

- In the German Federal Republic the instrument of free collective bargaining as the free negotiation of working conditions between employer associations and trade unions, in particular at the sectoral level, has proved to be productive, progressive and also flexible. Trade union membership density is (still) sufficiently high to enable the unions to use this instrument to counter government deregulation measures (which, it is true, have in most cases merely been announced, but have by no means resulted in such extensive intervention as in the United Kingdom, for example).
- The separation of political parties and trade unions as different pillars of the worker movement is likewise firmly established and has stood the test of time. Throughout Europe, trade unions with

definite political leanings have, without exception, greater problems of acceptance in society than do unions which are independent of political parties. When parties and trade unions are too closely linked, this is evidently harmful for both organisations in the long run.

- Although the dual system of representation of employees' interests through trade unions (collective bargaining policy and the right to strike) and works councils (company agreements involving the commitment to refrain from industrial action) now runs smoothly on the whole and is productive, there is the constant latent problem of the council members becoming independent of the trade unions. These problems are liable to become intensified as ideas of participation in decisions relating to the workplace become more definite. But the system does have the capacity to deal with problems flexibly as well as great capacity for compromise, owing to the fact that the authorisation bases of the two pillars on which it rests are different.

- The participation system which has been established by law in Germany is thus geared mainly to plants/companies and undertakings. In view of the growing need for employees to have a say in the introduction of technological innovations and new forms of work organisation, the demand for constant further qualification and the intensifying debate on a collective bargaining capacity which is co-ordinated at the European level, the German industrial relations system needs to be revised on at least two points. These are direct participation (participation at the workplace) and the introduction of European works councils.

SOCIAL PRODUCTIVITY AND DIRECT PARTICIPATION

The German trade unions have been considering a change of outlook in the past few years aimed at taking an active role in the planning, introduction and control of new technologies and the flexibility this involves regarding the organisation of work, qualifications and wages. Roth and Kohl (1985) pioneered trade union adoption of the topic, particularly in the largest German union, IG Metall. Cf. Lecher (1991) for further orientation of this discussion towards the flexibility and productivity potential of participation in decisions concerning the workplace.) This change has far-reaching consequences for the trade unions and their relations with employees and the structures for representing their interests in the company (and thus for the industrial relations system as a whole).

The company and the workplace are tending to become the most important context for taking a critical look at, and shaping, technology-induced work processes involving new forms of work organisation, even if it must be borne in mind that the company or plant is incorporated into the higher-level central planning and management system of the undertaking or group of undertakings. Within the framework of the dual system in Germany, works councils are becoming more significant than the trade union organisations operating above the company level. At the same time, however, they have to deal with the possibilities of non-representative, direct employee participation in decisions concerning the workplace. Trade union bargaining policy is tending to become a framework policy for differentiated company agreements between works councils and company management. The determination of wages, for instance, should no longer be linked only to the current job activity and performance of the individual, but should also be commensurate with the qualifications held and system-related (group) performance potential. Through participation at the workplace, which has hitherto been omitted to a large extent in the German system, it has now become possible to achieve decentralised flexibility, social productivity and the humanisation of work.

The move to open industrial relations systems and downwards towards direct participation is, incidentally, to be observed in all highly industrialised countries. (The problems of efficient coordination of indirect and direct participation which inevitably ensue and are crucial for works councils and trade unions are discussed in the European context by Krieger and Lange (1992).) In 1986, there were already four million quality circles involving some 40 million employees, and there has meanwhile been a tremendous increase in the United States, the 'Small Tigers' of East Asia and in Europe in particular. But it is not only the fact that the system has spread that clearly indicates that the participatory concept is successful; the fact that the quality circle concept has been developed further into new forms of production and work organisation, such as total quality management (TQM) – for example, approximately 1.8 million employees were involved in TQM at the beginning of the 1990s – is further proof of its success. When one considers further elements of group work (up to 8 per cent of the people employed in automobile production including the subcontracting industries were recorded in Germany in 1992) and financial participation in the results of the undertaking (just under 20 per cent of all workers in France are involved), then the trade unions are clearly facing a massive challenge to provide constructive answers. This means that they themselves and/or the traditional representative structure at the company level must join these new participation models, in order to avoid the situation where the workforce is reduced under the fashionable slogan of 'lean production', but also in order to be able to play a role in the shaping of humane working conditions.

The (re)discovery of the subjective factor of productivity – which has always been predominant with British classicists as living work as opposed to dead work (capital) – is, however, only one aspect of the issue. Further aspects, which are at least as interesting and important, are the market-related technical and qualification-related innovations which rank high in the developed industrialised countries and the relevant multinational subcontracting firms. These factors are as follows:

- the growing need for flexibility as the result of changing market requirements (keywords: diversified production of quality goods in small series);
- changes in the employment market owing to the growing supply of qualified and well-trained workers;
- the scope for rationalisation, organisation and flexibility offered by the new microelectronically aided technologies;
- the counter-productive elements of the classical Taylorist system of organising work (keywords: extremely short task cycles and excessive fragmentation of tasks);
- experiments and empirical examples of possibilities for linking individual employee interests with a new style of work organisation in the company (keywords: production islands, partially autonomous groups, team and group work).

The last point in particular refers to a concept of workplace participation as the point of departure for achieving 'alternative' quality circles. The following aspects could be quoted as essential points of such a model of work organisation which is geared to workers and socially oriented: the employees concerned should be represented through a combination of direct participation and (classical) representative participation, since it is not possible, particularly in the case of major projects (such as the introduction of CAD/CAM in the plant), for all of the persons concerned to participate in all tasks and decisions to the same extent. The representation should be carried out by union-oriented employees so as to ensure there is a link between participation in decisions concerning the workplace and the trade unions and works councils. As a general principle, individual participation must be integrated into the existing (works council/trade union related) system of collective representation of interests so as to avoid a situation where groups with varying involvement are played off against one another (rationalisation winners against rationalisation losers, the regular workforce against the fringe workforce). This will be one of the most difficult tasks of the trade unions and in particular of works councils.

Those affected by the introduction of new technologies, and thus by the work organisation and qualification measures this entails must, as a fundamental principle, be given the opportunity also to meet the management and the people in charge of developing the technology and work organisation systems in their own working groups, in addition to and independent of joint project groups, with a view to discussing and organising their objectives. A co-ordinated participation infrastructure must thus be built up within the company, the fundamental element being the participation of those concerned in decisions concerning the workplace. And finally, this complex model of participation must be regulated in some sort of binding form (eg through a company agreement between the management and the works council, where possible on the basis of a collective framework agreement between the trade unions and the employers' association). This would guarantee continuity and a habitual pattern of conduct, since these are the preconditions for the long-term success of such decentralised participation in decisions concerning the workplace.

These requirements entail both effects in the field of performance-related pay, which has predominated hitherto, and new problems for the trade union representation of interests:

- With the introduction of new integral work activities and the organisation of work in groups, the subjective aspect is likely to be enhanced. This will bring a departure from quantifiable performance scales relating solely to results (time-related piece-work systems, bonus pay, Time and Motion Measurements). On the other hand, subjective performance criteria related to an individual's conduct and motivation will become more important. This includes willingness to co-operate, loyalty to the company, identification with company objectives and other virtues which are deemed positive, ie social qualifications which are not related to any specific process and/or extra-functional social qualifications.
- This at the same time involves a development from result-related individual performance to group-related system performance. Labour qualifications which are not related directly to individual tasks are gaining importance.
- Time-related, performance-controlled forms of remuneration (prescribed time to be worked on standard pay) will become more significant. Performance requirements will be prescribed for the fixed hourly wage; these requirements will no longer apply to the individual worker but will be calculated for entire groups and departments as system-related production reference numbers (relating to production targets).
- With these trends the negotiation of agreements between employees and/or works councils and management, as a performance

programme which is accepted by both parties, will become more important than the traditional and often pseudo-scientific registration of quantified individual performance. Fairness standards and concepts of fair pay will become more important than the quantification of work performed, which has prevailed hitherto.

- If the traditional elements of performance registration and the corresponding assignment of pay lose significance, new forms of participation in the negotiation of the performance compromise must be implemented through collective bargaining and at company/plant level. New tasks facing trade unions and works councils are thus to shape this process of negotiation and to standardise the rules of the system accordingly. The essential factor is now to transform the piece-rate policy which has prevailed hitherto into a real performance policy for integral tasks and group work, within the framework of a collective bargaining policy geared to working time and technology. The requirement for trade unions and works councils to shape that policy actively is growing in comparison to the performance control activity which has prevailed hitherto.

Participation at the workplace will thus play an important role in the future as a socially oriented model of participation which complements, but also contrasts with, the relevant social techniques employed by management. What is important for trade unions is to combine these possibilities for direct participation sensibly and effectively with the representative participation which has prevailed hitherto.

THE FUTURE POSITION OF EUROPEAN WORKS COUNCILS IN THE GERMAN INDUSTRIAL RELATIONS SYSTEM

In addition to developing direct participation, the second challenge for the German industrial relations system is presented by the process of internationalisation, which has been institutionalised through the enactment of the European Commission Directive on European works councils (EWCs). Obtaining information from the transnational group of undertakings in question for the body representing employees' interests in the respective national sections of the group, however, is not the sole function of a European works council. These councils are just as much a channel through which knowledge of the various industrial relations and trade union representation systems in the different countries can be acquired, and the national industrial relations systems gradually integrated Europe-wide. Rehfeldt (1994) points expressly to this dual aspect, which is extremely important for building up a future European industrial relations structure.) The establishment of European works councils (EWCs) thus also affects the trade unions.

The following comments give a brief description of the directive and a critical assessment from the trade union point of view, as well as proposals for linking and/or integrating the future EWCs into the future decisive articulations of the industrial relations system: extended participation in decisions concerning the workplace and the ability to bargain at supranational level.

After many years of debate and after the failure of the 'compensatory social dialogue' of the two sides of industry at the EU level, the directive on the establishment of European works councils was adopted by the EU Council of Ministers of Social Affairs in September 1994 and should be nationally implemented two years later. (Blanpain and Windey (1994) give the best and most complete survey of the vicissitudes of the history of the directive right through to its adoption.) It lays down procedures for informing and consulting employees' representatives for the approximately 1500 undertakings currently operating on the European scale. To fall within the field of application of the directive, a group of undertakings must have a total of 1000 employees in the 11 EU Member States (except for the UK, which has opted out of these issues by declining to sign the Maastricht Social Protocol) and 150 employees in each of at least two member states.

Where this is the case, negotiations are held between the central management of the undertaking and a special body of employees' representatives on the forming of the EWC, provided, however, that this is requested by at least 100 employees and/or their representatives from at least two establishments in at least two different member states. The tasks, composition, term of office, frequency and length of sessions and, not least, the financial and material resources to be made available for the establishment and operation of the EWC are laid down by this negotiating body. Employees can consult trade union representatives, who act as experts. The cost of these negotiations is borne by the undertaking.

The German trade unions welcome the establishment of EWCs. The EWC directive will also stimulate the debate on the inclusion of the trade unions and thus, in the final analysis, of collective bargaining policy for crossfrontier undertakings. This applies especially to monistic systems (apart from the UK, the Scandinavian countries in particular and also Italy), where trade union bargaining policy takes place at the plant/company level and there is thus a direct combination of information and consultation rights deriving from the directive and the exercise of those rights for collective bargaining policy at the company level. But it is also clear that with the establishment of EWCs, the trade unions will be directing their attention not only to the supranational level, but also to the possible changes at the company level in the various groups of undertakings falling within the field of application of the directive.

The practical implementation of this directive in dual representation systems, such as the system in the Federal Republic of Germany, could also lead to the information possibilities thus acquired being used at two levels. On the one hand, the European works councils could try to reach a sort of European group company agreement with the management. The EWC level would probably play the weakest part in the works council/national works council/group works council/EWC hierarchy to begin with, and the employers' associations are still absolutely against the directive being used in that way. But it is by no means to be ruled out in the future, particularly in the context of the promotion of corporate identity. Arrangements of this nature would, however, have an inherent tendency to corporate trade unionism, which would mean a certain amount of exclusivity of industrial relations within the group as far as the national industrial relations environment is concerned. A mechanism of this nature could result, in the long term, in exclusion from the national industrial relations system.

However, it would also be conceivable, and most desirable for the trade unions and for the standardisation of industrial relations systems at the European level, if the national trade unions operating in the respective groups of undertakings would co-ordinate their activities and make the information received from the European works councils the basis of real collective bargaining talks and agreements with the competent employers' associations. But the precondition for this would be that the trade unions concerned collaborate constantly on group-related issues and that the employers' associations agree to this type of negotiating system. (It was J. van Rens (1991), the Head of the International Department of the Dutch trade union confederation FNV, who made this interesting forward-looking proposal, which has also been taken up in the programme of the European Trade Union Confederation.) Both prospects seem unreal for the time being, but they should not be ruled out completely given the novelty and openness of the EWC instrument.

A final aspect of the possibilities of EWCs results from the dual development of contemporary economic and production logic towards greater decentralisation (decentralisation down to the plant/company level, direct participation, participatory management) and at the same time greater globalisation (internationalisation, trans-border business structures, corporate identity, the development of European identity under the pressure of world market competition, particularly in the triad). In a forward-looking EWC model, the attempt should at least be made to bring these opposite poles closer together, primarily according to the three criteria of the structure of the institutions to be created, the procedure for electing the representative body and the good flow of information desired between the various levels: plant/company, undertaking, national group management (sub-group) and transnational group management.

The following problems have been identified on the basis of the limited experience gained to date with voluntarily agreed EWCs in several transnational European groups of undertakings (based mainly on the research fundings of Streeck and Vitols (1993) and Marginson (1994):

- the fact that the institutional rules depend on the goodwill of the management (there is no entitlement guaranteed by law);
- the fact that the quantity and quality of information is left to the discretion of the management (here again there are no legal guarantees);
- the uncertainty about one's own position, ie on the one hand mainly 'national identity' and thus national co-operation between the management and the body representing employees' interests, particularly in the relationship of parent companies and subsidiaries; and, on the other hand, the predominance of the international collaboration of European works councils over national interests;
- language-related communication problems and major problems in the building of confidence at supranational level between the various bodies representing employees' interests;
- familiarisation with the different respective national representation structures, their working methods and mentalities (eg German works council members' problems with the positions of British shop stewards and the non-organised members in France);
- assessment of the significance of information provided by the management, and the difficulties in disseminating this down to the plant/company level.

OUTLOOK

The dual system of employee representation through trade unions (collective bargaining, backed up by the right to strike) and works councils (workplace agreements and the obligation to maintain industrial peace) has proved to be effective both as a system of representation and in terms of economic efficiency. However, there are latent problems related to the issue of the autonomy of works councils, and their scope for pursuing localised and special interests, especially when placed under economic pressure. This issue has now emerged as an acute difficulty for the unions (and, in fact, for employers' organisations) in eastern Germany, where local managements and works councils have sought to be exempted from the wage rates specified in industry agreements. Moreover, this question could also take on greater significance in the longer term should hopes for enhanced co-determination at workplace level come to fruition. But the system does provide a relatively flexible mechanism for resolving problems and a relatively high capacity for achieving compromise, as each of the two components of the respective systems derives its legitimacy from different roots.

The existing system of statutory co-determination is primarily concerned with the individual establishment and the firm. Given the greater need for employee co-determination at the immediate workplace, on issues such as technical and organisational innovation and the need to develop regional and structural policies at European level, there is both scope and some imperative for the extension of co-determination to these, as yet untackled, fields of activity. Meeting the need and aspirations for individual and collective co-determination, and thus contributing to industrial peace and social harmony, requires a structure of employee, works council and trade union influence at all these levels.

Looking to the future, complex and highly industrialised societies, such as Germany, still have to grasp the full implications of the fact that their system of industrial relations, with its associated impact on employee motivation, represents a central, productive social force which is no less important than the customary technical and economic components of productivity. The crucial issue for the trade unions in the short and medium term is whether they can link the related issues of economic efficiency and social progress in a form which benefits working people and does not exclude unemployed and whether they can reach a European organisation and bargaining level. In view of German economic strength within the European Union, how these issues are resolved within Germany will also have a major impact on the rest of Europe. At the moment, the employers have accumulated years of experience in wielding the 'soft technologies' of quality circles, user involvement and corporate culture, and the internationalisation of capital is unequivocally predominant. The trade unions still have much ground to make up.

REFERENCES

Bispinck, R. (1993) 'Deutschland' in Bispinck, R. and Lecher, W. (ed.) *Tarifpolitik und Tarifsysteme in Europa* (Collective bargaining policy and collective bargaining systems in Europe), Cologne: pp. 48–79.

Blanpain, R. and Windey, F. (1994) *The European Directive on European Works Councils Information and Consultation of Employees in Multinational Enterprises in Europe*, Louvain:

Jacobi, O., Keller, B. and Müller Jentsch, W. (1992) 'Codetermining the future', in Ferner, A. and Hyman, R. (ed.) *Industrial Relations in the New Europe*, Oxford/Cambridge, MA: pp. 218–69.

Krieger, H. and Lange, R. (1992) 'Der "New Deal" für die neunziger Jahre: die Verzahnung repräsentativer und direkter Arbeitnehmerbeteiligung in Europa (The new deal for the nineties: Dovetailing representative and direct employee participation in Europe), *WSI-Mitteilungen*, 12, pp. 788–99.

Lecher, W. (1991) 'Den Tiger reiten Soziale Produktiviäat und direkte Partizipation' (Riding the tiger: Social productivity and direct participation), *Gewerhschaftliche Monatshefte*, 2, pp. 103–109.

Lecher, W. and Naumann, R. (1991) 'Bundesrepublik Deutschland' in Däubler, W. and Lecher, W. (eds) *Die Gewerkschaften in den 12 EG-Ländern Europäische Integration und Gewerkschaftsbewegung*. (The trade unions in the 12 EC countries, European integration and the trade union movement), Cologne: pp. 24–31.

Marginson, F. (1994) 'Freiwillig vereinbarte Europäische, Betriebsräte: Voraussetzungen und Probleme für Management und Gewerkschaften' in Lecher, W. and Platzer, H. W. *Europäische Union Europäische Arbeitubeziehungen? Nationale Vorraussetzungen und Internationaler Rasmen* (European Union European industrial relations? National preconditions and international framework), Cologne.

Rehfeldt, U. (1994) 'Die "europäischen Konzernräte": Bilanz der französischen Initiativen' (The European 'group councils: a survey of initiatives in France) in Lecher, W. and Platzer, H. W. (eds) *Europäische Union Europäische Arbeitsbeziehungen? Nationale Voraussetzungen und internationaler Rahmen* (European Union European industrial relations? National preconditions and international framework), Cologne.

Roth, S. and Kohl, H. (eds) (1988) *Perspective: Gruppenarbeit* (The group-work prospect), Cologne.

Streeck, W. and Vitols, S. (1993) *European Works Councils: Between Statutory Enactment and Voluntary Adaptation*, Discussion paper WZB.

Van Rens, J. (1991) 'Europa-weite Bündelung der Kräfte in gewerkschaftlichen Joint-Ventures' (Pan-European concentration of forces in trade union joint ventures), *Die Mitbestimmung* B, pp. 291–3.

13

The Market Research Market

Walter Tacke, Market Research and Communications Consultant

OVERALL DEVELOPMENT OF THE MARKET RESEARCH MARKET IN GERMANY

The market research market in Germany is growing at a rate that is above average. As a result of this, in 1998 a 14 per cent increase in turnover was achieved. At the same time the number of employees in this sector rose by 12 per cent.

In 1998 the German market research institutes generated a turnover of DM2.334 billion (1997 – DM2.032 billion) of which 64 per cent (1997 – 69 per cent) was domestic research, and 36 per cent (1997 – 31 per cent) foreign research.

In spite of this increase, Germany was overtaken for the first time by Great Britain in terms of turnover which was acknowledged during the ESOMAR Congress in Berlin October 1998. The following table shows the comparable development since 1993:

Table 13.1   *Turnover development Germany/ Great Britain 1993–1997*

Turnover (ECUmn)	1993	1994	1995	1996	1997
Germany	703	780	875	922	1035
Great Britain	599	675	730	823	1192

Britain's unusual increase in turnover value from 1996 to 1997 (45 per cent) was based mostly on the rising strength of the pound sterling.

The market research institutes' most important client is the consumer goods industry, which is responsible for 55 per cent of turnover, followed by media and publishing houses that account for 15 per cent, as the following table of trends shows:

Table 13.2   *Customer turnover distribution 1996–1998*

Customer	Turnover distribution 1996 (%)	Turnover distribution 1998 (%)
Consumer and durable goods industry	63	55
Media and publishing houses	17	15
Other customers (associations, service providers, authorities etc)	20	30
Total	100	100

The number of private research institutes, field organisations, market research consultants and studios is also increasing year by year.

The current list of the top ten German market research institutes is as follows:

Table 13.3   *The ten largest German market research institutes*

Number	Institute	Turnover (DM million)
1	GfK Group, Nuremberg	600.0
2	Infratest Burke, Munich	360.0
3	IMS, Frankfurt	180.0
4	AC Nielsen	149.0
5	INRA, Mölln	92.2
6	Icon, Nuremberg	65.4
7	Ipsos (GFM-Getas), Hamburg	55.4
8	IVE, Hamburg	50.5
9	EMNID, Bielefeld	50.0
10	Kehrmann, Hamburg	20.0

In particular, opinion research continually gains significance in the media because they talk more and more about how it is not so much the facts that are important, but rather the opinions about them. Nowadays, opinions are the facts.

This latest development caused the former federal president, Richard von Weizsäcker, to say that in Germany one no longer lives in a democracy, but rather a public opinion research democracy.

In spite of this market development in favour of opinion research there is no firm or state-recognised vocational training for public opinion researchers. This fact carries the great disadvantage that anyone who is attracted to this career can open a market research institute or set up a practice as a market research consultant overnight, without any appropriate qualification.

However, since market, opinion and social research services are exclusively carried out in accordance with set rules and regulations, and because the quality of services cannot be judged completely by clients, due to the complexity of the research process, standards for the professional competence of the research institute must surely be set.

These not new but important findings have resulted in a wide discussion about quality assurance being undertaken within German market research circles.

In particular the *Arbeitskreis Deutscher Markt- und Sozialforschungsinstitute e.V.* (ADM) (Association of German Market and Social Research Institutes) and the *Berufsverband Deutscher Markt- und Sozialforscher e.V.* (BVM) (Association of German Market and Social Researchers) are taking pains to bring to the fore that which is always facing them – quality assurance.

An article by the ADM, *Standards zur Qualitätssicherung in der Markt- und Sozialforschung*, ('Quality Assurance Standards in Market and Social Research') highlights a current agreement with the BVM, with regard to deepening the understanding of the quality of the research process and bringing to the fore the necessity for higher quality research results.

Further, these standards for quality assurance should form a scientific-methodical basis for the ISO 9000 certification of market and social research institutes.

This chapter deals with the following subject areas:

- working with the client;
- conceptual study management;
- obtaining data;
- data processing;
- client consultation.

SPECIFIC MARKET DEVELOPMENTS AND INFORMATION REQUIREMENTS

Market development is currently being shaped by a series of important demographic, economic, social and consumer trends. Market research has to take these varying developments into account.

The following identified trends are of prime importance:

- Shrinking of the population (increasing age; advanced education; proletarisation of academics; higher proportion of foreigners (guest workers); war refugees; growth of the single household, etc);
- Economic development is being held back by a series of restraints (huge tax charges because of the high state quota; increasing debt of public-owned industry; high payments to East Germany, Eastern Europe, the EU and the third world; Germany being an extortionately expensive production centre);
- Social development is being more strongly determined due to the following trends:
  - Society is becoming more complex and individualisation is increasing;
  - The change in values is becoming more dynamic and because of that consumer opinions, attitudes and behaviour change considerably;
  - Consumer needs are more varied, but also increasingly determined by irrational, incalculable and unpredictable factors;
  - The effects and consequences of societal, state and economic measures, such as laws, regulations, reforms and social requirements are more difficult to predict;
  - The information overload of the population is leading to a permanent increase in selection, but also to a lack of orientation.

In spite of this there are so-called 'megatrends' which dominate the market. These can be described as follows:

- Everything is becoming increasingly 'glocal': on the one hand the world is becoming more like a village, due to electronic media; on the other hand the motto 'all business is local' is becoming increasingly valid;

- Overall, regionalisation is coming to the fore. This is particularly apparent by the regional cakes and recipes that are highlighted;
- Geographically orientated target group concepts (micro-geographical analyses and market segmentation) are on the advance;
- We are confronted with a growing experience and free-time movement while simultaneously implementing strict economic, rational behaviour;
- Faith Popcorn's 'cocooning' trend (keeping yourself within your own four walls) has in the meantime caught hold of 40 per cent of German citizens, as an extensive, empirical survey discovered (*Das Kundenbaometer*, 1994, p.79);
- Since the consumer believes he has less time, he relies more and more on convenience. Railway station services, service station shops, kiosks and bistros are the modern 'docking places' for single people – both younger and older – and young couples without children;
- The breaking up of mass production is also being established, resulting in gourmet cat food and an increasing variety of tastes, eg tomato soup vs children's soup.

In the meantime, some sectors (air travel, motor vehicles) are talking about one-to-one marketing.

These development trends which have been described have a positive effect on market research because the market behaviour of consumers today is, in part, the rubbish of tomorrow.

The proximity of consumers and the need to be up-to-date with changing behaviour signifies the current development and the increasing importance of market research in Germany.

The indirect result is an increased demand for information that must be of a less theoretical nature and directed more towards the actual behaviour of consumers.

Convenience, the drawing on experience, and attractive prices are the fundamental drivers of current buying behaviour.

THE STRUCTURE OF GERMAN MARKET RESEARCH INSTITUTES

The structure of German market research institutes is quite different. Their diversity is characterised by the diversity of work, which varies in content and is sometimes highly specialised. It is a matter of differentiating between market research institutes, field organisations, market research consultants, studios and EDP (electronic data processing) service providers (see *BVM Handbuch der Marktforschungsunternehmen* 1996 and *Context*, 'Vertraulicher Informationsdienst zu Fragen der Kommunikation in Wirtschaft und Gesellschaft', (Confidential Information Service for Questions of Communication in Economy and Society).

The numbers can be broken down as follows:

- 426 market research institutes;
- 37 field organisations;
- 41 market research consultants;
- 152 test studios;
- 31 other service providers (EDP evaluation etc).

As far as market research institutes are concerned, predominantly they are so-called 'mixed institutes' ie most of them carry out all popular methods of market research, as opposed to just one. They offer:

- every single method which is useful to the investigation and collection of information, facts, opinions, attitudes and behavioural traits;
- fundamental studies on market sectors for consumer goods, durable consumer goods (utility goods) and industrial goods;
- the study of desires and needs, as well as expectations and fears etc towards producers, that is to say service providers, brands, products (so-called 'motivational studies');
- investigation into number of users, buyers' share and their change, as well as market fluctuation;
- investigations into the awareness of brands and companies, and assessments of the image of goods, brands and producers;
- product, price, packaging, marketing and advertising tests;
- studies into readership structures;
- control of advertising effects etc;
- investigations into the flow of goods from producer via trader (wholesaler or retailer) to the consumer in terms of different parameters (sales, turnover, market share, distribution, stock turn and others).

Some institutes have specialised and only deal with either panel research (Nielsen, IMS, GfK-Panelforschung) or certain sectors/methods (agricultural research, metal-working industry or retail research).

More detailed descriptions of these named institutes can be obtained from the *BVM Handbuch der Marktforschungsunternehmen* 1998 (BVM Handbook of Market Research Institutes), Deutscher Fachverlag GmbH, Frankfurt am Main, p.601.

In addition, further information can be obtained from the handbook, 'Who is Who in der Marktforschung 1996 ('Who's who in Market Research'), Deutscher Fachverlag GmbH, Frankfurt am Main.

PRIMARY RESEARCH: COSTS AND THE DURATION OF IMPLEMENTATION

The institutes listed in this chapter are, in the main, primary research institutes; secondary research (desk research) is predominantly carried out by in-house, corporate market researchers.

The costs of primary research are dependent on the following:

- extent of the work prior to the actual market research task (size of job, drawing up of questionnaires, target group identification etc);
- method of questioning (written, personal or telephone survey);
- sample size of surveys;
- normal surveys, set date or 'lightning' surveys;
- number of questions asked;
- difficulty in reaching target group and conducting interview;
- intensity and procedure applied to assess survey results;
- evaluation of results (yes/no) and possibly presentation.

It is easier to determine the costs of so-called 'multi-topic' (omnibus) surveys. They simply follow/comply with the type of question (open or closed), the methods (personal, telephone, CATI), and the size of the sample.

The following prices are, on average, those that are currently demanded:

Table 13.4 *Survey prices*

Method	Choice of electoral procedure	Number in sample	Costs (DM)		Duration
			closed questions	open questions	
CAPI-Bus[†]	Random	1000	1250	2000	2 weeks
Phone-Bus	CATI[‡]	500	900		2–3 days
	Random	1000	1300		
Face to face	Random	1000	1350	2100	3 weeks
Face to face	Quota	2500	2000	3000	3 weeks

Source: Planung und Analyse, Nr. 2/99 p.68ff 1999, Frankfurt.
[†] CAPI (Computer Assisted Personal Interviews)
[‡] CATI (Computer Assisted Telephone Interviews)

Aside from this there are average prices for group discussions[*], which are as follows:

Preparation of participants only   –   c.10,000DM + VAT
With presenter   –   c.15,300DM + VAT
With report   –   c.23,000DM + VAT
With simultaneous interpreter   –   c.25,300DM + VAT
[*]*Context*, Issue 13/96 p.11

OFFICIAL AND COMMERCIAL SECONDARY RESEARCH

The following can be named as sources of secondary research (desk research) in Germany:

Official statistics
Statistical Yearbook for the Federal Republic of Germany (annually)
Statistical Yearbook for the Lände
Statistical Yearbook for the German communities
Statistical Yearbook for the large towns

Commercial statistics
Desk research, Quellen- Lexikon der Marktforschung für Marketing, Kommunikation, Vertrieb und Einkauf aller Branchen, ('Desk Research Source Encyclopaedia of Market Research for Marketing, Communication, Sales and Purchases of all Sectors') Munich 1994/5.

This encyclopaedia contains all official and commercial secondary sources.

FINDING THE RIGHT MARKET RESEARCH INSTITUTE

For a company, finding a suitable market research institute to work with can be like an individual finding the right doctor.

The last statement is all the more accurate with regard to cross-border market research. How you structure the organisational side of things (direct contact with a foreign market research institute, or collaboration with a domestic institute that puts the appropriate foreign contacts at your disposal) always depends on finding a reliable institution.

There are three ways to get reliable market research partners, either abroad or in general:

1. If you engage in direct collaboration with a foreign institute, then you should have a checklist to assess to what extent the requirements for a successful collaboration are met.

    Some of the most important characteristics of quality ought to be further explained:

    ●   Reputation and the time an institute has been established are certainly no measures of ability. If however, an institute has successfully maintained its hold on the market for a lengthy period, it says a lot about the quality of its work;
    ●   The legal form of an institute together with its membership of associations and international market research chains says much about its financial standing and its following of certain standards, eg where confidentiality with regard to collaborations is concerned;
    ●   In market research, the professional quality of an institute's staff is of great importance. They are often engaged in teaching posts at universities and technical colleges, publications and advisory activities;
    ●   The technical standard (CATI-telephone studio, EDP equipment, interviewers etc) should not be disregarded, because that is what guarantees that jobs can be processed swiftly and varied methodically;
    ●   Because the age of the standardised exploration of the market has passed, and specialist or target group information is increasingly demanded, special sector knowledge can be an indication of specialist information.

All in all, it could be said that the German research institute environment has so far evaded any so-called 'black sheep'.

2. A different situation arises if a domestic institute is used for the purpose of undertaking foreign market research. Most of the larger German institutes are members of dependent and independent chains. These memberships are shown in the aforementioned *BVM Handbuch der Marktforschungsunternehmen* (BVM Handbook of Market Research Institutes), 1998.

    This type of approach has the following advantages:

    ●   only one communications partner;
    ●   minimal communication loss;
    ●   no language barrier;
    ●   identical survey methods;
    ●   comparable results through demographic standards;
    ●   identical survey period;

- simultaneous presentation of results;
- cost savings;
- clear legal accountability;
- evaluation and use of existing experiences.

3. The third route to achieve quality assurance and reliability of opinion polls in Germany is to obtain relevant information from the following institutes:

- *Arbeitskreis Deutscher Markt- und Sozialforschungsinstitute e.V.* (ADM) (Association of German Market and Social Research Institutes). Membership of this association is exclusively for those institutes that have undertaken several years of continuous work in the areas of market, opinion and social research, with more than five steady employees (excluding interviewer) at least one of whom has a completed university education.

- *Berufsverband deutscher Markt- und Sozialforscher e.V.* (BVM) (Association of German Market and Social Researchers). Membership of the BVM is safeguarded by its regulations in two different ways:

    (i) a professional register, in which personal members are listed if they have proven to the acceptance committee that they have at least three years work experience (for university graduates this period is reduced to two years) in the areas of market and/ or social research;

    (ii) the federal committee can expel members from the BVM if its reputation or interests are damaged.

As most market researchers are members of either the ADM or BVM – be it as individuals or as an institute – the meticulousness, merit, quality and reliability of the work of German market researchers are all, broadly speaking, guaranteed.

In Germany there is no recognised or known association for the protection or safeguarding of the interests of market research clients.

FURTHER IMPORTANT INFORMATION ON MARKET RESEARCH IN GERMANY

Data protection is of significance in the reworking of the 1994 IHK/ ESOMAR international code for the practice of market and social research, because there are necessary legal requirements that are not contained in the code.

To meet these additional demands a declaration was added to the code for the Federal Republic of Germany with regard to the practice of market and social research. This is also applicable if research is carried out abroad or under foreign instruction.

Furthermore, the ADM, BVM and also the *Arbeitsgemeinschaft sozialwissenschaftlicher Institute e.V.* (ASI) (Association of Social Science Institutes) have worked out and adopted a series of guidelines or principles, which, directly or indirectly apply to domestic as well as foreign clients/institutes if research is undertaken in Germany.

These guidelines cover:

- telephone surveys;
- peculiarities of pharmaceutical market research of German market research associations;
- the publication of results of research into choice;
- observations and observation methods by demoscopic surveys of German market research associations;
- interviewing minors;
- dealing with address data and addresses in market and social research;
- the recording and observation of group discussions and qualitative individual interviews;
- observations of demoscopic surveys.

Further guidelines are being prepared.

Aside from this, the guidelines published by ESOMAR (eg *Scheinkäufe*) likewise apply in Germany.

For further information on the field of market research a list of German-language market research literature is very useful. The same goes for the most important German language trade magazines, which are listed below:

Planung.und Analyse, Deutscher Fachverlag, Frankfurt am Main
Marketing-Journal, Verlag Marketingjournal, Hamburg
Die Absatzwirtschaft, Zeitschrift für Marketing, Verlagsgruppe Handelsblatt GmbH, Düsseldorf
Marketing, Zeitschrift für Forschung und Praxis, CH Beck, Vahlen, Munich.

14

Legal Considerations in the Appointment of Commercial Agents and Distributors

Angelika Baumgarte, German-British Chamber of Industry & Commerce, London

When a British company decides to establish a foothold for its products or services in the German market it has several options. The British company could, for example, appoint an agent or distributor, establish its own branch or subsidiary in Germany or enter into a joint venture agreement with a German company. Initially, the appointment of an agent or distributor is often the preferred option since it involves the least risk and financial commitment on the part of the British enterprise.

AGENTS AND DISTRIBUTORS DISTINGUISHED

In the English language the word 'agent' is often used in a much wider sense than to describe the commercial agent in a legal context. Moreover, it is sometimes used to include a distributor *(Vertragshändler)* as well. As from a legal point of view the term commercial agent *(Handelsvertreter)* is rather specific, I shall briefly describe the various legal and practical aspects that distinguish commercial agents from distributors.

Commercial agent	Distributor
Handelsvertreter	*Vertragshändler*

Definition

The agent is continuously entrusted to procure business transactions for the principal or to conclude them in the principal's name. The agent may be appointed in a buying or selling capacity for either goods or services.	The distributor buys goods on a continuous basis in his own name and on his own account from a manufacturer and sells them on his own account to his customers. The distributor forms part of the manufacturer's sales organisation.

Sales contract

There is only one sales contract, between the principal and his customers. The agent acts only as an intermediary, facilitating its conclusion.	There are two contracts: the manufacturer sells to the distributor and the distributor sells to his own customers. There is no direct contractual link between the manufacturer and the distributor's customers.

Market exposure

The principal will through direct exposure to both customers and risks gain considerable experience of the German market.	The manufacturer may not gather the same amount of information on Germany, as he is more remote. The manufacturer may not even know the distributor's customers.

Remuneration

Generally, the agent earns a commission. In most cases this will be a certain percentage of the sales price that the principal charges to his customers. During an initial start-up period the agent may well ask for a basic fixed retainer in addition to the commission.	The distributor will usually request a reduction on the manufacturer's list price. He will derive his income from the margin between the (reduced) manufacturer's price and the price he charges his own customers. He will not usually receive any additional remuneration from the manufacturer.

Price determination

The principal will determine the price which the customer in Germany has to pay.

The manufacturer determines the price that he charges to the distributor. But the distributor will determine the price he charges to his customer in Germany.

Financial risks

Usually, the principal will have many customers and therefore be exposed to several smaller financial risks.

The distributor is the supplier's main customer and may constitute one large risk. It is therefore essential to obtain a credit report before concluding the distribution agreement and again at regular intervals thereafter. The distributor should be covered by the manufacturer's credit insurance.

Termination of the contract

Upon termination of the agency agreement the principal will, as a rule, continue to supply the customers previously gained by the agent.

Upon termination of the distribution agreement the manufacturer may not gain any further benefit from the distributor's customers.

Regulation

The agent's rights and duties are laid down by statute law, ie in the Commercial Code.

The distributor's rights and duties are not fixed by statute law. But some of the rules relating to agents may, under certain circumstances, even apply to a distributor.

EU competition rules

The ordinary relationship between principal and agent is unlikely to be caught by EU competition rules.

The relationship between manufacturer and distributor may well be covered by EU competition rules and in-depth legal advice on this topic may be required.

SOURCES OF GERMAN AGENCY LAW

Agency contracts are governed by specific provisions in the German Commercial Code (*Handelsgesetzbuch*, which is referred to as HGB). The specific provisions relating to commercial agents are contained in sections 84–92c HGB. In addition, other more general sections of the same act apply to agency contracts, as the Commercial Code regulates a large variety of transactions between businessmen. The provisions of the HGB are supplemented by regulations contained in the German Civil Code (*Bürgerliches Gesetzbuch*, BGB), by German court decisions clarifying and interpreting the meaning of statutory provisions and by customary trade practice (*Handelsbrauch*).

If the agency contract is contained in a standard agreement, rather than an individually negotiated contract, the German Act on General Terms and Conditions (*Gesetz zur Regelung der Allgemeinen Geschäftsbedingungen*, AGBG) may become relevant. This act may render invalid those terms of the contract that are grossly unfair or detrimental to one party.

APPLICATION OF GERMAN LAW

If the principal is based in Britain and the agent or distributor is based and active in Germany, English or German law could apply to the agreement. German law will apply either because of the express or implicit choice of the parties or due to the rules on conflict of laws. If the agent or distributor is based and active in Germany, German law will automatically apply, unless the contract specifically stipulates English law.

German agents and distributors are reluctant to accept English law because they are familiar with the protection with which German law has provided them for a very long time. They are unfamiliar with English law but may be aware in many instances that it may be less favourable to them than German law.

All the acts mentioned above under the heading Sources of German Agency Law apply throughout the Federal Republic of Germany.

In an international agency or distributor relationship – just as in any other international contract – the applicable law, the place of jurisdiction and, in case of bilingual contracts, the language having priority should be specified. Ideally, all three should coincide.

Despite the implementation of the EC Council Directive on the Co-ordination of the Laws of the Member States relating to Self-employed Commercial Agents (Directive 86/653) in Germany and Britain, there still remain some substantial differences between the agency laws of both countries. I shall concentrate next on these differences as British companies are likely to be familiar with the main provisions and the general duties of principal and agents.

MAIN DIFFERENCES BETWEEN THE GERMAN AND ENGLISH RULES ON AGENTS

German law

English law

History

The current provisions on commercial agents have largely been in force since 1953. Most legal aspects on agents have since been clarified by court decisions.

The Commercial Agents (Council Directive) Regulations only came into force on 1 January 1994. This area of law is characterised by much uncertainty, given that up to now there have been very few decisions by English courts.

Scope of application of the rules

The rules contained in the Commercial Code (HGB) apply to all commercial agents, regardless of whether they are selling or buying goods or services. Certain modifications apply in respect of insurance and building society agents.

The Commercial Agents (Council Directive) Regulations only apply to agents dealing in goods, but not to those involved in the supply of services.

When commission falls due and entitlement to an advance

Commission falls due as soon as the principal has supplied goods or services. If a later point in time is contractually agreed, the German agent is by law entitled to receive an advance on his commission when the principal performs his obligation under the

Commission falls due at the latest when the customer pays the sales price. Before that point in time the agent does not have a right to an advance.

contract with the customer. The agent's entitlement to a reasonable advance may not be excluded by contract.

Debt collection commission

When the agent undertakes the special duty of collecting outstanding debts from the principal's customers, he is automatically entitled to a reasonable debt collection commission.

The English regulations do not provide for an automatic right to commission for the collection of debts.

Longest statutory period of notice to terminate the contract

Agency contracts that have run for more than *five* years may only be terminated by *six* months' notice to the end of the calendar month.

The longest notice period applicable in England amounts to *three* months for all contracts that have run for more than *three* years.

Agent's claim on termination

Upon termination of the agreement the agent may have a claim for an indemnity.

Upon termination of the agreement the agent may have a claim for an indemnity or compensation or both.

Post-contractual restraint of trade clause

If principal and agent contractually agree that the agent should refrain from competition with the principal *after* termination of the agency relationship, usually the agent is entitled to reasonable compensation throughout the duration of such a restriction.

English law does not provide for such an entitlement to compensation.

Period of limitation

In Germany contractual claims between the parties arising out of the agency agreement are time barred after *four years*. The period of time begins at the end of the year in which the claim has fallen due.

The Commercial Agents (Council Directive) Regulation 1993 does not contain special provisions for limitation. Therefore it has to be assumed that in Great Britain The Limitation Act 1980 applies, which in Section 5

However, the agent has to raise his claim for an indemnity within one year of termination.

provides for a *six-year* limitation period.

The claim for compensation or an indemnity must be notified to the principal within one year of termination.

MAIN ASPECTS WHEN TERMINATING THE AGREEMENT

As in many other legal relationships, problems often arise upon termination of the agency or distributor agreement. The British exporter needs to be aware of the minimum statutory notice periods under German law as well as the potential claim for an indemnity before he considers appointing a new agent or setting up his own sales office in Germany.

Notice periods

The length of the statutory notice periods depends on the duration of the contract. The notice periods mentioned below apply to the notice to be given by either the agent or the principal.

Notice period	Applicable in
1 month	the first year
2 months	the second year
3 months	the third, fourth and fifth year
6 months	the sixth and following years

The notice periods have to expire at the end of a calendar month. If the principal gives notice to his agent, who had been working for him for eight months, on 15 March, the notice will only expire at the end of April. The statutory notice periods may be extended by agreement, but not shortened.

These notice periods only apply to agents directly, but the German courts have in many instances also applied them to distributors. In these cases the distributors were closely integrated into the manufacturer's sales organisation and subject to agent-like duties. However, the circumstances of the individual relationship with a distributor may often justify a much longer notice period, eg one year. This is particularly the case where the distributor is only active for one manufacturer and where he undertakes substantial investments for a long-term relationship.

Claim for indemnity

Upon termination of the relationship the agent will usually be entitled to an indemnity (*Ausgleichsanspruch*). The claim for an indemnity is laid down in section 89b of the German Commercial Code (HGB). The purpose of this claim is to further reward the agent for having created a clientele that the principal can use after termination of the agency relationship.

The preconditions for the agent's claim for an indemnity are as follows:

- The agency must have been terminated. The means of termination are largely irrelevant; it is sufficient that a fixed-term contract has expired. However, no entitlement to a claim will be given if the contract is terminated by the principal with immediate effect because of the agent's culpable conduct. No claim arises either if the agent gives notice. However, the agent will still be entitled to an indemnity, if he gives notice and this is due to his age, or illness.
- After termination the principal will enjoy further substantial advantages from business relations with new customers recruited by the agent. Only 'new' customers will be considered, or those old customers the principal had before appointing the agent but with whom the business relationship has been so significantly enhanced that in economic terms they count as 'new'.
- By reason of termination of the contract the agent loses rights to commission that, had it continued, he would have had from business transactions already concluded or to be concluded in the future with customers recruited by him. In order to calculate the losses of commission a prognosis for several years after the end of the agency is made on the basis of the commission earned by the agent in the 12 months prior to termination of the agreement.
- Payment of an indemnity is fair, taking all the circumstances into account.

The maximum compensation payable is an annual percentage of the agent's commission calculated on the basis of the agent's average earnings during the five years prior to termination. The exact calculation of the indemnity is fairly complicated, given that it involves a prediction of future developments as well as a consideration of all circumstances of the individual case.

SIMILAR APPLICATION OF THE AGENCY RULES TO DISTRIBUTORS

Although the German provisions relating to commercial agents do not cover distributors, German courts have on numerous occasions decided that some of them may be similarly applied to distributors. This is particularly relevant in the case of the claim for an indemnity (*Ausgleichsanspruch*), as the termination of a distributor agreement may therefore become very expensive for the British manufacturer.

To recap on the definition given above under the heading Agents and Distributors Distinguished: a distributor (*Vertragshändler*) buys goods on a continuous basis in his own name from a manufacturer and sells them to his own customers. He has a contractual relationship with his customers; no direct contract exists between the distributor's customers and the manufacturer; and he is to some extent integrated into the manufacturer's sales organisation.

Although the preconditions for applying the rules protecting the commercial agent to a distributor have been changed by court decisions on several occasions, the crucial criteria for the application of the claim for the indemnity (*Ausgleichsanspruch*) appear to be the following:

- The distributor in the individual case has to be integrated into the manufacturer's distribution system in such a way that he can be compared to a commercial agent. Obviously the distributor does not have to fulfil all the duties that would be expected of an agent. Typically, he would however be obliged to represent the manufacturer's interests, to promote the manufacturer's products, to co-operate with the manufacturer's export department, to monitor the market and inform the manufacturer of developments, and not to sell any competitor's products.
- The distributor during the currency of the agreement or upon its termination has to make his customers known to the manufacturer, so that the manufacturer has the possibility to enter into a direct business relationship with the distributor's customers. If the manufacturer has access to the distributor's customers, either due to a contractual obligation on the distributor's part or because of the actual handling of customers (eg reporting requirements), the distributor will have fulfilled this criterion.

If the above preconditions are fulfilled, the distributor will be entitled to an indemnity upon termination of the agreement.

SOME PRACTICAL HINTS

The *Centralvereinigung Deutscher Handelsvertreter und Handelsmakler* (CDH) is the main German organisation of commercial agents – but not distributors. It represents agents' interests and gives assistance to them. Principals looking for an agent can advertise in a magazine published by the CDH.

CDH
Geleniusstraße 1
D 50931 Cologne
Tel: +49 221 51 40 43
Fax: +49 221 52 57 67

The German-British Chamber of Industry & Commerce is a membership organisation of German and British businesses and offers a variety of services to members and non-members alike. In the specific context of agents and distributors, it provides different means of finding a partner, from mere address lists via its own database research to an individual selection procedure based on your specific requirements. It offers credit reports on German companies as well as legal advice on agency contracts and assistance in solving problems informally, problems that may have arisen in the relationship with your German agent or distributor.

The German-British Chamber of Industry & Commerce
16 Buckingham Gate
London SW1E 6LB
Tel: 020 7976 4100
Fax: 020 7976 4101

The commercial officers at the British Embassies and Consulates in Germany also offer to find suitable agents in Germany. This research should be commissioned through your local Business Link.

CONCLUSION

When appointing someone in Germany you ought to provide him with a written contract clearly stating if his function is that of an agent (*Handelsvertreter*) or a distributor (*Vertragshändler*). Although it is in practice sometimes unavoidable, from a legal point of view it is not desirable to mix both functions.

If the agent or a distributor is based and active in Germany it is likely that German law will automatically apply to the relationship. If you wish English law to govern the contract, this should be especially agreed upon. It is noteworthy that despite the attempt to harmonise agency law throughout the EU by the EC Council Directive on the Co-ordination of the Laws of the Member States relating to Self-employed Commercial Agents, several important differences remain between the national German and English laws in this respect. These are most marked when it comes to the termination of the agreement. Moreover in Germany – unlike in England – a distributor may be protected by the rules applying to agents and may even be entitled to an indemnity.

15

Financial Incentives and the Funding of Investment Projects

John M Zindar, The New German Länder Industrial Investment Council (IIC), Berlin

INVESTMENT INCENTIVE POLITICS AND FORECAST

The political debate in Germany, and in Brussels, over the costs of investment promotion and other job-creating incentives continues. Budget tightening throughout the Euro-zone focuses the public's eyes more sharply on all expenditures. The EU appears more ready to challenge foul play and is exerting additional control through the European Commission's new Multisectoral Framework.

Moreover, the German government elected in September 1998 used its six-month (January–June 1999) turn at the Presidency of the European Council to push for reductions in the structural funds used to help develop the poorer regions of the EU, now accounting for one-third of the budget. This action was based on adjustments required before initiating membership of even poorer countries, and on the prognosis that the new eastern states of Germany will not need such support indefinitely.

But for the foreseeable future (or at least until a new structural funds budget commences in 2007), especially now that most of Europe has centre-left leadership, investment incentive subsidies will continue relatively unchanged.

This is good news for direct foreign investors in Germany who are, except in some minor respects, treated in the same manner as domestic investors when it comes to government financial support. Big advantages are still to be found in the new eastern German federal states (*Länder*); there remains a wide disparity between what public financial support investors can expect there and what is possible in the old western German states.

More good news for the investor can be found on the private side of financing an investment project in Germany; the banking system is restructuring within Europe's largest financial market and at the same time the venture capital market is growing faster than anywhere else in Europe.

Private and public financing go hand-in-hand in Germany. State investment incentives help to trigger access to funds from rapidly changing capital and equity markets. That should be the primary function of incentives. The strategic investor comparing alternatives for an international operation does not base final decisions on handouts. An investment rarely makes sense if it doesn't make sense without subsidies.

EASTERN GERMANY REMAINS 'CODE PINK'

Eastern Germany maintains its status among regions having the highest EU-allowable incentive rates. In 1999 the new German states were again awarded the EU's 'Objective One'[1] designation, depicted in pink on the European Commission's official map, for the period covering 2000–06. Western Berlin is not included in this grouping while eastern Berlin has been placed in a special 'transition' category which means that although the pace of economic development there no longer qualifies it for the Objective One category it will be eligible for special funds to ease its downgrading.

Other areas in the 'pink' during 2000–06 will include large parts of Ireland, Greece, Portugal Spain and Italy, small parts of Austria, Belgium, France, the Netherlands and the United Kingdom, as well as some overseas possessions.

---

[1]Objective One areas are currently defined as those with a GDP per capita which is 75 per cent or less of the European Union average for three consecutive years – altered to seven consecutive years for the policy period 2000–06.

Joining eastern Berlin in the loss of Objective One status are large areas of Ireland and smaller regions in Belgium, France (including all of Corsica), Italy, Spain, the Netherlands and Portugal (including Lisbon). While some small portions of England and Wales have been added to the Objective One grouping, parts of Scotland and all of Northern Ireland are no longer eligible. These changes are significant because eastern Germany's toughest competition for direct investment in yen and dollars is found in the British Isles, the Netherlands, France and Spain.

Altogether, the EU expects an approximate decrease of 7 per cent in the current number of 92.2 million inhabitants in Objective One areas under the new regulations. The overall structural fund recipient areas of the EU's population will be reduced in coverage from 51 per cent to 40 per cent. The EU is also simplifying the process by reducing the number of objective areas from six to three.

It is important to note that the EU structural funds policy can only maintain a level playing field with regard to setting percentage-of-investment incentive ceilings. However, because member countries and regions pool their own funds with those available from the EU, some countries are willing, and able, to offer much larger volumes of financial assistance to investors than others.

Germany, as the prime example, has, over a five year period, financed nearly as much manufacturing investment as Italy, France and the United Kingdom put together (see Table 15.1). This has proven especially beneficial for the new federal states, which have been on the receiving-end of the vast majority of investment subsidies in Germany (see Table 15.2).

Table 15.1 *State financial support for investment in manufacturing 1992–96*

Top six EU countries	Amount (€ billion)
Germany	83.1
Italy	55.2
France	21.1
Spain	8.9
United Kingdom	7.8
Belgium	4.8

Source: The Sixth Report on State Assistance for Manufacturing in the European Union, European Commission, 1998.

Table 15.2   *Funds committed for cash grants 2000–02*

Federal state	DM million
Eastern states	
Saxony	1,880
Saxony-Anhalt	1,121
Thuringia	1,002
Mecklenburg-Western Pomerania	980
Brandenburg	957
Berlin	657
Total	**6,597**
Western states	
North Rhine/Westphalia	220
Lower Saxony	198
Bavaria	80
Schleswig-Holstein	64
Rhineland-Palatinate	50
Saarland	50
Hesse	20
Bremen	18
Hamburg	0
Baden-Würtemberg	0
Total	**700**

Source: Achtundzwanzigster Rahmanplan der Gemeinschaftsaufgabe 'Verbesserung der regionalen Wirtschaftsstruktur' für den Zeitraum 1999 bis 2002 (2003), The German Parliament, April, 1999

INVESTMENT INCENTIVES FOR EASTERN GERMANY

Current German implementation regulations for the new states were approved on 14 April 1999 and in effect until the end of the year 2002. These allow most SME-sized[2] direct investors to receive up to the EU's Objective One maximum of 50 per cent (large firms 35 per cent) of the investment that can be subsidised in non-repayable grants known as 'GA Money'[3] (alone or sometimes calculated with the subsidised value of other programmes) almost everywhere in the new states.

[2] The EU definition of an SME applies, ie firms with up to 250 employees and a maximum turnover of €40 million or balance sheet sum of €27 million. SME eligibility is lost if a non-SME company holds a share of 25 per cent or more.

[3] The local business jargon for funds from the federal, state and EU budgets placed in the *Gemeinschaftsaufgabe* (regional economic structure improvement) programme.

Map 2   *Maximum investment incentive areas in Germany*

These incentive regions were last designated by the federal government on 1 January 1997. In much of western Germany, and some parts of eastern Germany, federal regulations lower the maximum levels allowed by the EU. Each of the 16 states have the final say and can further downgrade the levels of assistance available within their jurisdictions.

Source: Achtundzwanzigster Rahmanplan der Gemeinschaftsaufgabe 'Verbesserung der regionalen Wirtschaftsstruktur' für den Zeitraum 1999 bis 2002 (2003), The German Parliament, April, 1999

Table 15.3 *Investment incentive awards from major programmes in eastern Germany 1990–97*

Programme	Amount (DM billion)
GA Money for industry	38.0 granted
GA Money for infrastructure	24.0 granted
'Soft' loans & equity	71.5 loaned & invested
Federal guarantees	15.0 guaranteed
Tax credits/bonuses & special depreciation	28.0 in tax relief or cash bonuses
R&D promotion	5.5 granted
Environmental protection	2.0 granted

Source: *Bilanz der Wirtschaftsförderung des Bundes in Ostdeutschland bis Ende 1997*, Federal Economics Ministry, 1998.

German rules effective from 1 January 1997 state that the metropolitan areas of Berlin, Dresden, Eisenach, Erfurt, Gotha, Halle, Jena, Leipzig, Potsdam, Schwerin and Weimar as well as some rural areas can, with few exceptions, only offer grants with ceilings of 43 per cent (large firms 28 per cent)[4] (see Map 2).

Industry eligibility for these grants is widening, now allowing many services, but still largely excluding the agriculture, construction, energy and water utilities, forestry, mining, retail, storage and transport businesses.

Most of these industries on the negative-list[5] are, however, eligible for most other financial incentive programmes such as R&D, human capital and environmental grants, various 'soft' or below-market interest rate loans,[6] as well as state guarantees and equity infusions. Although these programmes have no expiry dates, annual budgets for each must be approved.

The negative-list for the potentially lucrative tax credit/cash bonus (*Investitionszulage*) programmes is similar but smaller than that for grants. Again, many services once excluded are now eligible. The

[4]The EU sets overall guidelines within which individual member states implement their own policy emphasising local development priorities. Thus, even though Bonn is allowed by Brussels to offer the 50 per cent (large firms 35 per cent) maximums for each of these Objective One areas except western Berlin (and eastern Berlin after 1999), Bonn can and does designate them as Objective Two.

[5]The concept of negative and positive lists is important. The EU has its general list of the types of firms that can and cannot receive structural grants. Each German state further defines those lists according to their priorities.

[6]It is interesting to note that much of this credit traces its origins to Marshall Plan seed money.

Investitionzulage offers either tax credits to profit-making firms which are investing in plant and capital equipment or cash bonus payments to investors still in the red. The current amounts of the credits/bonuses are 20 per cent of the capital equipment investment for SMEs, and 10 per cent for SME investment in plant and for large firm investments in both plant and equipment. This current scheme was approved on 18 August 1997, took effect on 1 January 1999, and will last until the end of the year 2004.

INVESTMENT INCENTIVES FOR WESTERN GERMANY

The maximum incentive thresholds to be hoped for in the maturely developed states of western Germany are 28 per cent for SMEs and 18 per cent for large companies, again with rare exceptions. The areas of eligibility for any GA Money within the old states are also shrinking, recently dropping from a coverage of 22 per cent to only 20.8 per cent of the western side's population.

The German government downgrades all of the few Objective Two areas designated by the EU in the old western states (see footnote 4). Western Berlin, the area hit hardest by post-unification economic trends, has always been the only exception, recognised as an Objective Two area by both Brussels and Bonn. Since 1 January 1997, eastern Berlin's status has been downgraded to match the western side of the city, resulting in a uniform 43 per cent (large firms 28 per cent) maximum subsidy.

However, many of the above-mentioned non-GA Money support programmes for eastern Germany are also on hand in western Germany. The major exception is found under the category of tax breaks. Unlike new states, the old states are unable to offer the generous *Investition-zulage* or tax credit/bonus.[7]

The only special tax programmes available for investors in western Germany are also available in eastern Germany: a special accelerated depreciation allowance (*Sonderabschreibung*) of 20 per cent which can be used in conjunction with regular depreciation methods,[8] and a capital reserves allowance (*Ansparabschreibung*).

---

[7]The old states had also been disadvantaged relative to the new states until the special accelerated depreciation allowance of 40 per cent (previously 50 per cent) of the investment was completely eliminated for the latter at the end of 1998.
[8]This special depreciation allowance is for small companies with a balance sheet sum of no more than DM400,000.

Table 15.4 *Summary of comparative major incentive programmes for eastern & western Germany*
(percentage for large firms given in brackets where applicable)

Programme	New federal states (NFS)[9]	Old federal states (OFS)	Recent changes
Tax incentives			
Tax credits or cash bonuses	up to 20% (10%) of investment amount	None	In effect until end of 2004. Until end of 1998 10% (5%) was for the NFS. Industry eligibility list widened
Depreciation allowance	20% accelerated on top of normal methods	As left	Until end of 1998 the NFS were allowed a special depreciation rate of 40%
Capital reserves allowance	Taxable profits can be reduced by 50% of investment	As left	
Capital asset tax exemptions	Net Worth & Municipal Trade taxes eliminated	As left	Prior to striking these tax codes only the NFS were exempt
Investment grants			
GA money	Up to 50% (35%) of investment amount. Most urban areas are limited to 43% (28%)	Up to 28% (18%) for small selected areas only	German implementation rules extend until end of 2002. Based on capital or labour expenditures. 10% of land costs are also eligible. Industry eligibility list widened
R&D support	6 major programmes	4 major programmes	More support for R&D is planned
'Soft' loans & equity infusions			
Kreditanstalt für Wiederaufbau (KfW) (reconstruction bank)	3 major programmes for SMEs, environment, and equity infusion	As left, 3 plus 2 more for venture capital and GA Money areas	Below-market interest rates are now largely same for both the NFS and OFS
Deutsche Ausgleichsbank (DtA) (equalisation bank)	7 major programmes for expansion, modernisation or start-up, the environment and equity infusion	Also 7 programmes for the same plus operating resources	As above

[9]Although unified Berlin is considered a new federal state, the situation can be complicated as there are eligibility variations between western and eastern Berlin.

Table 15.4   *(Continued)*

Programme	New federal states (NFS)	Old federal states (OFS)	Recent changes
Eastern Germany equity fund	Strengthens equity for SME expansion, market growth or product development	None	Renewed for NFS after end of 1998 expiration for an indefinite period
Consolidation funds	Emergency funds for SMEs with liquidity problems	None	
European Union	4 major programmes for GA areas, R&D, start-ups and intra-EU co-operation/JVs	As left plus 1 more for venture capital	
Loan Guarantees			
State & Federal Guarantee Banks	1 in each of the 6 states	1 in each of the 10 states	
DtA Guarantees	1 programme for SME expansion, modernisation or start-up	1 programme for the environment	
European Investment Bank (EIB)	For SMEs	None	
Labour-Related Subsidies			
Structural change support for unemployed	Up to 100% of total wage costs for 10% of workforce for up to 12 months	None	New, in effect from June 1998 until end of 2002
Long-term unemployed support	Up to 80% of total wage costs for up to 6 months	As left	Set to expire end of 1999. Renewal expected
Other programmes	19 other major programmes	10 other major programmes	

Source: IIC, Berlin, 1999

Another tax issue of importance to investors is that the two levies from which business in eastern Germany was exempt, and business in western Germany was not, have recently been abolished for the entire country – the net worth tax (*Vermögensteuer*) at the end of 1996, and the municipal trade tax (*Gewerbekapitalsteuer*) at the end of 1997. Both were to be reinstated for eastern Germany but were instead eliminated in an example of the country's slow but steady progress in the field of tax reform – in this case resulting in an advantage for the western states.

IMPORTANT NEW CHANGES IN GA GRANT ELIGIBILITY

GA grants were largely applicable only to capital goods expenditures. However, there are three very noteworthy changes for investors in the new implementation rules now valid for all of Germany until the end of 2002:

1. For the first time the purchase of land is eligible for GA subsidies. The investor can now calculate 10 per cent of the fair market price of land within (not in addition to) the investment incentive percentage ceiling;
2. In order to better support labour-intensive projects, investors can, for the first time, choose to base their GA grants either on capital expenditures or total wage costs over a two-year period. There are restrictions on where and what kind of jobs are created;
3. SMEs can now calculate the full costs of intangible goods such as software, patents and licenses. Non-SMEs can calculate only 25 per cent of their intangible costs, which was the limit previously set for firms of all sizes.

MORE SCRUTINY: THE EC'S NEW MULTISECTORAL FRAMEWORK

Not only is Brussels reducing the area and population covered by high investment subsidy allowances, it is also increasing its scrutiny of the incentive awards decided at local levels. Causing a stir and some anxiety within the investment incentive business, the European Commission instituted new oversight and approval procedures for incentives on 1 September 1998, grandfathering the new rules for any incentive application submitted as of 1 August 1998.

On the surface the new procedures, known as the Multisectoral Framework and initially in effect for three years, have dramatically changed the way things are done. The effect in the real world is still unknown, although it can be assumed that for most investors there will be few noticeable changes. In fact, the overall impact could be quite positive, as the Multisectoral Framework clarifies rules and results in final incentive package approvals at an earlier stage, significantly reducing uncertainties for an investor.

Before the new framework, most approvals were officially given by Brussels after the state government (in the case of Germany) itself had notified the investor of its response to an incentive application. In many cases, the approval from Brussels was not confirmed before the investor purchased equipment and subsequently received the actual subsidy payments. Most of the time this was not a problem as the European Commission, assuming that local authorities were acting within pre-approved rules and amounts, would simply rubber stamp the subsidy offer.

However, in a few cases, when the Commission decided to take a closer look, both the local authorities and the investor could be in for a nasty surprise if the approval was overruled. Brussels' rationale for its new oversight system was based on the growing caseload and the spiralling value of incentive offers as well as on the number of abuses that had been uncovered throughout the EU. Two of the headline-grabbing cases which brought Germany into conflict with Brussels in 1996 concerned Volkswagen in the state of Saxony and Bremer Vulkan in the state of Mecklenburg-Vorpommern, both discussed in the equivalent chapter in the previous edition of 'Doing Business with Germany'.

Under the new framework, the Commission must now routinely assess and notify approval of all state financial incentives exceeding €50 million for a project *before* the local authorities approve and disburse funds. The new EC assessment process could theoretically reduce the local offer of incentives by up to 85 per cent.

The process calculates three factors which can reduce or leave the value of the incentive package unchanged for the eligible investor. These factors are:

1. competition (how much would the aid distort a market);
2. capital/labour (the lower the ratio the less distortion);
3. regional impact (calculation of indirect job creation).

Factors 1 & 2 can be negative, reducing the incentive package. Factor 3 can be positive, offsetting negative factors by up to 50 per cent, but unable to increase the incentive offer. Factor 1 will likely have the most serious effect, possibly making it difficult for large, established firms in industries such as automotive, chemicals, pharmaceuticals, shipbuilding, steel and textiles to receive generous investment assistance.

Certain investment aid packages of less than €50 million could also face this new assessment and notification process. To qualify for early scrutiny the investment project must meet all three of the following criteria:

1. the project investment exceeds €50 million;
2. the aid intensity exceeds limits (when financial assistance is more than 50 per cent of the percentage of investment ceiling for the objective region);
3. the aid per job created is greater than €40,000.[10]

KEY PRIVATE FINANCING TRENDS

As noted at the beginning of this chapter, public financing must be matched correctly with private financing for an investment project to work best. Although the money and other finance markets in Germany are covered extensively in other parts of this book, it is worthwhile emphasising the very new trends in banking and elsewhere which can have a significant impact on the engineering of an optimal public incentive package. An optimal financing package in eastern Germany, for example, would in most cases only require the investor to bring approximately 15 per cent of the required capital to the table.

Besides the rapid growth in German venture capital markets (in 1997 venture capital start-up investments were ten times higher than in the UK) the most important trend for the direct foreign investor is the rapid progress towards internationalisation in German finance. The German banking system has always felt unfamiliar to foreign, especially Anglo-Saxon, business. Now that is all changing.

General globalisation trends, accelerated by the introduction of the euro and the placement of the European Central Bank in Frankfurt, have had a big impact. The debt market in Europe, riding a boom in new euro-denominated bonds, grew 80 per cent in the six months following the euro's inception at the beginning of 1999. There has also been a consolidation trend within German banking as a string of high and not so high-profile bank mergers were completed. Deutsche Bank's merger with Banker's Trust is leading the way in what should be the strong outward movement of other German banks.

These processes also bring restructuring and strengthening, helping to make German and European capital markets more transparent, competitive and specialised as well as less expensive. Know-how is building up and more creative financing instruments are being adopted.

---

[10]This should not be confused with the long-standing rule that only DM1 million of investment per job created (or DM500,000 per job saved) is eligible for GA Money grant consideration, eg a small firm in eastern Germany could only expect up to 50 per cent of DM10 million when investing DM20 million to create only 10 jobs.

Competition in credit markets will be further boosted if the EU follows through on its measures to stop the huge subsidy flows to the German *Sparkassen* (savings banks) and *Landesbanken* (state-owned banks) which account for a dominant 80 per cent of the retail banking market.

In the equity markets, the joint venture between the stock exchanges in Frankfurt and London solidifies them as the dominant players in Europe. A big generational change in business ownership is triggering an accelerating trend in IPOs (Initial Public Offerings). Germans are finally investing a growing amount of their significant savings in stocks and equity funds.

Deutsche Bank's entry on the New York Stock Exchange should also have pioneering repercussions, because in 1999 in order to perform better the bank placed DM47 billion of its holdings in large corporations into an autonomous subsidiary, known as DB Investor. The controversial German practice, in which banks own major shares of the big firms to which they lend, has always been open to criticism for dampening new competition, especially from abroad. Deutsche Bank's move falls short of divestment, which would trigger a heavy tax burden, but adds transparency and confidence to the system.

INVESTMENT ADVISORY SERVICES

The above discussion over trends in investment incentives attempts to simplify and describe a system which can be complicated. Most foreign investors, particularly those that have limited international experience, require substantial external support in the investment decision-making process. Of course all the best consultancy firms in the world are represented in Germany, and each will normally have a team of inward investment specialists.

In terms of free advice, there are a myriad of official ministries, agencies, banks, institutes and societies which offer information and assistance on putting incentive packages together. An exhaustive list of these groups can be found in Appendix 1. Many of these official entities are specialists in one form of assistance or another. Assistance is also available from local specialists in the economic development agencies (*Wirtschaftsförderungsgesellchaften* or *Wifos*), one of which is found in each state (except for Bremen, which has two).

Germany lags behind all of its major competitors in Europe in developing any kind of centralised inward investment promotion/assistance structure. For historical reasons, it runs most public business within a very decentralised, federalist system. In fact, Germany gave little priority to attracting and aiding foreign investment until after reunification when the rebuilding of the new states had begun.

Although there is a revenue-sharing scheme in Bonn which supports foreign investor assistance, the concept leaves each of the states largely on its own in fighting over potential investments. Each state can boast of its local expertise in helping investors, but very few promotion or assistance activities are co-ordinated for Germany as a whole.

An 'Invest in Quality' all-state marketing group was recently disbanded after agreeing upon a joint logo and website. Under the stewardship of the ZfA or Federal Centre for Foreign Investment in Germany, (in the Federal Ministry of Economics and Technology – BMWi) the *Wifos* continue, however, to attend joint strategy meetings in an effort to identify common goals.

The boldest step taken in investment promotion thus far is The New German Länder Industrial Investment Council, GmbH (IIC), which was activated in early 1997 to represent eastern Germany. Headed by the former Executive Board Chairman of Klöckner Werke AG, Hans Christoph von Rohr, the IIC's 35-strong team is the first official German agency to actively promote the interests of not just one state but a region. It has a mandate until the end of 2001, as well as the resources, to professionally develop a world-wide network to match investment opportunities with potential investors, while providing full-service support throughout, and after, the decision process.

In recent years there has been a slow growing movement cutting across the major German political parties which is urging the establishment of something akin to the Invest in Britain Bureau. It is likely that this could be established early in the next decade. The appointment of Hilmar Kopper, former Chairman and CEO of Deutsche Bank in June 1998 as the (part-time) Special Envoy for Foreign Investment in Germany was the latest cautious step in that direction. His four-person office began operations in January 1999.

20 PRACTICAL TIPS ON SERCURING FINANCIAL INCENTIVES

This list is intended to provide a summary of practical information to foreign investors seeking financial support from the government. It does not pretend to be all-inclusive nor guarantee success, but it does address many of the most often-asked questions and common concerns of prospective investors.

1. **Do not make any investment expenditures until the application process for incentives is initiated**. In most cases, other than for tax credits, money spent beforehand will be ineligible for consideration.
2. **Keep up to date on changing regulations** which can effect a financial plan, either in the short or long-term.
3. **Initial information** can be best gathered from the Federal Centre for Foreign Investment (ZfA) for all of Germany (offices in Berlin and Chicago) and The New German Länder Industrial Investment Council GmbH (IIC) for the six new states in eastern Germany (offices in Berlin, New York and London). German chambers of commerce, embassies, consulates and other representations can also help with preliminary information.
4. **Obtain an overview of eligible programmes** for each case. This can be done at the ZfA, the IIC or in each state. This information forms the basis for developing the optimum incentive package. There are a variety of computer programmes, as well as printed material, obtainable in English.
5. **Identify the necessary points of contact throughout the public sector.** Maintaining a high profile during the incentive application process is obviously important. In addition to the ZfA and the IIC, contacts include the state economics and finance ministries which are usually the most important decision-makers for grants. Other ministries such as those dealing with agriculture and technology can also be important. The development banks at the federal and state levels are the primary contacts for loan and equity support. Universities, technical schools and research institutes can also be valuable partners.
6. **The primary contacts for all investment incentive information** are the economic development agencies in each of the ten western German states, and the IIC for the six eastern German states.
7. **At the municipality level** the mayor and his/her development agency can be important players as well as the local chambers of commerce (*Industrie- und Handelskammer – IHK*). The local employment office (*Arbeitsamt*) needs to be contacted concerning wage, training and other labour-support programmes.
8. **Grant (GA Money) levels are decided** by the individual states with the approval of the European Commission. Normally, the highest investment amount that can be subsidised is DM1 million per new job created.
9. **There is healthy competition among and within the individual states**. Each can have numerous variations in the available incentive programmes. Depending on development agendas, states prioritise industries and locations for the limited pool of

support funds, and will tailor supplementary programmes to be added to the basic mix of incentives.

10. A local representative can shepherd applicants through the day-to-day activities of the incentive application process, but **high-level company team visits are very important** to raise the profile of the case. The firm should indicate early on its readiness to be a good corporate citizen.

11. All those in the process should attempt to **learn rudimentary German and basic cross-business cultural etiquette**. Negotiating style, for example can be very different in Germany than elsewhere. Basic company brochures and introductory letters should be translated into German.

12. **Enlist good local professional assistance**. Local accountants, lawyers and tax advisors with experience in the local area of the intended investment will be indispensable.

13. **Find a commercial house bank**. Identifying a bank legally operating within Germany which will fully support your efforts to obtain grants and loans is key. Most applications need to be submitted through a house bank. Some banks are more interested in servicing this type of clientele than others.

14. **A legal German business entity must be established in order to receive financial support**. This can be a subsidiary or a registered branch office. The most typical entity is the *GmbH* (limited liability company), for which the shareholder capital must amount to at least DM50,000. With a good lawyer the establishment of a GmbH can be accomplished within a few days.

15. **A new company must be entered in the commercial register** (*Handelsregister*) where the firm will be located. This should take about two weeks.

16. **Grant applications usually need to be accompanied by documentation** such as a description of the firm and its investment intentions, business and financial plans, financial records going back approximately two years, proof of *Handelsregister* entry, property titles, construction permits, leasing contracts and tax returns.

17. **The number of direct and indirect jobs created or saved are often the key consideration for grant levels**. Other considerations include the transferring of technologies and management know-how, innovative R&D planned and the level of development and the priority an industry has in the chosen location.

18. **There is an important distinction between SMEs and large firms when it comes to programme and support level eligibility**. The EU-approved definition is that SMEs have less than 250 employees and a maximum annual turnover of €40

million or a balance sheet sum of €20 million. If other firms own more than a 25 per cent share of the German company in question, then the size criteria are applied to the largest of those shareholders.

19. **The EU ceiling for total incentives as a percentage of investments is 50 per cent for SMEs and 35 per cent for large firms**. These highest-level ceilings are only allowed in eastern Germany. The entire amount can be in grant money; however, the benefits derived from tax and soft loan programmes can be calculated into the maximum percentage allowed.

20. **Final decisions on incentive packages are most often made within four months**. Approved grants and loans are usually disbursed within two months of making an investment expenditure.

The author wishes to acknowledge the research assistance of Mr Guido Schenk, IIC, Berlin.

16

The New Insolvency Code

*Dr Christof Schiller and Dr Eberhard Braun,
Schulze & Braun, Frankfurt*

On 1 January 1999, after more than two decades of often heated debate, the new German Insolvency Code came into effect.

The new Insolvency Code was meant to solve three problems:

- to unite the codes concerning insolvency into one law;
- to ensure that more insolvencies can be carried through;
- to change the scope of the Insolvency Code from a regulation of enforcement to a regulation permitting the recovery and reorganisation of enterprises.

The laws concerning insolvency in effect until recently mainly stemmed from the year 1877. The bankruptcy code (*Konkursordnung*) was one of the important codifications of the German private law and has to be appreciated as part of the major codifications of that time, together with the Commercial Code, the Civil Code and the code regarding the civil procedure.

The bankruptcy code of 1877 was considered a highly skilled codification. However, legislators considered insolvency law to be primarily a law for the enforcement of claims. Whereas the Code of civil procedure regulated the enforcement of one individual claim against the debtor, the bankruptcy code was meant to be the law of enforcement in cases where the debtor is unable to pay all his debts and thus becomes insolvent.

This concept of the law turned out to be quite problematic, because it failed to recognise the fact that companies often become insolvent for reasons that are beyond their influence, and that they should in many cases be kept alive and reorganised to secure jobs and the monetary interests of the creditors. An insolvent company sold as a going concern will in most cases produce larger realisations than a company sold at break-up value.

Other laws regarding insolvency in effect until recently were the *Vergleichsordnung* of 1935, which is comparable to the British Deed of Arrangement Act. This codification never had any practical use, because the return offered to the creditors had to be a minimum of 35 per cent, which in almost all cases was impossible to reach. Furthermore, since the reunification of Germany, the insolvency laws for the new German states were to be found in a seperate law (*Gesamtvollstreckungsordnung*). With the new insolvency code (*Insolvenzordnung*) these three codifications no longer exist and the rules regarding insolvency are to be found in the *Insolvenzordnung* alone.

The second problem the legislators meant to solve was the fact that most insolvency proceedings cannot be commenced because the company does not have any assets that would pay for costs of the court and the receiver. German law allows a wide range of opportunities for creditors to use assets of a company as collateral. Consequently, in almost all insolvency cases the assets 'belong' to the preferential or secured creditors and claims of unsecured creditors or costs cannot be covered.

This difficulty could have been dealt with by the legislators limiting the opportunities for using assets as security. The law makers could not find the courage to change these provisions, which would have entailed fundamental changes to the German civil law. The solution the legislators found is a compromise. The receiver has the right to liquidate the assets even if they are assigned to a creditor. He can charge a fee from the receipts of this liquidation. This right of the receiver is limited to assets belonging to preferential creditors that had assets asigned to them. The receiver has no right to liquidate assets belonging to creditors entitled to seperate satisfaction, which is mainly the case for suppliers who retained title to goods or for creditors who delivered assets to the bankrupt on loan. This new regulation facilitates the work of the receiver and also allows costs of the proceedings, and especially of the receiver, to be covered even in cases where all assets are used as collateral.

As already mentioned the third focus of the legislators was to change the insolvency law from a law of enforcement to one permitting and facilitating the recovery of enterprises and individuals.

Despite the fact that the *Konkursordnung* was never meant as a tool for reorganisation of troubled businesses practitioners had in past years worked towards this goal. The method used by the practitioners was mainly to use a new legal entity to buy the assets of the bankrupt with the approval of all the creditors having a lien on these assets. This new legal entity would be free from the burdens of the bankrupt, since all the liabilities would remain with the debtor. However, by law all the labour contracts would be transferred to the new legal entity. This mechanism for saving companies in insolvency became over the decades quite useful and was widely accepted. The new Insolvency Code does not change this method, however with the recovery plan it introduces a new possibility for the reorganisation of enterprises in insolvency. To a large extent the German legislators adopted the US Chapter 11 Procedure by allowing either the bankruptcy receiver or the debtor to draw up a recovery plan. With such a plan debts and securities can be reduced to reorganise a company.

The recovery plan has to be approved by the creditors; however the court has the right to deem a creditor to have approved it, if it can be established that the recovery plan is in the best interests of this creditor. With the introduction of recovery plans the German law makers not only created a new method to reorganise an enterprise, but also established it as a symbol for the new focus of the insolvency code on recovery rather than enforcement and liquidation.

What remains to be seen is how practitioners, meaning the courts, the receivers and the lawyers counselling debtors, will adopt this new method. To introduce a recovery plan is quite time-consuming and thus costly. These costs have to be paid at a time when the acceptance of the plan is uncertain, so it might be that the practitioners will mainly stick to their old methods of selling off the assets after extensive negotiations. However, the recovery plan will certainly be indispensable in cases where the actual legal entity has to be saved, or in cases where negotiations just do not lead to constructive results due to the resistance of individual creditors. In these cases, the recovery plan completely changes the position of opposing creditors, because it provides a tool to overrule their resistance.

Apart from the novelties mentioned above the insolvency code also empowers the 'debtor in possession'. The law is meant for cases where there is actually no mistrust of the debtor and thus allows him to 'be his own receiver'. It remains to be seen how the courts will make use of this new possibility.

A new regulation without any precedent in German law is also article 286 of the Insolvency Code. After a period of seven years a debtor may be released from his debts if for seven years he used his income to pay off creditors. For the duration of these seven years the debtor is only entitled to a minimum of funds, to cover his basic expenses. The old insolvency law of 1877 also allowed for private individuals to file for bankruptcy. However, the protection of the bankruptcy code ended once the bankruptcy proceedings had come to an end. This new regulation will probably have most effect in cases concerning individuals becoming insolvent due to extensive consumer spending. For companies going into insolvency proceedings the relief from old debts will most likely be achieved by a recovery plan, so there is no need for a seven-year period.

After 20 years of intensive debate, the new German insolvency law turned out to be a compromise. The legislators did not curtail the opportunities for using assets as collateral. Hardliners did not want to accept the possibility of relief from old debts at all. It can be concluded that, apart from unifying the insolvency regulations, the legislators successfully changed the focus of insolvency regulation from a law of enforcement to a law for recovery. At any rate, practitioners will have to live with the new law and the new law will have to prove its practical appeal in day-to-day work.

Part Three

Finance and
Banking Issues

17

The Structure of the Banking Sector

Jens A Roennberg, PricewaterhouseCoopers, London

UNIVERSAL BANKING SYSTEM

In Germany, a so-called universal banking system is in place in which most of the banks offer a full range of banking services, from retail to investment banking including mortgages, discount brokerage, telephone and internet banking. Additionally, they offer life insurance, investment funds and asset management services. The most common distribution channel is still the branch network, but so-called direct banking via telephone, mail or internet is becoming increasingly important. As these services are offered by the established banks, market entry for new banks is still very difficult.

GERMAN BANKING SECTORS

Apart from the central bank, the German banking sector can be divided into private sector banks, public sector banks, credit co-operatives, specialised banks and banks with special functions.

Central bank

The central bank in Germany is the Deutsche Bundesbank, which is based in Frankfurt am Main and has nine main branches in the German states (*Landeszentralbanken*).

Although the central bank is independent from the federal government, it is responsible for the stability of the currency and has to support the economic policies of the federal government.

The Deutsche Bundesbank is the only institution in Germany allowed to issue bank notes. Furthermore, it is lender of last resort for the banking system, holder of the country's monetary reserves and clearing house for payments like cheques, bills of exchange and other cashless payments through the accounts that banks are obliged to maintain with it.

Additionally, the central bank has limited responsibilities in banking supervision. It monitors the liquidity of individual banks and of the whole sector and compiles several banking statistics.

Since 1 January 1999 the responsibility for the stability of currency has been handed over to the European Central Bank (ECB) in Frankfurt for the 11 countries that joined the European Monetary Union (EMU-11).

The European Central Bank is an independent institution and is dedicated to monitoring the stability of the euro as its first priority. A subordinate task, together with the national central banks, is to support the economic policy of the member countries, so far as it is not contradictory to the stability of the currency.

Structure and members of the ECB council are set out opposite.

Private sector banks

Private sector banks are generally incorporated as private limited companies (AG, GmbH). The Deutsche Bundesbank monthly reporting divides this group into so-called large banks, regional banks, branches of foreign banks and private bankers. There are currently only three large banks – Deutsche Bank AG, Dresdner Bank AG and Commerzbank AG. Regional banks offer to those banks that have a presence within only a certain geographical area. Due to mergers within the private sector banks the current distinction between large and regional banks may have to be amended in the future. Although Postbank AG is always mentioned separately, it should be classified within the private sector banks, despite the fact that it is currently owned by the federal government. This bank offers, without any regional restriction, a limited range of banking services like current accounts, savings accounts and credit cards, and uses the post office, telephone and the Internet as distribution channels. The privatisation of Postbank AG is expected within the next few years.

Directorate

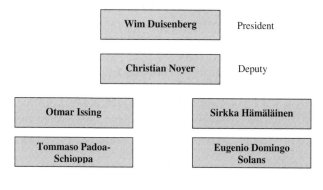

Governors of the national central banks of the EMU-11

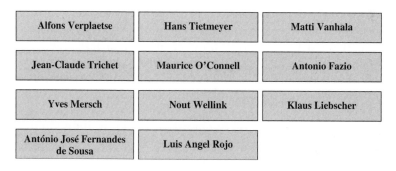

Figure 17.1 *Structure and members of the European Central Bank Council*

Public sector banks

This group of banks consists of the local savings banks (*Sparkassen*), their regional clearing institutions (*Landesbanken*) and a central institution (*Deutsche Girozentrale – Deutsche Kommunalbank – DGZ*). These banks are incorporated under public law by local authorities but they are fully independent entities. Basically they are supposed to operate only within the area in which they were founded in order to ensure cheap basic services like savings deposits, payment services and property lending for employed individuals and small business. Nowadays they offer generally the same product range and services as private banks. Larger commercial clients use the services of the Landesbanken and of DGZ.

Due to mergers the number of savings banks is declining, but on the other hand the merged savings banks are becoming more powerful competitors, taking advantage of their state background.

The central institutions act as central banks and clearing houses for all savings banks within a particular region. They also offer the full range of banking services and give their clients access to international services by maintaining a world-wide branch network. For this reason most of the Landesbanken are represented with branches in the main financial centres of the world. Mergers within the *Landesbanken* have created very large entities, which directly compete with the private banks. Whether the state background gives those banks an unfair advantage with regard to the private banks is still under discussion at the European Commission.

The DGZ acts as a central bank for the whole savings bank sector. Its future role within this sector is still under discussion.

Credit co-operatives

The credit co-operatives sector has a similar structure to the public sector. It consists of a larger number of more or less small credit co-operatives (*Volksbanken, Raiffeisenbanken*), which are incorporated under the co-operatives law, their regional institutions (*Genossenschaftszentralbanken*) and their central bank (DG Bank).

The typical client base of co-operative banks is individuals, small businesses and agricultural enterprises. The *Genossenschaftszentralbanken* act as central banks and clearing houses for the credit co-operatives in their region. DG Bank, incorporated as an AG with effect from 1 January 1998, operates as a central bank and clearing house for the whole sector. Both the regional institutions and DG Bank offer the full range of banking services and compete with the *Landesbanken* and the private sector banks. As far as international operations are concerned, the main difference to the public sector banks is that while most of the *Landesbanken* have their own branches in the main financial centres, for the co-operatives sector only DG Bank has branches abroad.

Specialised banks

In addition to the universal banks described above, there are several specialised financial institutions that provide only particular banking services. Most of them are subsidiaries of private banks and co-operative banks or are related to public sector banks.

Mortgage banks (*Hypothekenbanken*) play an important role in this sector. Their activities are restricted exclusively to mortgage lending and lending to public institutions. They raise funds by issuing mortgage-backed bonds or by issuing municipal bonds backed by their claims on public institutions. Therefore they normally have the best ratings from rating agencies.

Investment companies (*Kapitalanlagegesellschaften*), which are classified and regulated as banks in Germany, manage investment funds. Investment funds can consist of shares, bonds or property or a combination of all three. The funds issue investment certificates, which are traded, based on the daily value of the certificates.

Banks with special functions

Of the several banks with special functions, which are mainly public sector banks, the most important are *Kreditanstalt für Wiederaufbau* (KfW) and *Deutsche Ausgleichsbank*. KfW, initially formed to supply the West German industry with loans after the Second World War, is today engaged in financing export transactions and projects at home and abroad. Additionally, it provides services for the federal government in connection with the reunification of Germany and operates as the German development bank.

The *Deutsche Ausgleichsbank* (DAB) was formed after World War II in order to manage the funds of the European Recovery Plan (ERP), better known as the Marshall Plan. Since 1996, the funds are the responsibility of the German Federal Government. Today the DAB mainly supports the set up of new business, environmental protection programmes and integration schemes for German and foreign refugees.

MARKET SHARE

The number of banks and the market shares of the banking sectors based on total assets are shown in Table 17.1.

Within the private banks the three large banks (Deutsche Bank AG, Dresdner Bank AG and Commerzbank AG) have a market share of 50.4 per cent (1995: 44 per cent) and an overall market share of 15.4 per cent (1995: 12.1 per cent). The branches of foreign banks have a market share of 5.4 per cent and the private banks a market share of 1.6 per cent within the private sector banks.

The mortgage banks, which are included in the specialised banks, have a market share of 61.5 per cent (1995: 56.9 per cent) within the sector and of 13.1 per cent (1995: 11.8 per cent) overall.

Based on the total consolidated assets as of December 1997, there are the three large banks, three Landesbanken, three regional banks and

Table 17.1   *Banks and market shares of the banking sectors*

Banking Sectors	June 1998		December 1995	
	Number of banks	Market share (%)	Number of banks	Market share (%)
Private banks	329	30.4	335	27.4
Public banks	608	35.8	639	37.7
Credit co-operatives	2,380	12.4	2,595	14.2
Specialised banks	52	21.4	53	20.7
	3,369	100	3,622	100

Note: Assets and numbers of banks are taken from Bundesbank Bankenstatistik, September 1998.

DG Bank among the ten largest banks (excluding KfW). The next eight largest banks consist of one mortgage bank and seven Landesbanken.

COMPETITIVE SITUATION

The German banking sector is faced with increasing competition between the three banking sectors. Mergers not only take place within the savings banks and credit co-operatives but also within larger private banks. The results of this competition are that the number of banks declined from 8548 in 1970 to 6365 in 1980 and to 3369 in June 1998, but the remaining banks are becoming larger and stronger.

Competition also has an international focus. Following the globalisation of their commercial customers the German banks have to compete internationally as well. Therefore the big five started to acquire investment banks and asset management companies in the United States, the UK and France in order to become global players. Meanwhile, major UK banks are divesting from investment banking and from international presence.

BANKING SUPERVISION

Banks in Germany are supervised by the Federal Banking Supervisory Authority (*Bundesaufsichtsamt für das Kreditwesen*) and additionally by the Federal Securities Supervisory Office (*Bundesaufsichtsamt für das Wertpapierwesen*) if they provide services relating to securities (eg orders from individuals, custodial services etc).

The Federal Banking Supervisory Authority (FBSA) is an autonomous federal institution under the auspices of the Federal Ministry of Finance and recently relocated to Bonn from Berlin. Its main responsibility is to ensure that no undesirable developments in banking and financial services endanger the whole banking system or result in serious disadvantages for the national economy.

The FBSA has therefore been given wide-ranging powers that include granting and revoking banking licences, determining the principles governing capital and liquidity requirements, approval and rejection of members of the boards of directors of banks and of the external auditors. The FBSA is also allowed to intervene in cases of inadequate liquidity, threatened deposits or risk of bankruptcy, which means as well that a bank could be closed down by the regulators in serious cases. Furthermore, the FBSA is entitled to perform special audits in areas of concern according to Section 44 of the Banking Act, using specialists selected by themselves and charging the cost to the audited bank. The costs of the FBSA in general are shared by all banks.

18

The Private Equity Market

John Harper, HSBC Private Equity GmbH, Düsseldorf

INTRODUCTION

The past three years have witnessed a long-awaited increase in activity levels in the German private equity market. Although less mature than its Anglo-Saxon equivalents, the market (measured by total deal size) grew from less than DM2 billion in 1995 to almost DM7 billion in 1998, making it the largest in continental Europe. A number of high-profile deals, the increased local presence of private equity players and an attractive exit route through a revitalised stock market have combined to ensure that this form of transaction has become a feature of Germany's corporate landscape.

DEAL FLOW

The two main sources of private equity deals in Germany are divestments from large corporations and the sale of private companies from the *Mittelstand*. Both sectors have been undergoing great change recently as larger companies feel the effects of increased global competition, and the *Mittelstand* must face the challenge of a generation of owner–managers retiring.

Corporate divestments

Corporate spin-offs normally have similar characteristics to deals in the United Kingdom. They are marketed by investment banks that produce a sales memorandum and invite a number of parties to bid in an auction. Direct access to management and the vendor is limited and the price paid tends to be a full one. The main advantage of this type of transaction is that information is usually well ordered and the investment bank is used to dealing with private equity investors.

Even a few years ago the concept of selling subsidiaries to financial investors was anathema to many German companies, not least because few believed that the prices paid by industrial buyers could be matched. This has changed recently as more companies have embraced the concept of 'shareholder value' and focused on their core businesses. The composition of boards is changing as younger managers with international experience replace the previous generation of engineers and chemists. Private equity has been lent credibility as a result of several high profile transactions.

The *Mittelstand*

The *Mittelstand* forms a potentially large supply of deals but it is still in the early stages of its development as a private equity market.

One reason why so much attention has been focused on the *Mittelstand* is the problem of succession. Many of the owners are the original founders or their families, whose children cannot or will not take over the business. Acquisitions by financial investors, although still regarded with suspicion by some vendors, are establishing themselves as an attractive solution. Family shareholders often have strong emotional ties to their business and can be reluctant to sell to direct competitors. The management buy-out (MBO) model offers several advantages. The company retains its independence and the transaction can be carried out quickly and confidentially, which is a key consideration for many vendors. It is possible for the shareholders to reinvest in the new structure and share in the upside. A strong financial partner may also be willing to provide further funds for expansion or acquisitions.

What has led to this increased acceptance of (mainly foreign) investors buying large parts of Germany's *Mittelstand?* One of the drivers has been the birth of an equity culture in Germany. A process similar to that witnessed in the UK in the mid-1980s is taking place whereby the privatisation of well-known companies such as Lufthansa and Deutsche Telekom has increased the accessibility of the equity market to retail investors. This has coincided with the global bull run of the late 1990s and the launch of the *Neuer Markt*, a successful market for rapidly growing and young companies.

Investing in private companies can be rewarding as managers who are given entrepreneurial freedom can unlock substantial value for investors. There are drawbacks, however, such as difficulty in obtaining detailed financial information. In contrast to subsidiaries of larger companies, many *Mittelstand* reporting systems are not particularly advanced, as the owners have been content to simply receive their annual dividend. Due diligence can involve helping the management to construct a detailed business plan rather than checking a plan already in existence!

INTERMEDIARIES

Investment banks

The investment banking scene in Germany is dominated by the large US and German houses. Their modus operandi is similar to London-based banks, featuring auctions of larger corporate divestments. These auctions have tended to become broader and more competitive as the number of financial investors in Germany increases.

Several investment banks have expanded rapidly and there is now a good coverage of the larger deals in Frankfurt. Certain deals are still introduced to investors from London but these are diminishing in number as local operations take over. It is essential for a potential investor to cultivate relationships with individuals in the corporate finance area and certain private equity houses have developed a sector-based approach as a way to distinguish themselves from the opposition.

Mergers and acquisitions advisers

Unlike the UK, Germany has an extensive network of mergers and acquisitions (M&A) advisers that usually has a good flow of business from the *Mittelstand*. Most are lawyers, accountants or people with banking and investment experience. Private vendors approach these advisers rather than investment banks either because their company is relatively small, they are concerned about confidentiality or simply because they find it easier to deal with a German intermediary. Relationships with such advisers can be more difficult to build up than those with banks but, once their confidence is gained, access to the *Mittelstand* can be considerably enhanced.

Sales conducted by these houses differ from large investment bank auctions in that competition tends to be less fierce and one can usually gain direct access to the vendor. The process may however lack the rigorous organisation of the investment banks and the information provided is sometimes inadequate. One the whole though, the benefits of working with M&A advisers outweigh any disadvantages.

DUE DILIGENCE

In any private equity transaction a thorough due diligence exercise is vital. Until relatively recently there was a dearth of high quality due diligence providers in Germany due to the fact that the market was small and few people had direct experience of deals. The situation has improved as more deals have been processed and professional services companies focus upon due diligence.

A large number of German law firms have experience in structuring and negotiating commercial transactions and solving complex tax issues. Financial due diligence has traditionally been difficult to source in Germany; now most of the international accountancy firms are dedicating whole departments to this service. Management consultancy practices are also now well established and provide commercial and market studies for prospective targets.

One should be aware that due diligence exercises, especially for *Mittelstand* companies, can cause a degree of unease for the vendor and management. The high level of detail required by private equity investors and the considerable management time required can strain the relationship with the vendor. It should be made clear from the beginning what the process will involve so that both sides can minimise surprises.

THE PLAYERS

Competition has increased significantly in the past two years as most of the major UK and US private equity players have set up operations in Germany. They have been attracted by the extensive press coverage announcing an explosion in the size of the market, which has led to significant fund-raising exercises. It has become clear, however, that the supply of equity has outstripped demand and as a result prices have been pushed higher. It is to be expected that the balance between supply and demand will find its equilibrium in the medium term but for the moment there is considerable competition for every deal.

EXITS

The lack of exit opportunities has been one of the main factors holding back the development of the private equity market in Germany. This has changed considerably in the past few years, due to corporate restructuring and the emergence of the *Neuer Markt* as a viable exit route.

The first flotation in Germany of an MBO company, Tarkett, took place on the main market in 1994 at a time when there were only ten Initial Public Offerings (IPOs) each year. Due to the factors mentioned elsewhere in this chapter, the equity markets have since grown considerably. In the period from February to August 1998, for example, there were 26 *Neuer Markt* and 23 main market IPOs.

Several companies have been sold to domestic and international industrial buyers and this will continue to form an important exit route, driven to some extent by the general level of M & A activity in the market.

CONCLUSION

The German private equity market is now firmly established and most observers expect it to continue to grow, although perhaps at a more sedate pace than in the recent past. There is no shortage of institutional capital looking for a home and this will continue to drive deals in the corporate and *Mittelstand* markets. For the moment Germany is a seller's market, although with a good marketing strategy and contact base it is possible for private equity houses to unlock value from their investments.

19

The Structure of the Insurance Sector

Dr Andreas Freiling and Frank Viecens, PwC Deutsche Revision AG, Frankfurt

INSURANCE INDUSTRY OVERVIEW

Commercial environment

The German economy in 1997 experienced a slight upturn, and there were signs of a further slight upturn in 1998 and beyond. However, unemployment is high and investment returns low. Restructuring and cost cutting in Germany will continue for the foreseeable future.

Despite these unfavourable conditions, the insurance industry expected another year of high profits in 1997, after the recent record years, due to the absence of natural disasters, the falling number of claims and a still high level of premium rates. The trend of rate cutting that started in recent years is expected to continue, partly as a result of increasing competition from both outside and inside Germany.

The insurance market is highly developed, with a stable regime of regulation and low legal entry barriers.

Insurance industry structure

The German insurance market comprises some 2000 insurance companies, of which over 640 work on a national or international basis, the remaining being local mutuals. In addition, there are 77 branches of foreign insurance companies. Of the 640 larger ones, 260 are proprietary companies and 34 are government owned, the others being mutuals.

Foreign direct business totals about DM46 billion. The bulk of business is domestic.

Germany is experiencing an ongoing trend of concentration. On the other hand, new companies are being formed, mostly as niche players, and foreign insurers continue to enter the market.

The government social security insurance scheme, funded by employers and employees, covers a high level of retirement benefits, disability payments, health care costs and unemployment benefits. Premiums in this sector in 1997 were DM709 billion compared to a private direct market of DM239 billion. Based on a pay-as-you-go principle, the governmental system is in the long term unable to maintain the current level of benefits given the ageing population and medical inflation. Cover will therefore increasingly be provided by the private insurance sector.

The reinsurance sector is probably the strongest in the world, consisting of 35 professional reinsurers writing over DM60 billion in premiums (1997), of which 65 per cent was domestic business. German direct insurers continue to reinsure mainly with German and Swiss reinsurers.

Sources of business

Personal line business is provided mainly through tied agents or employed sales forces (over 75 per cent). They do not distinguish between life and property/casualty. The remainder splits into banks and brokers (10 per cent each) and direct selling. So far there is no evidence that brokers or direct sellers are gaining market share in a significant way.

Commercial business is generated either by brokers or directly. Brokers are experiencing a growth trend due to the demand of customers for high quality advice. Increasingly, compensation is being shifted from a commission basis to a fee basis.

REGULATION AND SUPERVISION

Regulatory authority

Regulation and supervision in Germany is split between two types of body, the Federal Regulator (*Bundesaufsichtsamt für das Versicherungs-wesen* – BAV) covering the national operators, and the various state regulators in each of the Bundesländer covering local insurers.

The regulatory rules are based on EU Directives and are similar to many other EU countries. Tight regulation is maintained only in health insurance in as far as it replaces the government health scheme (substitutional health insurance).

In life insurance, the maximum discount rate is set at 4 per cent and premiums in general have to be sufficient to cover all future benefits. Investments are restricted by class and debtor in order to spread the risk.

The BAV and the state regulators mainly apply the same rules and do not overlap. Insurers either fall under one or the other scheme depending on the size and geographic spread of business. The main focus of the regulators is on the financial stability of the carriers and proper profit sharing with the policy conditions or premium rates as required.

The regulators authorise insurance companies seeking to establish themselves in Germany, and perform ongoing supervision. The Insurance Regulation Act (*Versicherungsaufsichtsgesetz* – VAG) as amended in 1998 is the principal legislation governing insurance companies. This Act gives the BAV a wide range of powers including on-site audits, direct communication with the auditors, intervention in management, dismissal of management, run down of the company and closing down the insurer. The BAV is entitled to issue supplemental rules to specify in more detail the regulatory requirements.

Establishment and authorisation

Apart from EEA insurers operating under the single licence, no insurer may carry on direct insurance business in Germany unless authorised by the regulators under the VAG or the respective state Acts. With the exception of accident insurance and supplemental health insurance, separate legal entities are mandatory for life, health and property/ casualty in business. Life insurance includes pension insurance.

The authorisation process requires the provision of extensive and detailed information as set out in the Act. This information focuses on the articles of the company, its directors and shareholders, paid-up capital and any other funds available, the intended classes of business and reinsurance protection. Projections for premiums, losses, expenses and solvency are required for a three-year period. For life and substitutional health insurance, a qualified actuary, a premium trustee and an investment trustee have to be appointed. The actuary is responsible for the proper setting of reserves, the premium trustee for the adjustments of premiums and the investment trustee for the proper coverage of underwriting liabilities by qualified investments.

Reinsurance arrangements have to be appropriate to cover the direct insurance risk but no rules on the sort of reinsurers and the concentration of business are applied.

The authorisation process may take between 6 and 12 months depending on the complexity of the business and the type of policies to be offered.

Supervision and compliance

Ongoing supervision is carried out based on quarterly and annual reports to the regulator plus on-site inspections. In 1997 the BAV carried out 79 such inspections. Further information is gained from complaints and questions by insured or injured persons. In 1997 about 30,000 cases were recorded. Finally, the auditors' long form of report to the management must be forwarded to the BAV.

The returns to the regulator contain detailed information on the profitability of the company by segment, gross and net ceded reinsurance, investments and underwriting reserves and the solvency position. They are not available to the public.

The BAV may exercise its power of intervention in case of a risk of instability of the insurer as a whole and in case of significant mistreatment of policyholders. So far, the BAV has exercised its power via written recommendations and request or personal discussions. Any formal action of the BAV is subject to a decision of the courts governing the public authorities.

In Germany, reinsurers do not require any licensing and are not subject to any supervision other than providing information to the BAV, including annual returns, financial statements, auditors' reports and other information upon request.

The state insurers operate either as a public entity or a subsidiary of the government or of government-owned saving banks. They operate under the same conditions as private sector insurers. They have built strong mutual links and set up a joint reinsurance and a joint health insurance company. Distribution is through large branch networks and the savings bank system. Grouped together, they are the second largest insurance group in Germany after Allianz.

Neither brokers nor other intermediaries are required to be authorised. They are under no direct supervision but must comply with the legal system in general. Legally, no qualification or certification is required. However, the industry has created a training facility, a certificate for intermediaries that should demonstrate a basic qualification to the customers and a central register where all certified intermediaries are listed.

By far the largest area of compulsory insurance is the government social security scheme including health, long-term care, unemployment, workers' compensation and pension covers. All employees have to join this system. High earners can opt out of the health and long-term care element. The self-employed are not included in this system. In the private sector the only compulsory insurance for individuals is third party motor liability for car owners. Premium rates are based on claims experience by region and type of car, but are not regulated. Products have to cover a minimum standard but may offer higher limits of liability. In the commercial sector, certain types of activities require compulsory insurance cover. The main ones are operators of nuclear plants and aircraft, pharmaceutical companies, hospitals, doctors, lawyers, notaries, tax advisers, auditors and hunters.

POLICYHOLDER PROTECTION

Solvency requirements

Solvency requirements are governed by the EU Directives and have to be matched by sufficient amounts of capital. The regulators do not require any capital in excess of the minimum amount. The German market does not expect specific levels of capital or other funds.

Legislation allows for certain items to be recognised as capital, ie 50 per cent of the unpaid nominal share capital, hidden valuation reserves within an investment, unallocated amounts in the reserve for policyholders' dividends, and future profits of the life portfolio. Intangibles are not allowed.

Investment policy

Insurance companies are not restricted in their investments, so far as they cover underwriting liabilities, beyond the general restrictions set out in the Third EU Directives. In principle all assets are admitted as recorded in the balance sheet, except intangible assets. If insurers fail to have sufficient qualified investments they have to present a plan to the regulator showing how the differences will be made up. If the regulator is not satisfied he may ask the shareholders to pay in additional capital to avoid his closing down the company.

Various limits are stated by law to ensure the proper spread of investments. No class may exceed 50 per cent and no single debtor may exceed

5 per cent of all investments. Banks and government securities may not exceed 30 per cent of all investments. Properties are limited to 25 per cent and overall equity investments to 30 per cent of all assets. Each single participation may not exceed 10 per cent of the capital of the company invested in. Foreign currencies must be matched.

Insurance contracts

All insurance contracts must be based on the Insurance Contract Law (*Versicherungsvertragsgesetz* – VVG), which covers general basic rights and obligations of insurers and policyholders such as premium payments, claims payments, cancellation rights and provision of information to policyholders. It is supplemented by the general conditions of the company for each class of business and the individual wording of the policies. The VVG does not restrict the content and design of insurance products.

Insurance contracts usually renew automatically with a right of each party to cancel the policy at the renewal date. Most contracts are annual or for periods of several years. Together with the policy, extensive customer information must be provided by the insurer if this is not done in advance.

Other requirements

The minimum capital requirements are the solvency requirements. However, for start-up companies in the life sector BAV requires a minimum amount of DM10 million either in the form of cash or guarantee by the parent.

Policyholders are not protected by any compensation fund against the risk of failure of an insurance company or inability to pay the benefits due. Motor liability insurers, through a special society, provide compensation to victims of uninsured or untraced drivers.

FINANCIAL STATEMENTS AND AUDIT REQUIREMENTS

Accounting policies

Accounting principles are set up by law, amplified and interpreted by BAV regulations as to methods of valuing assets, technical reserves and accruals. These principles apply to both statutory accounts and BAV returns. Nonetheless, there is some divergence in accounting practice, especially for loss reserves and for the valuation of securities, but only within the scope of the Insurance Regulation Act and the BAV regulations. Supplementary recommendations have been published by both the BAV and an insurance auditors' committee, mainly with regard to details of valuation and presentation of assets and some technical reserves.

A generally accepted German accounting principle states that all realised investment profits and losses resulting from investments, as well as any unrealised losses, should be shown in the profit and loss account. No profit or loss may be credited or debited directly to the reserves or retained earnings (shareholders' funds). Furthermore, all increases and decreases of the shareholders' fund should be stated separately in the annual accounts and/or the management report. Only German professional reinsurers operating on a world-wide basis are allowed by a BAV regulation to credit some investment profit to their loss reserves, stating those amounts separately in the profit and loss account and reporting the respective amounts in the notes.

Direct writing companies have to adopt the normal annual basis of accounting whereby incurred claims, net of reinsurance recoveries, commissions and expenses for the financial year are charged against the earned portion of written premiums, net of reinsurance. Exceptionally, marine and aviation business may be accounted for on a two-year basis, in which the results of each underwriting year may be estimated and are not determined until the end of the first year of development after the year in which business is written.

Unearned premiums are usually computed for direct business on the 365th method, net of commissions. For indirect business, less precise methods are still in use, depending on the periods of notification. German tax regulations require that commissions be deducted from unearned premiums and computed in a manner similar to that accepted for statutory and BAV purposes. Acquisition costs, except for life insurance, are not specifically identified and are not shown separately in the balance sheet as a deferred asset. For direct life business such costs may be deferred and shown separately. These deferred amounts are computed annually by the actuary, in accordance with a formula approved by BAV and stated in the business plan.

When it is considered that unearned premiums are likely to be insufficient to meet losses arising after the balance sheet date during the expiry of business in force, a separate deficiency reserve must be set up for pending losses, which are no longer tax deductible since 1997. This is also mandatory for marine and aviation business in the first underwriting year for which the results have been estimated, especially when big losses have already been incurred. Loss reserves should include reasonable amounts of direct and overhead expenses for investigating and settling outstanding losses, and also for incurred but unreported claims calculated on the basis of experience. No discounting or recognition of future inflation is allowed.

Although reinsurance companies experience delays when waiting for their notification of premium income and claims, they should adopt the annual basis of accounting. Consequently many professional reinsurance companies use the 'non-coterminous underwriting and financial year method', where the financial year ending 30 June incorporates the underwriting results of the previous calendar year. Additional reserves for outstanding claims that are reported extremely late or for missing contract accounts from proportional business should be set up on the basis of experience. For excess of loss reinsurance, a certain percentage of the respective premium income is set up as an additional loss reserve in the balance sheet.

In general insurance, the result of indirect business is sometimes determined only after 24 months. All general insurers and reinsurers operating in Germany are obliged to accrue a fluctuation reserve for every line of direct and indirect non-life business, if the following three conditions apply:

1. Premiums earned, net of reinsurance, in a particular line of business are not less than DM250,000 (averaging the current and the two preceding years).
2. The loss ratio, net of reinsurance, plus the combined commission-and-expenses ratio (gross) in this line has reached 100 per cent in any one of the 15 preceding years.
3. The standard deviation of the loss ratio (net) of the 15 preceding years in this line is 5 per cent or more.

Life insurers in Germany have to prepare an income statement showing the results of operations and the main elements thereof, including investment income and expenses and, separately, the main results of the ceded portion. Actuarial valuations should be made every year (at least every three years for the smaller pension funds). The life fund reserve, as well as the deferred acquisition costs, should be computed actuarially in accordance with the formula of the business plans, using cautious assumptions, such as an interest rate of 4 per cent and conservative mortality tables.

All life insurers operating in Germany are obliged to state in their business plans that at least 90 per cent of the net income for the year (contracts before 30 June 1994) or 90 per cent of the investment income for the year (contracts after 30 June 1994) will be credited to a surplus reserve for policyholders' dividends. This reserve should normally be granted to them within a three-year period. As a consequence of market competition, 96–98 per cent of the life insurers net income is in part credited to the policyholders in the year of origin (*Direktgutschrift*), and the rest is credited to the reserve. The remaining 2–4 per cent are used for shareholders' dividends and income taxes.

Fixed interest-bearing securities and shares have to be valued at the lower of cost or market value; optionally, they may be valued at the lower book value of a preceding year. Mortgages, loans and bonds are carried at nominal values. The difference between the nominal value and the lower cost is deferred and credited proportionately to investment income. German commercial law, also applying to mutual companies, does not allow write-offs in the year of purchase for any fixed asset or equipment, with the exception of low-value assets costing up to DM800 for each item.

Disclosure

The management report published by the general insurance company should be made up separately for the directly or indirectly accepted business of each line (fire, liability, theft, aviation etc) and show the major elements of the underwriting results, net of reinsurance.

In addition, returns to BAV should disclose the results of the accepted as well as the ceded business for each directly or indirectly accepted line. These returns are not available to the public.

Auditing

The statutory annual accounts of all companies organised as stock corporations (*Aktiengesellschaften*), of all registered (larger) mutual companies and of all German branches of insurers registered abroad have to be audited annually by an independent chartered accountant (*Wirtschaftsprüfer*) in order to be approved by BAV.

Legal requirements (*Prüfberichtsverordnung*) specify the information to be disclosed in the German (long form) audit report and minimum audit requirements with respect to the loss reserve, the fluctuation reserve (non-life), the actuarial calculation of the premium reserve (life) and the EDP procedures.

TAXATION

Taxation is based on the published financial statements. No distinction is made between life, health and property/casualty insurers and reinsurers. The rules are the same as for all commercial enterprises. The basis for taxation is the net profit for the year as adjusted for certain unaccepted items such as overstatements of underwriting reserves according to estimates by the tax inspector.

The rate for stock companies is 45 per cent on retained profits and 30 per cent on distributed profits. For mutuals a rate of 42 per cent applies. An additional federal income tax surcharge of 7.5 per cent of the tax levy is also payable.

In addition, a local income tax ranging between 13 per cent and 21 per cent is charged by the municipalities. This is a deductible expense for corporation tax purposes. Grouping of companies is allowed under certain circumstances.

Insurance and reinsurance companies are generally exempt from VAT related to premiums and investment income. Consequently, VAT on related costs is not recoverable.

All direct property/casualty premiums are subject to a premium tax of 15 per cent. In addition, insurers covering fire risk are subject to a fire brigade tax at a rate of 8 per cent of the respective premium.

Part Four

Corporate Finance Issues

20

Raising Finance – Private Equity Funding

Wolfram Schmerl, PricewaterhouseCoopers Corporate Finance Beratung, Frankfurt

Compared to the UK and French markets the German private equity market has been slow to develop. Several factors including the attitudes of traditional lenders, a reluctance among firms to provide information regarding their financial standing to outside investors, and a general lack of information regarding the processes involved have combined to limit the progress of this form of financing in Germany.

In recent years, however, the size of the market has grown at an astonishing pace. This growth has been driven by the need to finance the generation change of a large number of *Mittelstand* firms, and by the growing acceptance among these firms of private equity as an acceptable form of finance. An additional important factor has been the pressure faced by foreign providers of private equity to achieve higher returns in the underdeveloped German markets in preference to their own maturing markets. The most important factor however, has been the increasing opportunities available to providers of private equity to obtain a profitable disposal or exit of their investment. Exit channels have expanded as merger and acquisition opportunities have increased and as European public stock markets for smaller companies have multiplied in the last few years.

The following article provides a short summary on the German private equity market and is intended to offer broad guidance to managers and entrepreneurs seeking an infusion into their business of this form of financing.

DEFINITIONS

Private equity (PE) is a form of equity capital provided to enterprises that are not traded in the public equity markets. For such companies PE can finance acquisitions or the development of new products and technologies as well as strengthen its balance sheet or expand its working capital. PE can also resolve ownership and management issues (succession-related problems in family-owned companies), or finance the buyout or buy-in (MBO/MBI) of a business by experienced managers. This financing is most commonly arranged and managed by investment companies, which invest this capital on behalf of mainly institutional investors such as insurance companies, pension funds, banks, publicly-owned development institutions, but also on behalf of wealthy private individuals or organisations.

The form of PE provided may be characterised by the stage of development of the company in which it is invested. Capital provided in early stages of the company's development may be defined as 'seed', 'start-up' or 'early stage' capital. This applies particularly to the IT, telecommunication and biotechnology sectors. Private equity may also be provided at a later stage to finance expansion plans, capital expenditure, bridging, buyouts/ins or turnarounds.

Private equity can be deployed in a wide variety of situations, which should not be viewed as strictly defined processes, but rather as loosely defined structures that must be altered to fit the requirements of each deal. Several examples of common structures are described below:

- A management buyout (MBO) is one form of a buyout where the existing management buys the company, business or undertaking that they have been managing from the owner;
- A management buy-in (MBI) is a transaction in which a team of experienced managers acquire a company or business to which they consider they can add value through their management expertise;
- A leveraged buyout (LBO) is any form of acquisition that is financed to a large extent by borrowings to be repaid out of the future cash flows of the business;
- An institutional buyout (IBO) is where a financial investor initiates the buyout;
- Another variation of a buyout is when a large number of employees subscribe for equity in the bought-out business (EBO). This type of buyout is popular where it is desirable to motivate a large number of highly skilled employees.

Table 20.1 *Buyouts 1995–97*

Country	1995 Value (£ million)	1995 Number of deals	1996 Value (£ million)	1996 Number of deals	1997 Value (£ million)	1997 Number of deals	Total change 1995–1997 (%) Change in value	Total change 1995–1997 (%) Change in number
Austria	32	3	79	6	77	6	141	100
Belgium	14	5	77	10	275	8	1864	60
Denmark	37	8	237	12	249	14	573	75
Finland	144	28	323	24	486	32	238	14
France	951	101	1076	103	3210	126	238	25
Germany	540	74	1148	62	2319	84	329	14
Ireland	104	6	60	6	49	7	–53	17
Italy	175	15	656	22	1813	20	936	33
Netherlands	523	57	684	56	661	61	26	7
Norway	11	6	100	5	105	5	855	–17
Portugal	93	7	99	5	39	2	–58	–71
Spain	145	13	160	11	217	19	50	46
Sweden	436	18	520	16	920	17	111	–6
Switzerland	406	41	922	52	1511	63	272	54
Total excl. UK	**3611**	**382**	**6141**	**390**	**11,931**	**464**	**230**	**21**
UK	5547	577	7833	610	10,380	660	87	14
Total	**9158**	**959**	**13,974**	**1000**	**22,311**	**1124**	**144**	**17**

Source: Europe Buyout Review, 1999 and PricewaterhouseCoopers

THE BUYOUT MARKET IN GERMANY IN A EUROPEAN CONTEXT

The European buyout market developed exceptionally well between 1995 and 1997. In continental Europe, the transaction volume climbed by 230 per cent during this period, rising to a total of £11.9 billion. In 1997 the total volume in continental Europe exceeded that of the UK for the first time.

In 1997, Germany was the third largest buyout market in Europe by value. The UK still dominates the European market place with a value of some £10.4 billion representing 47 per cent of the total European transaction size. The German buyout market accounted for some 10 per cent in 1997 with a value of £2.3 billion.

Between 1995 and 1997, the German buyout market grew by more than 320 per cent in value. Although the number of buyouts in Germany increased only moderately from 62 to 84, the rise in volume reflects the growing interest of financial investors in Germany's buyout market. In addition, the average transaction volume increased from £7.3 million in 1995 to £27.6 million in 1997. This underlines the trend that institutional investors are investing in larger transactions.

The growth potential for the German buyout market is tremendous. Although gross domestic product in Germany in 1997 was more than double that of the UK, the buyout volume in the UK totalled over £10 billion, or 4.5 times the German level, providing an indication of the potential for growth in the German buyout market.

The growth described above was maintained in 1998 and is expected to continue. The performance in German buyouts is mainly driven by large privatisations of state-owned businesses (eg Tank und Rast) and disposals of family-owned businesses. In addition, Germany's buyout market will be further influenced by the strategies of large corporations (such as Hoechst and Siemens) to increase profitability by concentrating on core activities and to increase their focus on shareholder value.

THE ROLE OF MANAGEMENT IN BUYOUTS

A critical feature in the success of a buyout is the quality of the management team. Financial investors must be convinced that the team is sufficiently experienced, entrepreneurial and committed to the buyout before investing their funds. Traditionally, management in Germany has been risk averse, which has been a major handicap to the development of the German buyout market in the past. Recently however, a noticeable entrepreneurial culture is slowly emerging in Germany.

A buyout involves a degree of risk for the management team. Whilst managers are generally not expected to invest a substantial amount of funds, they will be expected to make a commitment to the funding of the buyout and be prepared to forego this investment if the business fails.

One of the major tasks of the management team is the preparation of the business plan. This is not only part of the financing process but also an aid to management in focusing their efforts on determining the future path of the business, steps needed to ensure success along this path, and their financial implications. A clear, concise and well-presented business plan is an important factor in securing investors' confidence in the management team and the buyout proposal.

The focus of management has traditionally been on profitability rather than cash flow. An important aspect of a buyout is the cash flow potential of the business. Management therefore need to come to terms with the cash flow concept and implications of the transaction's particular financing.

In every buyout, the existing management will face a conflict of interest. On the one hand, it is responsible for the operational aspects of the business and should try to maximise the value of the business to existing shareholders; on the other hand, it assumes the role of a co-buyer who has insider information on the business and an understandable interest in not overpaying for the business. This conflict of interest should be addressed at an early stage of the proposed transaction and be handled carefully. A potential solution of the management's conflict is the appointment of an advisor who has in-depth experience of management buyouts/ins. In addition, the advisor will help to achieve the best possible deal from debt and equity providers and maximise the management's shareholding. Further, a competent advisor will allow management to concentrate upon the operational aspects of the business during the MBO process.

USUAL STRUCTURE OF A BUYOUT

The financing of a buyout will normally involve equity and debt financing. In addition, markets have developed for more innovative financial products such as mezzanine or high-yield debt to finance acquisitions and meet financial providers' needs.

An MBO/MBI will always require some equity investment from the management. This may not be significant in the view of the acquisition price but is simply intended to ensure management's commitment to the proposed buyout. At an early stage in the buyout process, management and institutions have to agree on how much of the equity each will be allocated.

The cheapest form of debt finance is bank borrowings secured on the assets of the company, which is generally known as 'senior debt'. Senior debt may typically take the form of a medium term loan with a fixed repayment schedule. The more senior debt that can be raised the less equity finance is required which in turn increases the likely returns enjoyed by the financial investors. However, there is a limit to how much debt can be supported by the cash flow of the company. It is important that the level of debt and its servicing costs do not impair the viability of the business.

The financing structure of an acquisition also needs to take account of the so-called 'thin capitalisation' rule of the German Corporation Tax Act. According to that rule, interest payable by a German company (ie the acquisition vehicle) to its foreign shareholder is, under certain circumstances, treated as hidden profits distribution. This applies to interest exceeding the 'safe haven' of 3:1 (debt: equity), which is extended to 9:1 for holding companies.

The more expensive type of debt, which is an increasingly common feature of larger buyouts, is subordinated borrowing known as 'mezzanine finance'. Mezzanine finance generally attracts a higher rate of interest than senior debt. Mezzanine finance may also provide a higher return for the opportunity via the premium on redemption or an equity kicker.

The most expensive type of finance is Institutional Equity. There are currently extensive funds focused on the German market, giving rise to an extremely competitive environment. Financial investors require returns substantially in excess of the cost of borrowing in order to reflect the risks of investing in a highly geared, unquoted private company. They measure their potential success on an investment by reference to the Internal Rate of Return (IRR), which is the rate of return on their total investment represented by the discounted value of future income and capital cash flows.

The form of equity interest injected by institutional investors is varied and depends as much on investor preferences as on the structure of the business. Equity investors normally subscribe for some form of ordinary shares, preference shares, loan stock or a combination thereof. The precise terms vary from deal to deal.

In recent years, ratchets have become common features of buyouts. A ratchet is an arrangement whereby the managers progressively receive a greater proportion of the shares if the company performs well. The philosophy behind a ratchet is that it motivates management and reduces the financial investors' risk.

ADVANTAGES OF PRIVATE EQUITY/ APPROPRIATENESS OF A BUYOUT

The success of a buyout will depend not only on the industry in which the business operates, but also on the ability of the management team and on several characteristics of the company:

- It should be able to generate predictable positive cash flows that will normally be used to repay acquisition debt as rapidly as possible to de-gear the company. Typically these cash flows will be generated from operating profits and working capital improvements;
- A buyout company should be able to support significant borrowings to enable it to gear up. The more the purchase price that can be borrowed without risking the stability of the business, the less equity investors will need to finance, which means that management will be able to own a larger share of the company;
- Ideally the business should have a strong position in its market and have an established product range.

Financial investors prefer buyout targets to be in industries with established technologies and strong surplus cash flows. Suitable buyout targets are therefore those which fit in the following categories:

- non-core businesses;
- profitable subsidiaries of a cash-starved group;
- businesses which do not generate sufficient returns on capital employed;
- family-owned businesses with succession problems.

EXITS

Any buyout will normally incorporate a proposed exit route for the management and the financial investor. Different financial investors have different time scales within which they need to realise their investment. Usually, financial investors plan to exit between three and seven years after investment. There are generally three types of exits:

- flotation;
- trade sale;
- institutional sale.

The most common exit route of financial investors in the US and UK is a flotation or an IPO. Flotations are also becoming popular in Germany, as Germans pay increasingly more attention to stocks as a profitable form of investment.

A trade sale may allow investors to realise a value for the entire investment. In some cases, a high price is achievable for strategic reasons. However, a major disadvantage of trade sales faced by management is that they may lose their independence or indeed their employment with the company.

Institutional sales or secondary purchases have been used as exits in the past only to a minor extent. However, this exit route may also gain significance in the future, because financial investors are increasingly identifying disinvestments to other financial investors as an exit opportunity.

OUTLOOK

The German buyout market is expected to continue its rapid growth as there is an increasing acceptance for private equity deals, both from corporate and private shareholders of businesses. Increasingly, German buyouts will be driven by managers seeing the once in a lifetime opportunity of becoming owners of the business they manage. However, the proposed tax reform by the new German government may have a significant impact on the treatment of private equity and acquisition finance (ie the taxation of the NewCo and private equity funds in connection with capital gain on exit and management). Even taking into account this slight constraint, the market for private equity and the opportunities for management teams that the market's development can create, will most definitely be among the most important factors driving Germany's future economic growth at the heart of Europe.

21

The Mergers and Acquisitions Market

*Anita Davisson and Astrid Schmidt,
PricewaterhouseCoopers Corporate
Finance Beratung, Frankfurt*

Since 1994 the German mergers and acquisitions (M&A) market has been constantly growing. From 1994 to 1997 the number of deals with German participation increased from some 2600 to 3000 per annum. In 1997 the number of deals increased by more than 7 per cent. The total number of deals was 3283 with an estimated 3000 deals in 1998, in that year whereas due to restricted disclosure, only 2206 deals have to date been notified officially in 1998.

The German M&A market is becoming more and more international and the interest in German targets is still very high. The percentage of German-German deals has been decreasing over the last few years yet still accounts for more than half of all deals registered. More than 600 companies were taken over by foreign investors in 1997. The most active buyers came from the United States, UK and the Netherlands. German acquisitions were mainly in France followed by the United States and the Netherlands. Overall the German market is developing rapidly, albeit with a time lag of a few years compared to countries such as the US and UK.

The value of transactions involving German companies doubled to DM150 billion in 1997. Adjusted by the so-called mega deals, the transaction value is DM60 billion implying that Germany represents 30 per cent of total European M&A activity by value.

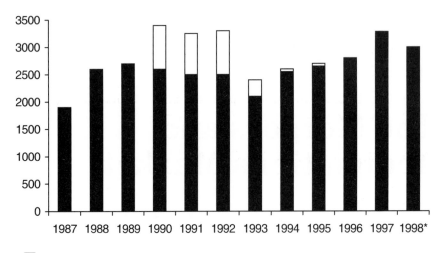

☐ Privatisations of Treuhandastalt

*1998 estimated; 2206 transactions until 31 December 1998 announced; estimated
transactions in total, 3000
Source: based on M&A Review, 1998

Figure 21.1   *M&A transactions in Germany over the last ten years*

Germany is becoming increasingly important in terms of world-wide
M&A activity. Transactions such as Daimler-Chrysler, Deutsche
Bank-Bankers Trust and Hoechst-Rhone-Poulenc were important cross-
border deals with German participation. Additionally, there were some
major German-German deals, such as Thyssen-Krupp which took place
in 1998. Furthermore, the M&A activity in the middle market has been
increasing.

The trend to larger deals involving German participation can be
demonstrated by the figures for the first half of 1998: although the
number of deals increased by only 5 per cent, the published deal volume
increased by more than 140 per cent. This trend continued in the second
half of 1998 with a significantly higher average deal size than in 1997.

STRUCTURE OF GERMAN INDUSTRY

German industry is characterised by some large conglomerates and
about 300,000 companies in the *Mittelstand* (middle market).

Overall, German industry still has a fragmented structure with a
generally low concentration level. Therefore, and as a result of increasing

competition from the European market, the trend to mergers and acquisitions has been increasing. In only a few industries is the concentration level very high. For example, in the retail sector, the top ten companies account for more than 80 per cent of total turnover and the top 50 for 99 per cent of total turnover. Therefore smaller companies have to be either in a niche position, grow through mergers and acquisitions or dispose of their business to one of the major players.

REASONS/WILLINGNESS TO SELL A COMPANY

The German M&A market has become increasingly sophisticated, although not yet comparable with Anglo-Saxon standards. In the past a large number of deals were completed without involving an M&A specialist; in many cases, only a local tax adviser or lawyer was involved. However, the German M&A market has been changing and it has become more popular to sell or buy a company with the support of a professional M&A adviser. Furthermore, only a few companies have their own M&A departments and therefore the shareholders and management are often directly involved.

Due to the *Mittelstand* mentality of the German market, the private owners of a company tend to be conservative, and consider the disposal of the company as a last option only. As a result, in many instances the company owners are more likely to have missed the optimum timing for disposal and may therefore have to sell the company under worse conditions at a later time. Many *Mittelstand* companies are now owned by a younger generation. These inheritors usually have an international education and are, in principle, more willing to sell off the family business than the older generation of business founders.

Over the last few years concentration on core business has been another reason for disposals. Additionally, the increasing focus on shareholder value concepts has resulted in big groups identifying subsidiaries or business units that are non-core businesses.

Also, the German government is increasingly disposing of state-owned companies. The privatisation of these companies is generally by way of an auction.

TARGET IDENTIFICATION

The first step in an acquisition process is to define a clear strategic vision and establish acquisition criteria (eg size, products, location).

There are two major groups of potential targets in Germany: *Mittelstand* companies (totalling some 300,000) and the subsidiaries of larger groups. A number of the family owners of the *Mittelstand* companies have succession issues that can be overcome by disposing of their business. However, some owners are hesitant about selling off their business to a direct competitor against whom they have competed in the past. In larger German groups the increasing focus on shareholder value concepts is leading to restructuring processes and such companies are willing to dispose of their non-core businesses.

Prior to approaching the target, adequate information needs to be gathered. However, family-owned companies tend to be loath to disclose any kind of information. Public companies and sizeable German limited companies (*Gesellschaft mit beschränkter Haftung* or GmbH) are required to file financial information. However, the majority of companies do not disclose anything more than the basic financial information such as turnover and number of employees. Additionally, the common corporate structure, limited liability partnership company (GmbH & Co KG) is exempt from disclosing financial information. For public companies such as *Aktiengesellschaft* (AG), it is much easier to obtain detailed financial information. The number of publicly quoted companies is increasing constantly: by the end of 1997, 817 were listed.

Identifying a target can be done through the acquiror's local subsidiary, through the relevant business unit, through publicly available databases or through a local market expert. In an auction process, the acquiror may be approached directly by the target or its advisers.

Subsequently, the acquisition strategy for each of the targets identified should be defined. The strategy should also include tax structuring considerations for acquiring the target and a preliminary consideration of anti-trust aspects as to whether the merger or acquisition could be subject to German (or European) anti-trust laws.

APPROACH OF TARGETS

The preparation of an appropriate information package on the target forms a basis for making an approach. There are major cultural differences in approaching targets in Germany and abroad. With the German *Mittelstand* mentality, private owners are principally not receptive to 'cold' approaches as they are, for example, in the United States.

The approach of the target depends on the structure of the disposal process. If the target is approached on an exclusive basis, the acquiror may influence the structure of the process. In an auction process, the acquiror has to follow the process, including any restrictions laid down by the target and its advisers. The probability of success tends to be higher within a private process.

VALUATION TECHNIQUES FOR ACQUISITIONS

After receiving an initial, albeit limited, information pack on the target and discussing its contents with the target, an indicative valuation will be the basis for the first offer letter by the acquiror.

With shareholder value concepts gaining more acceptance by sizeable companies, the discounted cash flow method is becoming increasingly common in Germany. A market valuation based on comparable transactions or based on comparable listed companies may also be used as a benchmark. It is very difficult to identify comparable transactions with German participation or with comparable German listed companies and to obtain comparable financial information from the target of the transaction. These issues are starting to change as the number of listings is increasing.

Other valuation methods are the discounted earnings method, which is defined as a standard by the German Institute of Accountants and accepted by the German legal and tax authorities as well as the *Stuttgarter Verfahren*, which is mainly applied by tax authorities for certain tax purposes.

The initial valuation of the identified target is a stand-alone valuation of the target and a stand-alone value of the acquiror's strategic business unit (pre-acquisition). The value of potential synergies has to be added and transaction and integration costs (post-acquisition) taken into account. The purchase price for the target is often influenced by the planned tax structuring of the acquiror.

Such a valuation of the target will form the basis for final price negotiations. During the acquisition process, the acquiror will receive further information which will potentially impact the valuation model and thereby price negotiations. Key to ensuring a successful conclusion to a transaction, is bridging the value gap of vendor and acquiror which tends to be rather significant in the German market place.

COMPETITIVE SITUATION IN AN ACQUISITION PROCESS

Trade buyers have been the most popular buyers in Germany to date; but over the last few years financial buyers have shown increasing interest in German companies as well. Even if the disposal process is organised as an auction, financial investors have often submitted the best bid and have finally been the successful acquiror. Additionally, the numbers of management buyouts (MBOs) and management buy-ins (MBIs) is increasing. The attraction of a financial investor is the continued independence of the business, this playing a major role in the decision process of *Mittelstand* companies.

On the other hand, *Mittelstand* companies have the opportunity of an Initial Public Offering (IPO). The newly established *Neuer Markt* forms the basis for even smaller companies to float on the stock market.

DUE DILIGENCE

A proper due diligence investigation usually enhances the chances of an acquisition's success, especially with non-German investors. The due diligence should identify any inherent risk in the following major areas: financial, legal, tax, commercial and environmental. The due diligence may take place before or after signing the contract. Sellers in Germany are increasingly open to due diligence procedures as part of the acquisition process. In general, German sellers seek to have the due diligence process as late in the process as possible, sometimes preferably after the signing of the purchase agreement.

CLOSING

The general terms of the purchase agreement may be negotiated during the due diligence process. The appropriate capital and finance structure for the target should be defined. After the purchase agreement has been signed, the exchange of shares of the target and the purchase price takes place (closing). Thereafter, the integration of the target, which is critical *inter alia*, to the realisation of value, commences.

Part Five

Accounting and Taxation Issues

22

Company Formation – Tax and Legal Implications

Christoph Schreiber, PricewaterhouseCoopers, New York, and Adrian Yeeles, PricewaterhouseCoopers, London

REGISTRATION AND FISCAL REQUIREMENTS ON FORMATION OF A BUSINESS

Individuals and corporations planning to carry out a business activity in Germany must cope with a number of formal requirements as set forth by administrative, civil and tax laws.

The term 'business' normally includes any engagement in a trade or business that is aimed to recognise gain, is conducted not just incidentally and goes beyond the scope of a mere administration of property. Prior to engaging in such a business, entrepreneurs both foreign and domestic need to obtain a general trade permit (*Gewerbeschein*) which is issued, upon application, by the local trade agency (*Gewerbeamt*) for a small fee. Certain activities which are either deemed dangerous, eg the distribution of fire arms, or are believed to presuppose specific knowledge and abilities such as the rendering of services as a solicitor, a physician, an architect etc, as well as most handicraft trades, require a well-defined professional education, the receipt of a corresponding degree and/or a thorough examination of the candidate's character. Finally, a few jobs, especially in the banking and insurance sector, can be done only if the applicant, in addition, has proven to be of extraordinary personal reliability. In some cases, professional associations watch strictly over the observance of the applicable rules and, in exercising their duties, demand disclosure of company data and other information.

An entrepreneur who carries on a business activity in Germany must, as a general rule, be entered in the public trade register (*Handelsregister*) irrespective of his/her legal organisational form either as a sole proprietor, a partnership, a branch office or as a corporation. Public trade registers are kept for each municipality by the appropriate District Court. Basically, all documents that are submitted by an applicant for registration need to be in notarially certified form. A number of defined business transactions such as the setting-up of a corporation, the appointment of a managing director of a German Limited Liability Company (*Gesellschaft mit beschränkter Haftung* – GmbH) as well as certain amendments to the articles of association of an existing company, eg the increase of the nominal share capital, shall be executed before a public notary and become legally effective only when they have been entered in the public trade register. Hence, registration and notarial fees, which are usually based on the value of the underlying transaction, add cost to the formation of a business in Germany. It must further be considered by an investor that, depending on the individual workload, local courts sometimes do not complete a registration until several months after application; so, depending on the circumstances, an unlimited liability for the founders of a business can turn out to be inevitable.

Upon engaging in a trade or business, the entrepreneur or business entity is obliged to notify the German Inland Revenue of its activity by contacting the local tax department. Upon such notification, the authority will send a questionnaire asking the taxpayer for details regarding the kind and size of the new business, precise business address, projected turnover and estimated profit for the current year, number of employees, filing of an opening balance sheet etc. The information so ascertained enables the local tax department to determine reasonable quarterly income and trade tax prepayments, to establish a payroll tax account and to issue an individual taxpayer identification number (*Steuernummer*), plus a specific VAT number if the taxpayer anticipates carrying out intra-European Community deliveries or supplies.

Assuming that the new business employs staff, further notice shall be given to the appropriate social security authorities ie the local health department (*Allgemeine Ortskrankenkasse*), which will collect the monthly social security contributions, and the industry specific fellowship association (*Berufsgenossenschaft*), which provides the mandatory professional accident insurance. While, as a general principle, all workers and employees who perform their duties in Germany become compulsory members of the German state-controlled social security system, foreign individuals on a temporary secondment to Germany may be eligible for an exemption from German social security taxes. Secondees from an EU country need to obtain an E101 form that is issued upon application by their home country social security department.

A foreign company which engages in a German trade or business but shall not be deemed to maintain a taxable presence in Germany under the relevant provision of a bilateral tax treaty (see below for details) can still be required to make prompt monthly payments of German payroll and social security taxes if it acts through an associate who habitually exercises his employment services in Germany.

Since stamp duties and capital transfer taxes on the issuance of new shares were repealed several years ago, no tax whatsoever will normally fall due upon formation or alteration of a business in Germany. However, an investor who purchases German real property (either directly or through a partnership) will be liable to real property transfer tax. Under the existing laws the transfer of shares in a company that owns German real property triggers real property transfer tax only if the buyer acquires the total outstanding stock, but after December 31 1999 a change in ownership of at least 95 per cent will be sufficient. Real property tax amounts to 3.5 per cent of a specific real property value which in most cases represents about 80 per cent of the present fair market value.

ORGANISATIONAL FORMS OF DOING BUSINESS IN GERMANY

An investor has a choice between a variety of organisational forms of which the most common are briefly explained below. The various business forms differ substantially in terms of legal characterisation, accounting requirements, set-up procedures, liability issues and tax treatment, so the identification of the best alternative represents one of the crucial commercial decisions.

Sole proprietor

An individual operating a trade or business on his own, ie not through a separate legal entity and without any partners, shall automatically be considered a sole proprietor. A sole proprietorship is easy to establish and often proves to be the appropriate organisational form for craftspeople and small businesses. There are fewer comprehensive accounting requirements and little administrative work, but personal liability for all debts and legal obligations incurred in connection with the business is unlimited. Income derived from a sole proprietorship is taxed together with earnings from all other income categories, although a reduced marginal rate applies to the business income. Under a newly introduced minimum tax mechanism, losses from certain passive investments may, with effect from 1999, be offset against income from an active trade or business, but only up to certain amounts.

Partnership

For a trade or business the German civil laws offer two different partnership versions, the general partnership (*Offene Handelsgesell-schaft* – OHG) and the limited partnership (*Kommanditgesellschaft* – KG). A general partnership is an association for business purposes formed by two or more general partners. These general partners can be either individuals or corporations and either domestic or foreign. A limited partnership has at least one general and one limited partner. An increasingly popular form of a limited partnership is the GmbH & Co KG, often structured with the GmbH being the general partner and another corporation as the sole limited partner. Partnerships are easy to set up; a written partnership agreement is not required although highly advisable. Partnerships engaged in a German trade or business, however, need to be registered in the public trade register. Even though they do not qualify as separate legal entities, partnerships themselves may conclude contracts; they can own assets and incur liabilities and they can sue others or be sued. A general partner will be held personally liable with the entire business and private property for the debts of the partnership, but this liability can be limited by using a corporation as a general partner.

Partnerships are considered flow-through entities for income/corporate tax purposes, ie profits will be allocated to the partners and taxed at their level. However, as far as VAT and trade taxes are concerned, the partnership itself is the tax subject and, thus, is treated as if it is a company.

General and limited partnerships are vehicles often used by craftspeople and small to medium sized family businesses. However, they have gained importance dramatically as joint venture and holding companies; the GmbH & Co KG especially plays a significant role within German acquisition strategies.

Companies

The German limited liability company (GmbH) and the stock corporation (AG) are the most important business corporations. While a GmbH must have a minimum nominal share capital (*Stammkapital*) of DM50,000 (of which DM25,000 shall be paid in upon registration), the equity of a standard AG *(Grundkapital)* must amount to at least DM100,000. The taxation of German corporations is discussed in greater detail in Chapter 24.

The GmbH represents the most popular form of doing business in Germany, on the grounds that it appears as a highly flexible and rather informal type of corporation. Transactions such as the assignment of shares and certain amendments to the articles may require notarial form but are easy to accomplish. The GmbH is frequently used as both operating entity and holding company and, in general, grants to the foreign investor the lowest possible tax burden.

BASIC TAX CONSIDERATIONS ON FORMATION OF A BUSINESS IN GERMANY

Besides commercial and business driven demands there are just a few basic tax considerations to which thought should be given by an investor prior to determining the right organisational form for the German trade or business.

Representative office versus permanent establishment

Foreign entrepreneurs sometimes wish to avoid the creation of a taxable presence in Germany. In this case, it is of crucial importance that the German business operations are conducted through a pure representative office and no permanent establishment is maintained. Britain's bilateral tax treaty with Germany precisely defines the prerequisites for a permanent establishment which constitutes such a taxable presence. In a nutshell, where a foreign company maintains a fixed place of business in Germany that does not exclusively perform auxiliary and supplementary functions, or where the foreign investor uses a dependent agent who habitually exercises a power of attorney to act on behalf of the investor, a liability to German taxes cannot be avoided. Accordingly, the scope of activities which are deemed not to constitute a permanent establishment (eg pure storage of goods in a German warehouse) is extremely small. In any event, the distinction between a (taxable) permanent establishment and a (non-taxable) representative office is complex and without exception exposed to a tax risk, so intense professional advice should be sought prior to implementing any structure.

Branch or partnership engagement versus subsidiary

Perhaps the most important decision to be taken by a foreign investor who plans to run a business in Germany is whether to set up a local subsidiary, engage as a partner in a German partnership or merely act through a branch, ie a permanent establishment, of the foreign head office.

In the case of a branch, all business operations are looked on as activities carried on by the head office. Thus, claims and obligations relating to the branch business expose the head office to liability to the full extent of its assets. Although inter-company agreements between head office and branch are legally impossible, the allocation of branch profits and the segregation of expenses follow arm's length considerations. In practice, a double taxation can occur when the two jurisdictions undertake inconsistent allocations. Although there are basically no restrictions as to the activities which a branch can carry on, the constitution of a branch often becomes costly and time-consuming if it has to be entered in the public trade register. This is primarily due to the fact that many documents need to be procured from abroad, officially translated and certified. Under present tax laws a foreign corporation acting through a branch is taxed on its German profits at a higher corporate tax rate than a domestic corporation but, on the other hand, no withholding tax is imposed on remittances to the head office.

A German partnership can be structured so that the liability is actually limited to the entity's assets, in particular by setting up a GmbH & Co KG. Provided the partnership is engaged in a trade or business and maintains a fixed place of business, the tax consequences for the foreign investor are similar to those of a branch. Notably, however, a partnership can borrow funds under its own name and obtain a tax deduction for interest paid. German partnership tax laws also allow the deduction of interest incurred by the (foreign) partner in connection with the acquisition of the partnership interest.

 Most investments in Germany so far are structured in the form of a local subsidiary, mostly as a GmbH, as this corporate vehicle provides a high degree of flexibility and, in addition, qualifies for a lower corporate tax rate upon distribution of profits. On the other hand, start-up losses cannot normally be utilised in the parent company's jurisdiction but only carried forward at the level of the domestic German entity. Further, if a leverage of the German business operations is envisaged, certain limits as to the deductibility of interest on shareholder loans must be observed. Finally, the founders and/or the managing director of the company can be held personally liable for all obligations entered into by the company during the transitional period between the establishment of the company's business and its definite registration in the public trade register.

The key feature of the three alternative organisational forms are compared in the following table:

Table 22.1 *Organisational forms and their key feature*

Key feature	Branch	Partnership	Subsidiary
Separate legal entity	No	Partly yes	Yes
Civil law liability	Unlimited at branch level	Unlimited at partnership level	Limited at company level
Trade tax on income	Yes	Yes	Yes
Corporate tax on income	40%	40%	40% (30% upon distribution)
German dividend withholding tax	No	No	Yes/no depending on bilateral/multi-lateral agreement
Look-through for income/corporate tax purposes	Yes	Yes	No
Losses deductible in head office jurisdiction	Normally Yes	Normally Yes	No
German capital gains tax upon disposition	Yes	Yes	No if tax treaty applies
Deductibility of interest payments on shareholder loans	n/a (expense allocation)	Unlimited	Limited

Direct investment versus holding company structure

Finally, prior to implementing a structure for his German business activities, the investor needs to determine whether he should own the investment directly or interpose a holding company. Relevant criteria for this decision normally include, inter alia, the designated functions to be performed by the German business entity, any already existing structure, the intent to shift debt into Germany, profit repatriation policies, exit strategies and the potential acquisition of a German target company.

A direct investment through a German operating partnership or corporation is easy to establish and, as a straight-forward structure, normally not exposed to significant tax risks. In addition, it involves little ongoing administrative efforts and should require only moderate tax compliance work. On the other hand, a direct investment provides a much lower flexibility when it comes to the repatriation of profits and the disposition of the investment. For instance, an investor who wants to utilise the German profits for financing other group companies might consider owning the investment through a (German or non-German) holding company. Further, in case of a direct investment it can prove difficult to shift interest expense into Germany at a later stage. Most importantly, pursuant to the German revenue service when the stock of a German target company is acquired, a tax effective basis step-up of the underlying assets, if at all feasible, requires that the target company is held by a domestic corporation or a taxable branch of a foreign corporation.

Financial Reporting and Accounting

Wolfgang Suchanek and Sven Rosorius, PwC Deutsche Revision AG, Hamburg

In spite of the existence of EU directives, International Accounting Standards and the ever-increasing number of international business transactions, German accounting is still not widely understood outside Germany. Considerable attention has been devoted to gaining a better understanding of German accounts, and this remains an important task for anyone engaged in or contemplating doing business with Germany. This chapter covers the most important rules regarding financial reporting and accounting in Germany and highlights some of the most frequently encountered differences from UK, US or international practice.

REPORTING

Source of generally accepted accounting principles

German accounting principles are derived predominantly from the German Commercial Code (*Handelsgesetzbuch* – HGB), the generally accepted accounting principles (*Grundsätze ordnungsmäßiger Buch-führung* – GoB), tax law and tax court rulings and the pronouncements of the *Institut der Wirtschaftsprüfer* (German Institute of Certified Public Accountants). In addition, there are other laws that contain rules for certain specific types of entity (for example, public companies, banks and insurance companies).

Contents of financial statements

With regard to the content of financial statements there are certain differences between companies (*Aktiengesellschaften*, AG, stock corporations; and *Gesellschaften mit beschränker Haftung*, GmbH, limited liability companies) and other types of business organisations.

The financial statements of all German companies contain a balance sheet, an income statement and notes to the accounts. A statement of retained earnings and a statement of cash flows or statement of changes in financial position are generally not required, although cash flow statements have been required for group accounts of listed companies for periods beginning after 1998.

Whereas companies must follow the prescribed balance sheet format, they have a choice between two income statement formats. The more common of the two follows the *Gesamtkostenverfahren*, which classifies costs by their nature (eg total wages and salaries, total depreciation) and might be called the 'cost categories format'. With this format cost of sales and gross profit cannot be calculated. The other format is the *Umsatzkostenverfahren* and might be called the 'operations-oriented format'. This classifies items by function, is similar to the most common UK and US formats and does calculate cost of sales and gross profit.

The HGB requires that financial statements are prepared in a clear, understandable and complete manner; that both the balance sheet and the income statement are presented for the current and preceding years; and that the opening balance sheet agrees with the closing balance sheet of the preceding year (thus ruling out prior year adjustments).

The notes to the financial statements must provide an adequate explanation of the balance sheet items and all additional details necessary for the financial statements to give a true and fair view of the net worth, financial position and results of the reporting entity. All companies are required by the HGB to disclose certain basic information in the notes; large companies (see below) are required to make additional disclosures, while medium-sized and, in particular, small companies may omit some disclosures.

Furthermore, all medium-sized and large companies are required to prepare an annual management report on the company's economic condition and circumstances (*Lagebericht*), which does not, however, constitute part of the financial statements. The management report must give a true and fair view of the company's economic progress and position and must also cover significant events that occurred subsequent to the balance sheet date, expected developments within the company and its markets and any associated risks. The management report is covered by the independent auditors' report.

Statutory reporting and audit requirements

The extent and form of the publication of the financial statements and management report depend on the size of the company.

Two of the three requirements in Table 23.1 must be met for two consecutive years to determine the size of a company.

Table 23.1 *Requirements to determine size of company*

Companies	Total assets in millions (DM)	Total sales in millions (DM)	Total average number of employees
Small	≤ 5.31	≤ 10.62	≤ 50
Medium-sized	5.31–21.24	10.62–42.48	51–250
Large	> 21.24	> 42.48	> 250

Quoted companies, shares of which or other securities of which are regularly traded on a stock exchange are always deemed to be large companies.

Table 23.2 briefly summarises the requirements for each size category.

Table 23.2 *Preparation of financial statements*

	Large companies	Medium-sized companies	Small companies
Balance sheet	Unabbreviated presentation	Unabbreviated presentation	Abbreviated presentation
Income statement	Unabbreviated presentation	Abbreviated presentation	Abbreviated presentation
Notes to the financial statements	Full disclosure	Limited disclosure	Limited disclosure

All companies must file their financial statements and management report with the local Commercial Register within nine months (small companies 12 months) of the year end and notice of their compliance must be published in the *Bundesanzeiger* (Federal Gazette). Small companies do not need to file the income statement. Large companies must in addition publish their full financial statements and management report in the *Bundesanzeiger*.

It should be noted that the penalties for non-compliance with the publication requirements are minor and in any case very difficult to enforce. For this reason the great majority of small and medium-sized and even many large companies tend not to file or publish their financial statements. However, it is expected that the rules will be more rigidly enforced in future following a decision in 1998 by the European Court of Justice after pressure from businesses in other states.

Audit

All medium-sized and large limited liability companies and stock corporations are required to have their annual financial statements audited. Only qualified auditors are eligible to perform audits: certified public accountants (*Wirtschaftsprüfer*), who are authorised to perform all kinds of statutory audit, and certified auditors (*vereidigte Buchprüfer*), who are allowed to audit only medium-sized companies. As at January 1998 there were 9156 *Wirtschaftsprüfer* in 1759 firms and 4238 *vereidigte Buchprüfer* in 135 firms registered in Germany.

Partnerships and sole proprietorships

Some partnerships and sole proprietorships, because of their size, are regulated by the Law on Disclosure Requirements for Large Enterprises (*Publizitätsgesetz*). The size thresholds are as follows:

- Total assets (DM millions)   125
- Total sales (DM millions)   250
- Total employees   5000

If these thresholds are exceeded for two consecutive years, then these types of businesses also require annual audits and the financial statements must be published in the *Bundesanzeiger* and filed with the local Commercial Register. In this case, however, financial statements consist of balance sheet and income statement only – notes to the accounts are not legally required.

ACCOUNTING

General accounting principles

The generally accepted accounting principles apply to all types of business organisations. However, in the HGB there are special requirements for companies, so the detailed comments that follow do not in all cases apply to sole proprietorships or partnerships.

Besides the HGB there are in addition certain specific laws for individual types of companies. Examples are the *Aktiengesetz* (AktG) for public limited companies, shares of which are often traded at the stock exchange, or the *Gesetz betreffend die Gesellschaften mit beschränkter Haftung* (GmbHG) for private limited companies. Other specific laws relate to business types such as banks and insurance companies. All these specific company laws contain, amongst other matters, certain specific accounting regulations that have to be observed by the relevant companies.

The Fourth, Seventh and Eighth European Directives dealing with accounting and audit were implemented into German law in 1985.

Annual financial statements must be prepared using the historical cost basis of measurement and must strictly adhere to the going concern and accrual concepts. The prudence concept also has to be observed. This requires the recognition of all anticipated risks and losses arising up to the date of the balance sheet and becoming known up to the time of preparation of the financial statements and prohibits recognition of any unrealised profits. Revenue is only recognised when the delivery of the goods or the provision of the service has been completed.

In any system of accounting there are occasions when the accruals principle conflicts with that of prudence, but it is clear that in Germany prudence takes precedence. This is apparent from professional commentaries but also in the practical application of the principles. For example, no particular method of foreign currency translation is specified in the HGB; however, in accordance with the prudence concept, and unlike in the UK or United States, unrealised exchange gains may not be recognised as income. The precise method used must be disclosed in the notes.

The principle of individual valuation requires that an item-by-item approach be applied in any measuring process; offsetting assets against liabilities and income against expenses is not allowed.

German accounting also includes one particular concept that is almost unknown in other countries, this being that commercial financial statements are the authoritative basis for the tax accounts, which are not an independent set of accounts. On the other hand, most tax incentives can be claimed only if the treatment of a particular item in the commercial financial statements and in the tax accounts is identical (the 'conformity rule'). This principle results in a strong interaction between tax law and the accounting requirements, and this chapter gives several examples of its practical impact.

There is, however, a trend towards greater differences between commercial accounts and tax accounts as illustrated by recent tax regulations introduced by the German government. For example, provisions for pending losses on onerous contracts are no longer allowed for tax purposes even if deemed necessary for the accounts to give a true and fair view.

The HGB requires that the financial statements give a true and fair view. However, in contrast to the position in the UK, in Germany this requirement is not an overriding principle. The HGB assumes that compliance with detailed rules will generally ensure truth and fairness, but if that is not the case then the position has to be explained in the notes to the accounts.

ACCOUNTING PRINCIPLES FOR SPECIFIC ITEMS

Intangible fixed assets

Intangible assets such as franchises, patents, licences and similar rights must be capitalised at cost if they have been acquired. Capitalisation of self-generated intangibles, that is those not acquired from third parties, is not permitted. Perhaps the most important result of this rule is that research and development expenses may not be capitalised; these must, however, be commented on in the management report.

The HGB requires amortisation of capitalised intangible fixed assets over their estimated useful life.

If the value of an intangible asset is lower than the carrying amount, the carrying amount must be written down to the current value if the decrease in value is permanent (extraordinary depreciation). A write-down must be reversed under the same conditions as for tangible fixed assets (see below).

Expenses incurred in starting up or expanding a business

Under a special concession, expenses incurred in starting up or expanding a business may be capitalised. This amount must be amortised in each following year by at least 25 per cent. Profits may be distributed only to the extent that distributable revenue reserves and retained earnings exceed the amount capitalised. The capitalisation of start up or business expansion expenses is not permitted for tax purposes.

Goodwill

Capitalisation of purchased goodwill is optional in commercial accounts (mandatory in tax accounts). If goodwill has been capitalised, it is amortised over four years or systematically over the years in which the company is likely to benefit from it. For tax purposes, the amortisation period is fixed at 15 years starting with the year of initial capitalisation, so many companies also adopt the 15-year amortisation period for their commercial financial statements.

Tangible fixed assets

Fixed assets are carried at their historical acquisition or construction cost, net of accumulated systematic depreciation. Carrying fixed assets at revalued amounts is not permitted.

Fixed assets costing DM800 or less may be fully written off immediately (effectively taken straight to expenses).

Expenditure for improvements and replacement is capitalised, whereas expenditure for maintenance and repairs is expensed immediately.

Depreciation

A variety of different depreciation methods is acceptable in Germany including straight line, reducing balance, sum of the digits, units of production and hours of use. However, any methods that initially result in a lower annual charge than the amount determined by the straight-line method are not permitted. The maximum reducing-balance rate is three times the straight-line rate and, if used for buildings, the depreciation rate is systematically reduced as time goes on. For movable tangible fixed assets, reducing-balance depreciation rates remain unchanged. In order to obtain the maximum possible tax deductions however, it is common practice to switch to the straight-line method as soon as this method results in a higher depreciation charge for the year than would the reducing-balance method.

The useful life assigned to a fixed asset should be based on the asset's prudently estimated useful economic life. Guidance on useful lives is provided by tables issued by the tax authorities. Since German commercial law is flexible on the subject of systematic depreciation, companies usually use the tax tables for general accounting purposes as well. In determining the annual depreciation charges, the cost of the asset is not reduced by its expected residual value at the end of the assigned useful life, unless the residual value is expected to be very material.

In the year in which an asset is placed in service, depreciation is time-apportioned. For movable tangible fixed assets, however, tax rules permit companies to take a full year's depreciation charge for items acquired in the first half of the year and half the annual charge on those acquired in the second half; this has now become common practice in Germany.

While there is an option to recognise temporary diminutions in the value of a fixed asset to below its carrying amount by charging extraordinary depreciation, this is compulsory where the diminution is anticipated to be permanent. A reversal of the extraordinary depreciation is required if the reasons that gave rise to the charge no longer exist.

Tax regulations permit special accelerated depreciation for various reasons, for instance to encourage investment in former East Germany or for environmental protection. For this accelerated depreciation to be tax deductible, it must be charged against income in the commercial accounts.

While depreciation rules for accounting and tax purposes are based on entirely separate systems in the UK and differ significantly for certain assets in the United States, often leading to large amounts of deferred tax, depreciation reflected in the financial statements of German companies, substantially tax driven as it is, is often considered excessive when compared with that charged in British or US accounts. Therefore, when financial statements of German subsidiaries of British or US companies are to be prepared for consolidation purposes abroad, it frequently becomes necessary to adjust the depreciation expense downwards. The tax effect of such adjustments may need to be reflected in the calculation of any deferred tax balances at group level.

Government grants

There is no codified accounting standard covering government grants. In practice, the accounting treatment of grants related to capital expenditure is different from financial assistance towards current expenses.

To the extent that grants related to capital expenditure are subject to income tax, they are usually netted against the cost of the related fixed assets or deferred in the balance sheet and released over the expected useful life of the assets. This has the effect of reducing future (net) depreciation charges. If they are income tax free, they are usually included directly in other operating income. Financial assistance received towards current expenses is generally included directly in other operating income in the same period in which the corresponding expense is recorded.

Leases

Accounting for leases is not dealt with in the HGB. Whether the leased asset is to be capitalised by the lessor or the lessee depends on a number of different criteria, but in most cases the accounting treatment of a lease follows its treatment for income tax reporting purposes. The tax rules allow capitalisation only in rare circumstances, so in practice in Germany leases are generally treated as operating leases.

The decision as to whether the lease is a finance lease depends on a number of criteria, including:

- whether there is full payout during the non-cancellable period;
- whether the non-cancellable lease period covers less than 40 per cent or more than 90 per cent of the leased asset's normal useful life;
- whether the lease agreement includes a purchase or lease renewal option at the end of the non-cancellable period; if it does, the accounting treatment depends on the terms of the option.

Whether capitalisation is by lessor or lessee is further dependent on the nature of the leased asset; that is, whether it is land, a building or a movable asset.

For operating leases, the rental payments are expensed by the lessee and recorded as income by the lessor in the periods to which they relate. Lease commitments that do not appear on the balance sheet are required by the HGB to be disclosed in the notes.

Investments

The valuation of investments depends on their classification as current or fixed asset investments:

- *Current asset investments:* these are investments that are not intended as permanent investments of capital, are marketable and are carried at the lower of acquisition cost or market value.

- *Fixed asset investments:* these are carried at acquisition cost. Equity accounting is not used in single-entity financial statements. If an investment has declined in value, it may be written down to current value and must be if the decline is considered permanent. Should the reasons for the write-down cease to apply in subsequent years, commercial law requires that the write-down be reversed, unless the lower value is allowed for tax purposes, that is, unless a reversal would have tax consequences. Until 1998 all write-backs of fixed asset investments had a tax effect, such reversals were, in effect, optional. However, the latest tax changes mean that from 1 January 1999 reversals are mandatory for tax purposes so they will also be necessary for the commercial accounts. This is another example of the 'conformity rule' in operation.

Current assets

Inventories

The cost of inventory consists of the purchase or manufacturing cost. Purchase cost is calculated net of discounts and allowances. Manufacturing cost includes the cost of direct material and labour and any specific production costs such as special moulds and tools and manufacturing licence expenses; it may, and generally does, include manufacturing and materials overheads. Certain general administrative expenses may also be included, but selling expenses are not allowed.

Inventory cost should in principle be determined on an item-by-item basis. In practice, however, the moving average method, FIFO and, unlike in the UK, LIFO methods are also permitted.

The HGB requires inventories to be carried at the lower of cost or market value. Market value is generally represented by:

- replacement cost for raw materials and supplies;
- net realisable value (sales value less costs of completion and disposal and, at the company's option, profit margin) for work in progress and finished goods;
- for goods purchased for resale, the lower of replacement cost and net realisable value.

Provision may be made for fluctuations in value in the near future. Furthermore, a lower value can be used optionally if permitted by tax law.

Long-term contract work in progress is valued at cost (completed contract method), less any provisions necessary, and not by the percentage of completion method. This is an example of prudence in

German accounting since it means no profits are taken on unfinished contracts.

ebtors

The key points relating to accounting for debtors in Germany are as follows:

- Receivables due after more than one year that are non-interest bearing or bear interest at a rate lower than the prevailing commercial rate should be discounted to their present value.
- Foreign currency debtors are translated at the lower of the transaction rate and the year-end rate, so no exchange gains arise.
- In addition to specific bad debt provisions, flat rate provisions may be established for general credit risks; since these are also tax deductible they have been more common (and perhaps larger) than in the UK or United States. This may change in the future, however, since from 1 January 1999 provisions against debtors are only allowable for tax purposes when the losses actually materialise and not when anticipated as a matter of accounting prudence. This is another indication of the increasing trend towards differences between the commercial and tax accounts.

iabilities and accruals

General accounting treatment

There is no authoritative distinction between current and non-current liabilities. The HGB subdivides liabilities into accruals or 'provisions' (with separate items for pension, tax and other accrued liabilities) and accounts payable (with separate items for debenture loans, amounts owed to credit institutions, trade payables, notes payables, amounts owed to affiliates and other payables). Since 1 January 1999 long-term non-interest bearing liabilities and accruals and also non-cash liabilities have to be discounted at a rate of 5.5 per cent for tax purposes.

If there is certainty as to the existence and amount of an obligation, the item must be included in accounts payable; if there is any uncertainty about either existence or amount, the item must be included in other accruals. If only the due date of an obligation is uncertain, it is presented as a payable.

While the concept of matching expenditure with related income is fundamental in Germany, the concept of prudence has priority. Accordingly, accruals must be set up for uncertain liabilities and impending losses. Uncertain liabilities are estimated liabilities for which it is either known or probable that an asset has been impaired or a liability incurred as at the balance sheet date.

Accruals

In general, accruals must be set up for foreseeable losses. The following specific accruals are mandatory:

- uncertain liabilities and impending losses from uncompleted business transactions;
- deferred maintenance or waste removal costs to be incurred within 3 months (maintenance) or 12 months (waste removal) after the end of the business year;
- guarantee costs not incurred under a legal obligation;
- pension commitments entered into from 1 January 1987 (also see below).

In addition, the following accruals are optional:

- maintenance deferred from the current year, to be carried out more than three months after the year end;
- future major repairs, limited to specific conditions.

In many countries, including the UK, accruals for items where there is no current obligation (such as deferred maintenance) would not be established.

It should be noted that following the recent changes in tax law there are now more limitations on what can be accrued for tax purposes; it is possible that this will also tend to limit what companies accrue in their commercial accounts in future.

Dividends paid or payable

Proposed dividends are not accrued for at the balance sheet date but shown as a transfer from retained profits in the following year's accounts.

Pension accruals

In contrast to the position in the UK and the United States, where companies provide against their future pension obligations by irrevocably contributing funds to outside, non-controlled pension funds, German companies with few exceptions accrue for all future pension obligations under a related heading in their balance sheet.

Generally, there are no assets specifically designated to cover future pension payments; management uses the resources for the operations of the company and in this sense pension schemes are often a major source of funds for German companies. The accrual must cover all pension rights granted to individuals after 31 December 1986 and all subsequent increases. An accrual for obligations entered into before that date is optional but any amount not booked must be disclosed in the notes to the accounts.

While the actuarial method of providing pension accruals in Germany in many respects resembles the 'entry age method' used in Anglo-Saxon countries, it is largely influenced by German tax regulations. It measures the total obligation for each pension plan participant individually as the present value of future benefits, net of the present value of assumed future premiums that would be payable if a life insurance policy had been purchased.

The difference in the sum of these actuarial calculations for all pension plan participants between the current year and the preceding year constitutes one part of the annual pension expense. The other part consists of the actual pension payments made during the current year. Actuarial gains and losses are recognised currently as adjustments of pension expense rather than spread over a number of years, as they would be in the UK. This leads to greater fluctuations in pension costs.

There are several significant differences from UK/US practice in the detailed actuarial calculations. These have a direct bearing on the amount accrued and can be summarised as follows:

- The actuarial calculations do not normally take personnel fluctuations into account.
- The minimum entry age into the plan is assumed to be 30 years for all participants.
- The calculations are based on current salaries, ie future increases are not taken into account even though pensions are usually based on final salaries. Although pension indexation is mandatory by law, future pension increases are not taken into account unless specifically prescribed in the plan rules.
- The assumed interest factor used to compute present values is set by the tax authorities at 6 per cent.

From what has been said it is evident that the calculation of pension cost in Germany is significantly different from the Anglo-Saxon approach and, in fact, the pension accruals of German companies are often found to be deficient when they are compared with the sum of future obligations determined on the basis of British or US accounting principles.

In the context of post-retirement benefits in general, it should be noted that benefits other than pension payments are not common in Germany.

Taxation

The accrual for taxation should be calculated on the basis of the proposed profit distribution or of the shareholders' resolution concerning the appropriation of the results if already available. The reason is that different tax rates are applicable depending on whether the profit is retained (in which case the higher corporation tax rate is applied) or distributed as a dividend (in which case the lower rate is applied).

In the profit and loss account taxes on income or profits are separately disclosed from other taxes.

Deferred taxes

There are many areas in the German income tax regulations where an accounting method chosen for income tax purposes is also required to be used for financial reporting purposes. Accordingly, there are relatively few differences in Germany between taxable income for financial reporting purposes and that for tax reporting purposes, although, as already indicated, this may change in future.

The HGB requires a net deferred tax liability to be recorded using the full liability method when taxable income under tax regulations is lower than pre-tax accounting income due to timing differences. The recording of a deferred tax asset is optional, but if it is done profits may be distributed only if, after such distribution, the freely available revenue reserves plus retained profits less any accumulated losses brought forward are at least equal to the recorded tax asset.

Reserves

German rules require a larger number of subdivisions of reserves than do UK or US rules. Under the first overall division, as provided for in the European Fourth Directive, reserves are classified as either capital or revenue reserves.

Capital reserves include:

- amounts received for the issue of shares or warrants in excess of their nominal value;
- amounts received that are related to conversion rights or options attached to debentures issued;
- amounts paid in by shareholders in consideration of preferences awarded by the company;
- any other capital contributions from shareholders.

Revenue reserves include only such amounts as are created by transfer from the profits of any financial year. They would generally include:

- legal reserve;
- reserve for own shares/shares in a controlling company;
- reserves prescribed by the company's articles;
- other revenue reserves.

Legal reserve

German stock corporations must allocate 5 per cent of each year's profit to the legal reserve until, together with certain components of the capital reserves, the legal reserve is equal to 10 per cent of the par value of share capital; the articles may prescribe a higher reserve amount. The legal reserve may, substantially, be utilised only to compensate for losses that the company has incurred or to increase the company's share capital.

Reserve for own shares

It is a requirement that any holding of a company's own shares or any investment in shares of a controlling company must be offset by a reserve of the same amount. This reserve may only be released in tandem with a reduction of the corresponding asset.

Reserves prescribed by the company's articles

These comprise appropriations of earnings as prescribed by a company's articles and may, but need not, be earmarked for certain purposes.

All activities during the year in the reserve accounts must be disclosed in the balance sheet or the notes to the financial statements.

German accounting and disclosure standards or prevailing practices surrounding reserves substantially comply with International Accounting Standards.

Special items with an equity portion

A peculiar feature of many German balance sheets are special items with an equity portion (*Sonderposten mit Rücklageanteil*). Such items may be recorded only to the extent that tax recognition of certain transactions is dependent on their inclusion in the balance sheet. They have the attributes of both an accrued liability and a reserve: one portion is an accrued liability in that income taxes will have to be paid in the future when the item is dissolved; the other portion is in the nature of a reserve (equity).

For example, German income tax law permits taxpayers under certain circumstances to defer for tax purposes gains on the sale of certain fixed assets until they are applied against qualifying reinvestments within a limited period of time (rollover relief). This is only possible, however, if the gain is posted to 'special items' rather than to income. On the purchase of eligible new assets, an amount equivalent to the gain realised earlier on the sale of the old asset is deducted from the cost of the new asset as a depreciation charge against current income, while the previously deferred gain is restored to taxable income. Thus the net carrying value of the new asset is reduced by the earlier gain without an effect on income.

Other examples include crediting government grants to 'special items' rather than recording them as a reduction of the carrying value of the related asset, and crediting special depreciation for tax purposes here rather than to provisions for depreciation.

Special items with an equity portion are shown on the liability side of the balance sheet between equity and current liabilities.

Items of this nature are not recognised on balance sheets in the UK or the United States; to the extent that tax-free gains arise from disposals of certain assets these would be recognised as income, but would be taken account of in the determination of any deferred tax balances.

Contingencies

Practice regarding contingencies is relatively straightforward:

- Contingent gains are normally not recorded or disclosed.
- For contingent losses the accounting treatment (accrual or disclosure only) is governed by the concept of prudence. Accordingly, all contingent losses that are likely to occur must be accrued on an estimated basis. A contingent liability that has not been accrued must be disclosed on the face of the balance sheet or in the notes.

Extraordinary and exceptional items and prior year adjustments

Extraordinary items are items that are material in size, not regularly recurring and of unusual character. Items such as gains and losses on the sale of major assets or investments or of part of a business could be disclosed as extraordinary items under German rules, as could items related to mergers, acquisitions or restructuring.

All extraordinary items must be explained in the notes to the financial statements and extraordinary gains and losses should be disclosed separately, gross of tax, in the profit and loss account.

Unlike in certain other countries, including the UK, no distinction is made between extraordinary and exceptional items.

In general, German accounting does not recognise the concept of prior year adjustments. Any adjustments relating to prior years are normally included in the current year's profit and loss account, disclosed as extraordinary if significant. Only in very rare circumstances are changes made by adjusting the prior year's balance sheet. An example might be if an accounting policy had been used that was not permitted by law and the results or net assets of the company had been significantly affected by the use of this policy. There are also specific tax regulations that have to be observed in such cases.

Consolidation requirements

German parent companies meeting certain size criteria are required to publish consolidated statements comprising all group companies under common control, both domestic and foreign. The uniform German accounting principles, which may well differ from the ones used for local statutory accounts, must be applied for all companies included in the consolidation and all intra-group profits and losses must be eliminated.

For investments in companies in which 20 per cent or more is held, but not the majority of the voting rights, the equity method must be used. However, it should be noted that the equity method is allowed only in consolidated statements, not in single-entity financial statements.

Further detail on group accounting and developments in public financial reporting is provided in Chapter 26.

24

Business Taxation

Christoph Schreiber, PricewaterhouseCoopers, New York, and Adrian Yeeles, PricewaterhouseCoopers, London

INTRODUCTION

The taxation of businesses is split into two sections. In this first section the general tax treatment of businesses in Germany is considered and the matters that affect all businesses, regardless of their legal status, are discussed. The second section deals with the specific issues arising in the taxation of companies and the taxation of partnerships.

GENERAL INFORMATION

Business income is derived by any taxpayer that engages in a trade or business with the intention of generating earnings and profits. While individuals are taxed on the sum of income from seven different income categories (business income, self-employment income, employment income, capital investment income, rental income, agricultural income and specified other income), corporations are always considered to receive business income even if their revenues, in fact, stem from investment eg rented property or from a portfolio investment. German partnerships, and respectively their partners, generate business income provided the partnership is either engaged in an actual trade or business or qualifies as a deemed business entity under the domestic tax laws. The status of a deemed business entity is assumed if the partnership is legally represented, not by an individual who is also a partner, and if all general partners are companies and thus not exposed to an unlimited liability. Under this rule most GmbH & Co KG limited partnerships shall be deemed business entities. The distinction between business and non-business income appears crucial as trade tax is imposed on business income only.

The excess of revenues generated by the trade or business over all deductible expenses is, on a recurring basis, subject to income or corporate income tax, trade tax, solidarity tax and, where applicable, capital yields or withholding tax and church tax. Other important taxes include a value added tax (VAT) of at present 16 per cent and a 3.5 per cent real property transfer tax. Germany abandoned capital and stamp duties several years ago; since 1998 and 1997 respectively trade tax on capital and wealth taxes are no longer levied. Any taxes payable are finally determined, not via self-assessment but by the German Inland Revenue, after a review of the annual tax returns as submitted by the taxpayer. The general filing deadline for all annual returns is 15 May of the following year; upon a taxpayer's request the authorities usually grant an extension until 30 September. In extraordinary cases, the local tax department may even permit a filing as late as 28 February of the next year but one. Particular due dates apply to the remittance of withholding tax, payroll tax, VAT and prepayments on the estimated income, corporate income and trade tax liability. The tax assessment period generally equals the calendar year. However, businesses may opt for a fiscal year different from the calendar year; restrictions apply.

The taxation of business income in Germany is significantly affected by the major tax reform that the new federal government introduced in November 1998 and that was finally approved by the legislative bodies in March 1999. The tax reform bill contains numerous changes that are scheduled to become effective in three steps – 1999, 2000 and 2002. A modest relief in personal income tax rates and a reduction of the corporate tax rate on retained earnings from 45 per cent to 40 per cent are contrasted primarily by cut-backs of tax incentives, the disallowance of numerous tax deductions and the adjustment of calculation methods for the evaluation of liabilities. Considering that the corporate tax rate on distributed earnings remains unchanged at 30 per cent for the time being, the foreign investor merely faces a broader tax base and, therefore, will end up paying German taxes at a higher effective rate (for more details see below). The other part of the tax reform provides for an increase of indirect taxes on fuel and electric power in order to finance a moderate cut in the contribution rates for the state-provided social security system. Pursuant to the government's far-reaching plans, as from the year 2002 onwards (or even earlier) all business income, regardless of the legal form of the business, is intended to be subject to a uniform business tax at a rate of approximately 35 per cent but the details of this have still to be worked out. A switch to a uniform rate applying to both retained and distributed earnings would be so fundamental to the existing tax system that almost every foreign investor would have to rethink the structure of his business activities.

Applicable tax rates

Table 24.1 outlines the most important taxes on business income and the respective rates under the previous and the proposed law.

Table 24.1   *Taxes on business income and notes*

Tax	Tax base	Previous rate %	New rate %	Effective date
Resident corporation tax on retained earnings	Taxable income	45	40	1999
Resident corporation tax on distributed earnings	Distributed income	30	30	n/a
Non-resident corporation tax	German source taxable income	42	40	1999
Personal income tax (business income only)	Proportional business income	up to 47	up to 45 (43)	1999 (2000)
Personal income tax (non-business income)	Taxable income	up to 53	up to 51 (48.5)	2000 (2002)
Trade tax on income	Trade income	16– 20	16–20	n/a
Withholding tax (capital yields tax)	Dividends, interest, royalty	25/30 (lower treaty rate may apply)	25/30 (lower treaty rate may apply)	n/a
Solidarity tax	Income/corporate income and with-holding tax	5.5	5.5	n/a
Real property transfer tax	Specified value (deemed market value)	3.5	3.5	n/a

Determination of taxable business income

As explained in greater detail in Chapter 23 corporations and individuals who engage in a trade or business are required by law to keep accurate books and records and to prepare annual statutory financial statements that comply with German accounting principles. The principle according to which the treatment of a transaction and the valuation of an asset in the tax balance sheet shall follow the methodology applied in the commercial books is known as *Maßgeblichkeitsgrundsatz*. Hence, as a basic rule of the present tax law, the profit or loss ascertained under the German accounting rules forms the starting point for the determination of the taxable income.

Since taxation of business income in Germany is based on individual performance, generally all business-related expenses can be deducted in computing taxable profits, provided they have actually been incurred and are not on capital account. Taxes on income including the solidarity surtax may generally not reduce the amount of taxable income, so they must be added back if treated as an expense for accounting purposes (actually paid trade taxes, however, are deductible for corporate income tax purposes). Limitations apply to the deductibility of entertainment expenses (at least 20 per cent non-deductible), business gifts to non-employees (if the net value per person exceeds DM75), charitable donations (deductible up to certain income percentages only), director's fees paid to a supervisory board member, the private use of a company-owned or leased car and other specified expenses. Expenses that have been incurred to create an intangible asset may generally not be capitalised and can thus be deducted immediately.

Interest payments made on a business-related loan, eg acquisition debt, basically qualify as fully tax-deductible expenses for income and corporate income tax purposes. Restrictions apply, however, where expenditure relates to tax-exempt income; in particular, with effect from 1999 foreign dividends derived tax-free by a German corporation under the affiliation privilege shall be recharacterised, at 15 per cent, as a non-deductible expense. Further restrictions are posted by the German thin capitalisation rules on shareholder and shareholder guaranteed loans. This is further explained in Chapter 24. Notably, in computing the amount of taxable trade income generated by a sole proprietor, a partnership or a corporation, interest on any long-term loan (*Dauerschuldzinsen*) can be deducted at 50 per cent only.

The German tax laws also allow for the set up of non-taxable reserves in limited circumstances. The most important provisions are those dealing with pension reserves and clearly defined uncertain liabilities such as audit fees. Tax-deductible provisions may be made in respect of these items. In a few cases the capital gain recognised on the disposition of an asset can be deducted from the cost of its replacement, thus resulting in a tax deferral. Other than these, general accruals and provisions recorded in the commercial books are not permitted for tax purposes.

Depreciation is the major non-cash cost that qualifies as a deductible expense and thus reduces taxable profit in Germany. In line with general principles, fixed assets used in the business can be depreciated provided they are subject to normal wear and tear (eg machinery and other equipment but not land and financial assets). The amount of depreciation depends on both the expected useful life and the depreciation method chosen by the taxpayer. The federal fiscal authorities have published a list setting out the standard periods of useful life for most depreciable assets and it is common practice to adopt these for both book and tax purposes.

Under German income tax law there are two different depreciation methods available, the use of which depends on whether the asset in question is movable, immovable, tangible or intangible. For tangible movable assets the taxpayer may choose between:

- **straight-line method,** under which a fixed percentage is applied annually to the asset's acquisition cost; and
- **reducing-balance method,** under which a fixed percentage is applied to the opening book value each year.

The percentage rate used under the reducing-balance method may not exceed three times the percentage under the straight-line method or a maximum annual percentage rate of 30 per cent, whichever is the lower. A change from the reducing-balance method to the straight-line method is allowed but not vice versa. Movable assets being subject to wear and tear but costing not more than DM800 each (exclusive of VAT) can be fully depreciated in the year of acquisition or construction.

In contrast to the depreciation rules for movable assets, the useful life doctrine does not apply to immovable tangible property such as buildings. Rather, standard straight-line percentage rates must be used according to the rules of the German income tax code, whereby the applicable rates primarily depend on the date of acquisition or construction of the building. Buildings completed before 1 January 1925 shall be depreciated at 2.5 per cent per annum, whereas the rate for those completed after 31 December 1924 is 2 per cent. Where a building is used exclusively for business purposes and a construction permit was applied for after 31 March 1985, a rate of 4 per cent per annum is granted.

Intangible assets such as franchises, patents, licences, know-how, similar rights and also goodwill can be capitalised and depreciated only if they have been acquired for consideration. The amortisation period in this case shall equal the estimated economic useful life of the intangible, with the exception of goodwill, which must be depreciated over a period of 15 years.

Under the present tax laws taxpayers are permitted to write-down or even write-off an asset, eg an investment in another company or seasonal goods, either if the value has dropped permanently below the book basis or in case of exceptional wear and tear. In doing so an immediately deductible expense is created. However, as a practical matter, most write-downs and write-offs are thoroughly examined by the German Inland Revenue at a later tax field audit; for instance, the authorities will not normally approve a write-off of a loss-making investment during its start-up phase.

In determining the final taxation basis, losses either derived from another income category or incurred during a preceding or succeeding tax year will be considered, depending on the circumstances. As a general rule, individuals are taxed on the sum of profits and losses derived from all income categories. Restrictions apply to the crediting of speculative gains/losses and, effective 1999, the utilisation of losses from portfolio investments against profits from an active trade or business. Corporations are not affected by this limitation as they shall be deemed to generate income from one and the same category only. Profits not compensated horizontally, ie with losses incurred during the same assessment period, can be offset against loss carry-forwards from previous tax years. Until 1998 losses up to DM10 million could also be carried back into the two preceding years. Effective 1999, the loss carry-back is limited to one year and DM2 million; as from 2001 the maximum amount will be further reduced to DM1 million. The loss carry-forward under both the previous and the new law is indefinite. A separate set of rules covers the utilisation of trade tax losses.

For most businesses the proposed tax reform will lead to a decline in tax-deductible expenses and thus to a higher taxation basis. In particular, effective for fiscal years starting on or after 1 January 1999, all fixed assets shall be recorded for tax purposes at their original costs less regular depreciation, if applicable. Extraordinary write-offs and write-downs to a lower fair market value will only be permitted if it can be presumed that the fair market value has permanently dropped below the book value. Any write-down or write-off that has been performed in the past shall be recaptured, in any one year, unless the taxpayer can demonstrate that the fair market value is still lower than acquisition cost minus regular depreciation. If the latter is the case, the lower value may be entered. Accruals for future expenditure such as warranties, refurbishing etc may be calculated on a variable rather than a full cost basis only. Provisions for bad debts can no longer be built; any lump-sum depreciation will be disallowed. Accruals for certain cash liabilities shall be discounted under a mark-to-market concept. The tax-free rollover of capital gains to a new asset will henceforth be confined to land and buildings.

Table 24.2 *Sample computation of taxable income*

	Trade income	Corporate income
Profit according to commercial books	100	100
Current year tax prepayments treated as book expense	80	80
Adjustment due to non-deductibility of expenses (eg entertainment)	20	20
Adjusted income	200	200
50% of long-term interest	40	
Taxable trade income	240	n/a
Trade tax payable (est. 20%)	48	(48)
Taxable income for corporate tax purposes	n/a	152

Transfer pricing rules

Germany has been a leading proponent of the arm's length principle in transactions between related parties. Section 1 of the Foreign Tax Act (*Außensteuergesetz*) requires that arm's length prices be used for all inter-company transactions. The provisions are similar to transfer pricing rules in most of the industrialised countries. It is the intention of Section 1 of the Foreign Tax Act to place the controlled taxpayer on a par with an unrelated taxpayer and to determine the appropriate taxable income, should the controlled taxpayer have agreed terms and conditions that deviate from those an unrelated taxpayer would have agreed.

The *Administration Principles on Income Allocation* were published by the Federal Minister of Finance in 1983 as an interpretation of Section 1 of the Foreign Tax Act and have been a standard bearer for the development of transfer pricing as an international tax issue. They include general guidelines on the determination of an appropriate transfer price and also contain detailed comments on various inter-company transactions such as the delivery of goods, granting of loans, rendering of services, transfer of intangibles etc. Technically, the guidelines merely serve as directives for the evaluation of transfer prices at a tax audit in that the tax authorities are required to apply the principles when they audit a controlled taxpayer and review his or her transfer pricing policy. Accordingly, the guidelines are not legally binding. However, due to the scarcity of case law on transfer pricing issues and considering the strict enforcement of the principles by the tax authorities, related companies in Germany and their tax consultants also use the administration principles as the yardstick for measuring the appropriateness of transfer prices.

In general, the administration principles stipulate that inter-company transactions will only be approved for tax purposes if the parties have acted as though they were unrelated (dealing at arm's length principle). The yardstick for the arm's length character of a transaction among related entities is the standard of customary care employed by an orderly and prudent manager when dealing with unrelated persons.

The administration principles provide three specific methods for determining an arm's length consideration:

1. **Comparable uncontrolled price method** – adopting with any necessary modification the uncontrolled market price for the same or similar transaction, or adopting the internal price for the same or similar transaction to independent third parties.
2. **Resale price method** – taking the price at which the goods or services are sold by the related purchaser (reseller) to independent customers and subtracting an arm's length mark-up equivalent to the functions performed and risks borne by the reseller.
3. **Cost-plus method** determining the supplier's or vendor's cost by using the cost accounting concepts of the supplier or vendor applied towards independent parties or, if no uncontrolled transactions occur, another acknowledged accounting method and adding a mark-up that is customary in this industry or trade.

The German administration principles do not provide for either a comparable profit or profit split method as used in some countries, most noticeably the United States, of which Germany has been a consistent critic. However, as can be seen from the tax administration's approach during tax audits and from recent statements of German fiscal courts, the relevant criteria for the evaluation of inter-company business relationships have been continually broadened during the past decade. In particular, the Supreme Fiscal Court holds – and the tax authorities have apparently adopted this doctrine – that, irrespective of the appropriateness of the applied pricing method pursuant to the administration principles, a controlled distributor of intra-group manufactured products must always be left with a reasonable pre-tax profit. The philosophy behind this additional arm's length requirement is that, according to the federal judges, an unrelated reseller would not continue its distribution activities if it could market a certain product only at minimal or no profit.

Germany is a signatory to the OECD Transfer Pricing Guidelines for multinational enterprises and tax administrations. These do not contain binding rules but represent merely an international consensus on the application of the arm's length standard to test the appropriateness of inter-company prices. Yet, even though the guidelines are not law, they encourage member countries to follow them; in fact, prior OECD guidelines were traditionally well received (as they enhance the level of consistency) and partly even transferred into national legislation of single member countries. The revised OECD guidelines as issued in July 1995 take into account practical experience as well as interim developments in the member countries. Even though they still express a strong preference for the use of one of the three standard methods for testing the arm's length character of a transfer of tangible property, the new guidelines emphasise the importance of comparability as to functions performed, risks assumed and assets employed. Further, they introduce a so-called transactional net margin method that compares the operating profit of the controlled enterprise to a similar measure of operating profit realised by comparable uncontrolled parties. To a certain extent matching up with the approach described in the above paragraph, the (new) net margin approach makes clear that an accurate review of inter-company prices amounts to more than the determination of the right pricing method. The German tax administration has announced that it will review, and amend, the 1983 guidelines (which have remained unchanged since) probably in late 1999.

Trade tax

Trade tax is by far the most important municipal tax levied in Germany. It is imposed on any taxable trade income derived by enterprises both incorporated and unincorporated. Trade tax on capital *(Gewerbekapital-steuer)* was repealed with effect from 1997.

Trade income basically equals the amount of income to be determined under corporate income tax law. However, a number of further adjustments are required, of which the most important are as follows:

- Interest on long-term debts is deductible at 50 per cent only. A liability qualifies as long-term debt if it has been incurred either in connection with the setting up, the acquisition and the expansion of the business or if the term of the liability exceeds 12 months.
- Payments to a typical silent partner are excluded from deduction unless the partner himself is subject to trade tax.
- Profits and losses derived from foreign permanent establishments, as well as dividends received from both domestic and foreign subsidiaries (restrictions apply), are not taken into consideration when the basis for trade income tax is calculated.

Business income so ascertained forms the basis for the trade tax levy. Trade tax on income is calculated by multiplying the federal rate of 5 per cent (lower percentage brackets apply to unincorporated businesses) by a percentage factor set by the municipality (local multiplier). These multipliers currently range from about 360–515 per cent, leading to trade income tax rates between 18 and 25.75 per cent. Confusingly, the trade tax is itself deductible from the trade tax basis, so that the effective trade income tax rate might vary between 15 and 20.5 per cent depending on the municipality in which the business is run. The final burden is further reduced by the fact that trade tax is also a deductible expense for income and corporate income tax purposes. Trade tax losses may be carried forward for an indefinite period, whereby the computation of the loss carry,forward varies from that for income and corporate income tax purposes. A loss carry-back is not possible.

Interestingly, capital gains recognised from the sale of a partnership interest are presently not considered taxable trade income, irrespective of whether the partner is an individual or a corporation. Hence, a foreign investor can exit an engagement in a German partnership and would be liable to income taxes on the gain only. Further, a partnership can function as the dominating entity of a German fiscal unity (*Organschaft*).

Value added tax

As a member of the EU, Germany's VAT regime is very similar to that of the other member states. In principle, all transactions – both the supply of goods and the rendering of services – performed by an entrepreneur are subject to VAT. Depending on the individual circumstances of the transaction and the legal criteria, ie terms of delivery, type of service, residence of recipient etc, the transaction may be either taxable, tax exempt or even outside the scope of German taxation. Exports are often tax free as the transaction is considered to be performed outside Germany, while a number of other specified transactions are explicitly declared tax exempt although the supply takes place in Germany.

The standard tax rate is 16 per cent. A reduced rate of 7 per cent applies in certain cases. Specific rules may apply to transactions within the EU according to EU Directives.

Goods that have been imported from countries outside the EU are subject to import VAT at the same rates as the regular turnover tax. Entrepreneurs may deduct import VAT from their output tax liability if they utilise the imported items within their businesses or resell them.

One of the most important features of the VAT system is the entitlement of an entrepreneur to a deduction of any input VAT incurred on supplies of goods or services by other businesses. Entrepreneurs in Germany are in general obliged to prepare monthly preliminary VAT returns in which they offset input VAT against output VAT. Where the balance results in excess input VAT, a refund in cash is obtained from the authorities. The entitlement to input VAT deduction is subject to limitations and whether the resident entrepreneur carries out tax-exempt transactions. The performance of exports from Germany does not affect the right to deduct input VAT. Foreign entrepreneurs who do not perform taxable transactions in Germany but have, for whatever reasons, incurred business-related input VAT are eligible to a recovery of input VAT. An application must be submitted to the federal VAT office not later than six months after the end of the respective calendar year. Effective 1996, the refund option has been linked to reciprocity from the foreign entrepreneur's own tax administration.

Real property taxes

On transfer of real property, a real property transfer tax (*Grunder-werbsteuer*) at a rate of 3.5 per cent is levied. This rate is generally applied to the consideration as determined in the purchase agreement. Where no such consideration is payable, ie in case of mergers and spin-offs when only shares are transferred, the relevant value shall be determined on the basis of the actual or estimated gross rent to be derived from the actual or an assumed lease of the real property. If an appropriate rent cannot even be estimated, such as in the case of industrial properties, the taxation basis is the sum of the classified value of the land and the tax book value of the buildings. As a rule of thumb, the value so determined is in most cases slightly lower than the actual fair market value. An assignment of 100 per cent (as from 2000: 95 per cent) of the shares in a company that owns real property is considered a taxable transfer of the property. Where a partnership owns real property, a transfer of 95 per cent of the partnership interests to other persons is already treated as a taxable event. Although, according to the laws, both parties are liable to real property transfer tax as joint debtors, it is common practice in Germany that, pursuant to the individual purchase agreement, the buyer bears the entire burden.

German municipalities also charge a relatively moderate real property tax (*Grundsteuer*), which has to be remitted annually by owners of land. The amount payable depends on the value of the property, its intended use and a local multiplier.

TAXATION OF COMPANIES

Resident and non-resident corporations

German resident corporations, of which the *Aktiengesellschaft* and the *Gesellschaft mit beschränkter Haftung* are the most important, are in principle subject to trade, corporate income and solidarity tax on their world-wide earnings. Tax residence is established where a company has either its registered seat or place of central management in Germany. Potentially, an entity that was established under the corporate laws of a foreign country can qualify as a resident corporation if it maintains its central management in Germany.

Effective 1999, the corporate income tax rate for resident corporations amounts to 40 per cent (down from 45 per cent) on retained earnings. The rate is reduced to 30 per cent on distribution of the profits by way of dividend to shareholders. Mechanically, where tax has been paid at the higher rate, a refund of tax down to the lower rate is given to the distributing company. The refund is considered part of the dividend. The regular dividend withholding tax amounts to 25 per cent. Under most German tax treaties this rate is reduced to 15 per cent, 10 cent or even 5 per cent. Pursuant to the European Parent Subsidiary Directive dividends paid to an EU parent company do not trigger any withholding taxes at all; restrictions apply.

Finally, a 5.5 per cent solidarity tax surcharge relating to the financial burden resulting from German unification is levied on the assessed corporate income tax after deducting an imputation tax credit, if any, received by the corporation from its German subsidiaries. The tax reform bill does not address when the solidarity tax may be repealed.

Benefits granted to the shareholder of a corporation other than ordinary dividends qualify as a deemed dividend provided they are driven by shareholder rather than business considerations. Major examples include excess salaries paid to directors who are simultaneously share-holders and inter-company business transactions that deviate from arm's length standards. Deemed dividends lead to an adjustment of the corporation's taxable income. While trade taxes on the amount of the deemed dividend can normally not be avoided, the additional corporate tax burden depends on the earnings and profit pools available for distribution (see below).

A non-resident corporation, ie a company that has neither its seat nor its place of central management in Germany, is generally taxed on its German source income as defined in the domestic tax laws. Accordingly, apart from withholding taxes on income items such as portfolio income and royalties, a foreign corporation will normally be taxed on business income only if its German activities constitute a permanent establishment or branch. Where the non-resident corporation enjoys protection under a bilateral tax treaty the scope of German taxation is even more restricted, as only certain activities are deemed to create a taxable presence. German branch income generated by a foreign corporation is taxed at a rate of 40 per cent (effective 1999) irrespective of whether the earnings are reinvested at the branch level or remitted to the headquarters. The lower distribution rate of 30 per cent is not available. On the other hand, Germany does not levy any withholding tax, branch profits tax or ACT on remittances of branch profits.

Imputation system

A rather complex full imputation system *(körperschaftsteuerliches Anrechnungsverfahren)* forms the backbone of the German corporate income tax law. In a nutshell, it means that a resident shareholder receiving a dividend from a German corporation is taxed on the gross dividend, including withholding tax and the underlying corporate income tax. In return, the shareholder is entitled to an imputation tax credit for corporate income tax and withholding taxes paid by the distributing company. Where the tax credit available on a distribution exceeds the shareholder's own tax liability, a refund of the excess tax is given. Therefore, the interposing of a qualifying holding company that takes out an interest-bearing loan for the acquisition of a target company has become an attractive investment structure. Dividend income received by the holding company is set off against interest expense, which may result in a refund of taxes paid by the subsidiary. Non-resident corporations are not eligible for the imputation credit. Thus, when dividends are paid to a foreign shareholder, the 30 per cent rate converts into a final burden.

The imputation credit mechanism must be seen in concert with the system of the different pools of earnings of which *Eigenkapital* (EK) 40 and EK0 are the most important. EK40 (as well as the former EK45) contains those retained earnings that have been taxed at the higher corporate income tax rate. Dividend distributions made from EK40 or EK45 hence lead to a tax refund of 10 and 15 percentage points respectively. Profits pooled at one of the four EK0 baskets do not carry any corporate tax burden but a dividend funded from an EK0 basket may, or may not, trigger corporate tax at a rate of 30 per cent. For instance, certain foreign source income such as tax-free dividends and tax-exempt branch income qualify for the EK01 pool; dividend distributions made out of EK01 do not result in any German corporate taxes payable by the distributing company. In contrast, tax-free domestic earnings shall be categorised as EK02. Dividends funded from EK02 do trigger corporate tax at 30 per cent and thereby reduce the distributable amount. EK04 is actually not an earnings pool as it tracks shareholder contributions made to the capital surplus account. The German corporate income tax laws stipulate that dividends shall be funded top to bottom, ie starting from the basket with the highest tax burden.

Treatment of foreign source income

Resident corporations are generally subject to tax on foreign source branch and dividend income under domestic laws, but most German double tax treaties provide for an exemption (participation exemption). As far as branch profits are concerned, the exemption is given to avoid double taxation, as international treaty practice is to give taxing rights to the country in which the branch is established. In the case of dividends, the tax exemption at treaty level normally requires a stake of at least 25 per cent in the subsidiary, although this is reduced under German domestic law to 10 per cent. Where an exemption is given there is no indirect credit for underlying taxes paid by the foreign subsidiary. However, foreign dividend withholding taxes charged on dividends that are not eligible for participation exemption qualify for a tax credit, irrespective of the percentage of the shareholding. In addition, a few treaties grant a tax credit rather than an exemption, and some contain the proviso that treaty benefit depends on the activity of the foreign company.

Under rules introduced in 1999, tax may be levied on an amount up to 15 per cent of dividends received under a participation exemption in a double tax treaty. The scope of the new rule is, at the time of going to press, somewhat unclear, but in the worst case could impose a tax burden on 15 per cent of treaty protected dividends.

In addition to treaty benefits, unilateral relief for foreign tax, including underlying tax, is provided for in the corporate income tax laws. Broadly, the requirements are that the German corporation holds at least 10 per cent of the subsidiary for an unbroken period of not less than 12 months prior to the end of the fiscal year; in addition, the subsidiary must be engaged in an active trade or business. Depending on individual circumstances, this credit opportunity is also available for foreign profit taxes incurred by a second-tier subsidiary. Alternatively, the company may opt to deduct foreign taxes in computing taxable profits, for example where it has losses and is not taxpaying. These unilateral relief rules are only relevant in practice if the foreign earnings stem from a non-treaty country.

Table 24.3 *Sample of tax credit mechanism*

	Income/dividend	Corporate tax
Domestic subsidiary level		
Taxable income of subsidiary after trade tax	100	
Corporate tax payable	(40)	40
Tax refund upon dividend distribution	10	(10)
Dividend to parent corporation	70	
Domestic parent corporation level		
Net dividend income	70	
Tax credit	30	
Total dividend income	100	
Corporate tax payable	(40)	40
Corporate tax credit		(30)
Tax refund upon subsequent dividend distribution	10	(10)
Dividend to individual shareholder	70	
Individual shareholder level		
Net dividend income	70	
Tax credit	30	
Total dividend income	100	
Personal income tax payable (assumed 50%)	(50)	50
Corporate tax credit		(30)
Total tax on profit		50
Total net income	50	

The above sample ignores German withholding and solidarity taxes. It assumes a distribution of fully taxed profits.

While capital gains are basically taxed at the regular rate, gains recognised by a resident corporation from the disposition of a qualifying foreign subsidiary are exempt from both trade and corporate income tax provided a dividend paid by that subsidiary would be eligible for participation exemption. Effective 1999, capital losses resulting from such a transaction cannot, in turn, be deducted anymore.

TAXATION OF PARTNERSHIPS

Partnerships are a common feature of business life in Germany and have also provided flexibility in cross-border tax planning structures. The most important partnership vehicles for a business activity are the general partnership (oHG) and the limited partnership (KG). The latter is often managed by a GmbH as the general partner, thus forming a so-called GmbH & Co KG.

Since a partnership is not a separate legal entity federal taxes on income are imposed at the level of the partners, who can be either individuals or corporations. As the partners generally qualify as business entrepreneurs, any salaries and other benefits in kind granted to them as consideration for the performance of management duties are not respected as tax-deductible business expenses. The same is true for pension reserves referring to a pension commitment made by the partnership *vis-à-vis* its partners. On the other hand, certain assets put at the partnership's disposal by a partner as well as debt incurred by a partner in connection with the acquisition of the partnership interest need to be shown in a special item balance sheet of the respective partner. Expenses relating to these assets, such as interest on the acquisition loan, create a deductible expense at the partnership level. If structured properly, a foreign investor who engages as a partner in a German partnership may therefore get a double deduction of interest. There are several other specific regulations and principles, in particular with regard to the transfer and the acquisition of a partnership interest.

The partners are taxed on their share of the partnership's adjusted taxable profits in proportion to their share in the partnership capital (unless provided otherwise in the partnership agreement). Accordingly, if a partner is a domestic corporation, corporate income tax at a rate of 40 per cent or 30 per cent falls due. For individuals the regular straight-line progressive income tax tariff applies. However, while the maximum marginal income tax rate is currently 53 per cent, the maximum rate for income from business has been reduced from 47 per cent to 45 per cent, effective 1999. Non-resident partners in a German partnership pay, depending on their legal organisational form, German tax at 40 per cent (non-resident corporation) or up to 45 per cent (foreign individual) provided, however, the activities of the partnership constitute a taxable presence within the meaning of either the domestic laws or under the applicable tax treaty. For the purpose of trade tax, partnerships are treated as if they were separate legal entities, ie the partnership must itself file a trade tax return and pay the trade tax due.

25

Key Tax Planning Issues

Christoph Schreiber, PricewaterhouseCoopers, New York, and Adrian Yeeles, PricewaterhouseCoopers, London

INTRODUCTION

This chapter describes some key German tax planning issues concerning investing in Germany, using an example involving the acquisition of a German company by a foreign investor. Some of the relevant issues have already been discussed in previous chapters, for example whether to carry on the business in the form of a branch or a subsidiary. New issues discussed in this chapter include:

- obtaining and maximising the tax deduction in Germany for financing costs incurred in relation to a German investment, including a description of the thin capitalisation rules;
- forming a tax group (*Organschaft*) to pool profits and losses for tax purposes;
- maximising tax allowances in respect of the purchase price of an investment.

The chapter also highlights key anti-avoidance provisions, in particular the loss carry-forward rules on the change of ownership of a company.

Example

Foxtrot Ltd, a UK resident company, is in negotiations with the owners of Oskar GmbH, a German resident company, to acquire the Oskar business. Oskar GmbH is a family business that has been owned and managed for the last 15 years by two brothers, who are both resident for tax purposes in Germany.

The parties have agreed a price of DM10 million for the sale of the Oskar business, which represents a premium of DM6 million on the net asset value of the company of DM4 million. The parties have not yet agreed whether the deal will involve a share purchase or a trade and assets purchase. Foxtrot Ltd will finance the acquisition by way of a loan from a UK bank. Interest on the DM-denominated loan will be payable at a fixed rate of 4 per cent pa.

Oskar GmbH and Foxtrot Ltd are both expected to be profitable in the foreseeable future. Foxtrot Ltd has one subsidiary, Romeo SpA, an Italian company with a current market value of DM5 million. Oskar GmbH does not have any subsidiaries.

The date is now 1 June 1999 and the deal is set to complete on 30 June 1999.

DOES FOXTROT WISH TO ACQUIRE THE SHARES OR ASSETS?

Foxtrot would ideally like to acquire the assets of the business in order to maximise the tax allowances that it can claim on the cost of the investment in Germany. If Foxtrot acquires the shares in Oskar GmbH, it will not obtain any immediate tax relief in Germany for its DM10 million cost. Oskar GmbH will continue to depreciate its assets, which have a tax basis of DM4 million, at their current rate.

If Foxtrot acquires the trade and assets of the business, including goodwill, from Oskar GmbH, it should be able to obtain relief for the full cost of its investment. This is because goodwill amortisation is tax deductible in Germany. Goodwill is generally amortised on a straight-line basis over 15 years. Assuming the DM6 million premium on net asset value, which Foxtrot is paying, relates entirely to goodwill, the benefit to Foxtrot of acquiring the assets of the Oskar business, as opposed to the shares, will be approximately DM180,000 pa in German tax terms (DM400,000 pa amortisation at an assumed effective tax rate, corporation tax plus trade tax, of 45 per cent).

German income tax rules have in the past strongly favoured a sale of shares by German-resident individuals as opposed to a sale of assets. Although the major tax incentives to sell shares have now been virtually abolished, one significant incentive remains in that the sale of assets by a company is subject to trade tax, whereas the sale of shares by an individual is not. *Given the trade tax cost and their wish to make a clean legal break with the company, the Oskar brothers strongly favour a share deal.*

Initially, Foxtrot proposes a DM1 million reduction in the purchase price to compensate them for the extra German tax they will have to pay on the profits of the Oskar business under a share deal. Tax advisers for the Oskar brothers outline a structure for achieving the tax benefits of an assets deal, albeit for corporation tax purposes only, by converting Oskar GmbH into a limited partnership (GmbH & Co KG) post-acquisition. The conversion and its benefit, known as a 'step up', are outlined in further detail below. Given its urgent need to establish a presence in Germany, Foxtrot agrees to pay DM10 million for the shares in Oskar GmbH.

DOES FOXTROT WISH TO CARRY ON BUSINESS IN GERMANY THROUGH A BRANCH OF A UK COMPANY, A PARTNERSHIP OR A SUBSIDIARY?

The main legal and tax issues that need to be considered in deciding whether to carry on a business in Germany through a branch, partnership or a limited company are outlined in Chapter 22. The main point on which the Foxtrot directors focus is the difference between the corporation tax rate for a German branch of a foreign company (or for a foreign partner in a German partnership) of 40 per cent, compared with the rate for distributed profits of a German limited company of 30 per cent. The directors consequently decide to carry on the Oskar business through a German limited company, a GmbH.

HOW CAN FOXTROT OBTAIN TAX RELIEF IN GERMANY FOR ITS FINANCING COSTS?

In the light of the higher effective tax rates in Germany compared to the UK, Foxtrot wishes to maximise the tax relief that they can obtain in Germany for their financing costs of DM400,000 pa.

In order to obtain a deduction for this interest expense in Germany, Foxtrot decides to set up a new German subsidiary, Foxtrot Holdings GmbH, to acquire the shares in Oskar GmbH. Foxtrot Ltd will take out a loan from its UK bank and inject the funds in the form of debt (the maximum allowable) and equity into Foxtrot Holdings GmbH. Foxtrot Holdings GmbH will then acquire the shares in Oskar GmbH from the vendors.

Under the above structure, all interest payable by Foxtrot Holdings GmbH to Foxtrot Ltd will initially be disallowable for corporation tax purposes under the thin capitalisation rules. The structure therefore needs to be revised. The reason for this is that the book value of participations does not count as equity for the purposes of the thin capitalisation rules, unless the company qualifies as a holding company.

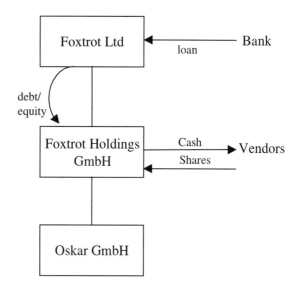

Figure 25.1 *Structure for maximisation of tax relief*

This is discussed in further detail in the thin capitalisation section below.

It is important to remember that loan interest payable by a German company is only 50 per cent deductible for trade tax purposes (with the exception of short term loan interest), regardless of the gearing level of the company.

WHAT IS THE MAXIMUM AMOUNT OF DEBT WHICH CAN BE INJECTED INTO FOXTROT HOLDINGS GMBH UNDER GERMAN THIN CAPITALISATION RULES?

Germany's thin capitalisation rules apply to loans to a German company from foreign related parties and also to loans from third parties that have been guaranteed by a related party. Loans from third parties fall outside the scope of the rules if interest receivable in the hands of the third party lender is taxed in Germany and is not drained out of Germany by way of a back-to-back loan arrangement or otherwise.

Where related party debt exceeds the so-called safe haven, interest payable on the excess debt is disallowed for corporation tax purposes and treated as a deemed distribution. Interest payable on related party loans is not disallowed, if it can be shown that the loan could have been obtained on the same terms from a third party (unless the interest is calculated by reference to profits or sales), regardless of whether the safe haven is exceeded.

The safe haven for companies other than holding companies is equal to three times shareholders' equity (subject to certain adjustments) per the accounts at the end of the previous accounting period. Where a company is in its first accounting period, the opening balance sheet is taken. Where interest on a loan is calculated by reference to the profits or sales of the German company, the safe haven is one half of the equity figure.

The main adjustment to the shareholders' equity figure per the accounts is that the book value of participations in other companies must be deducted. For example, if a company has equity of DM10 million, including participations in other companies of DM5 million, its safe haven for thin capitalisation purposes will only be DM15 million (3 × 5 million). It is important to note that this reduction in the safe haven does not apply to qualifying holding companies described below.

There are a number of other potential pitfalls within the thin capitalisation rules, particularly when setting up companies or transferring shares, and careful planning is required to avoid them.

Holding companies

The safe haven for qualifying holding companies is nine times the shareholders' equity, unless interest is calculated by reference to profits or sales, in which case the safe haven is one half of attributable equity. As mentioned above, the book value of participations is not deducted from the equity figure in calculating the safe haven of a holding company.

One of the conditions that must be satisfied to qualify as a holding company is that the company must hold participations in at least two companies. Foxtrot Holdings GmbH would not immediately satisfy this requirement, as it would only hold a single participation in Oskar GmbH.

In order to benefit from the more favourable treatment applicable to holding companies, Foxtrot Ltd could transfer its shares in Romeo SpA, an Italian subsidiary, to Foxtrot Holdings GmbH in return for an issue of shares by Foxtrot Holdings GmbH as shown in Figure 25.2.

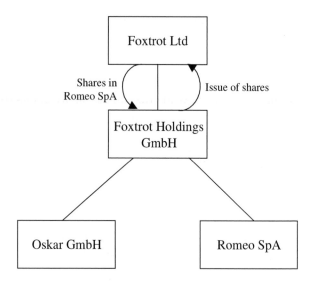

Figure 25.2 *Share transfer to qualify as holding company*

Following the injection of Romeo SpA, Foxtrot Holdings GmbH could now finance its acquisition of Oskar GmbH entirely by an issue of debt to Foxtrot Ltd. The safe haven for thin capitalisation purposes of Foxtrot Holdings GmbH would be calculated as shown in Table 25.1.

Table 25.1 *Calculation of safe haven for thin capitalisation purposes of Foxtrot Holdings GmbH*

	DM (million)
Investments in subsidiaries:	
Oskar GmbH	10
Romeo SpA	5
Less: Loan from Foxtrot Ltd	(10)
Equity under thin capitalisation rules	5
Safe haven (9 x equity)	45

Foxtrot Holdings GmbH would therefore have additional debt capacity of DM35 million on the basis of the above figures.

In order to ensure that interest on the loans to acquire the shares in Oskar GmbH is allowable in Germany, the transactions should be carefully structured and agreements carefully worded to ensure that it is clear that the loan from Foxtrot Ltd to Foxtrot Holdings GmbH relates entirely to the acquisition of the shares in Oskar GmbH and not the shares in Romeo SpA.

For German corporation and trade tax purposes, dividends from Romeo SpA and any capital gain on a subsequent sale of the shares in Romeo SpA would be exempt from tax at the level of Foxtrot Holdings GmbH under the German participation exemption, subject to satisfying conditions in the Germany–Italy tax treaty. An amount up to 15 per cent of dividends received would, however, be subject to tax under new rules described in Chapter 24 (foreign source income section).

HOW CAN TAX RELIEF BE OBTAINED FOR THE INTEREST EXPENSE IN FOXTROT HOLDINGS GMBH AGAINST THE OPERATING PROFITS OF OSKAR GMBH?

The next question to consider is how to obtain tax relief for the DM400,000 pa interest deduction in Foxtrot Holdings GmbH against the operating profits of Oskar GmbH. This could be achieved by forming a tax group, known as an *Organschaft*, between Foxtrot Holdings GmbH and Oskar GmbH.

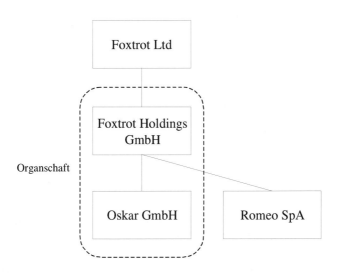

Figure 25.3   *Formation of a tax group to obtain tax relief*

Where an *Organschaft* is in place, all the profits and losses of the entities comprising it are treated as profits and losses of the so-called dominant entity, ie they are all pooled together in this entity.

German tax group rules require two entities to be integrated to a certain extent in substance; a tax group is not formed merely by holding the required percentage of a subsidiary's share capital. The integration criteria fall into three categories: financial, economic and organisational integration.

The integration criteria require a level of integration above that normally found between a holding company and a subsidiary in that it requires the holding company to actively participate in the management of the subsidiary.

In order for an *Organschaft* to be effective for corporation tax purposes, Foxtrot Holdings GmbH and Oskar GmbH would have to conclude a 'profit and loss transfer agreement'. Under this Oskar GmbH would agree to transfer its entire annual profit to Foxtrot Holdings GmbH at the end of each accounting period. In return, Foxtrot Holdings GmbH would agree to reimburse Oskar GmbH should it incur an annual loss.

A profit and loss transfer agreement is not required for an *Organschaft* to be effective for trade tax purposes or for VAT purposes.

The profit and loss pooling benefits could, alternatively, be achieved for corporation tax purposes by paying up dividends from Oskar GmbH to Foxtrot Holdings GmbH. Foxtrot Holdings GmbH could then reclaim the corporation tax credit attached to the dividends and thereby obtain full credit for its interest expense. There may, however, be a time lapse between payment of the corporation tax at the level of Oskar GmbH and the refund of the tax credit at the level of Foxtrot Holdings GmbH.

A considerable level of attention would need to be paid by Foxtrot and Oskar management to ensure that the integration criteria were met on an ongoing basis. A future tax audit would potentially reverse all profit and loss pooling benefits claimed in an accounting period, if managers were unable to demonstrate that the companies were sufficiently integrated throughout the accounting period under scrutiny.

Foxtrot decides to convert Oskar GmbH into a partnership in order to obtain a tax deduction for the DM6 million goodwill element of the purchase price. Under this structure, which is outlined below, the operating profits of the partnership will be offset by the interest expense in Foxtrot Holdings GmbH automatically. An *Organschaft* will therefore not be required between Foxtrot Holdings GmbH and Oskar GmbH & Co KG, the limited partnership.

HOW DOES FOXTROT OBTAIN A TAX DEDUCTION FOR THE DM6 MILLION GOODWILL ELEMENT OF THE PURCHASE PRICE (SO-CALLED 'STEP UP' IN THE TAX BASIS OF ASSETS)?

In order to obtain a tax deduction for the goodwill element of the purchase price, Oskar GmbH will be converted into a limited partnership, a GmbH & Co KG, as shown in Figure 25.4.

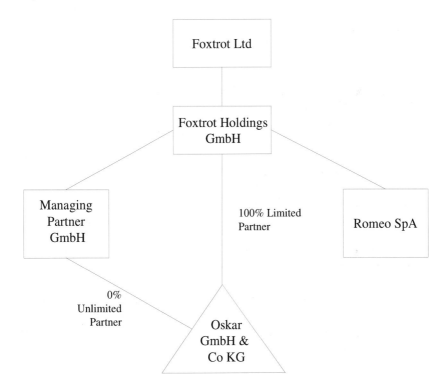

Figure 25.4   *Oskar GmbH's conversion to a limited partnership*

Under the Reorganisation Tax Act, the conversion can be carried out retroactively for tax purposes with effect from the acquisition date, ie 30 June 1999, provided there is a balance sheet for Oskar GmbH at that date and all relevant papers are filed with the Commercial Register within eight months of the acquisition, ie by 29 February 2000.

The tax deduction for the goodwill element of the purchase price will arise as follows:

- Foxtrot Holdings GmbH's shares in Oskar GmbH, which have a book value and tax basis of DM10 million (but which are not depreciable for tax purposes), will cease to exist on conversion and will be replaced:
  - in Foxtrot Holdings GmbH's commercial accounts, by a partnership interest with a book value of DM10 million; and
  - in Foxtrot Holdings GmbH's tax balance sheet, by a direct interest in the assets of Oskar GmbH with a tax basis of DM4 million.

- The potential loss for tax purposes of DM6 million will not be realised immediately, rather the tax basis of the assets of Oskar will be stepped up to their market value of DM10 million, which will give rise to increased tax allowances in the future.

- Assuming the DM6 million premium on net asset value relates entirely to goodwill, which is depreciable over 15 years, the step up will generate extra tax allowances of DM400,000 pa.

- The step up will be effective for corporation tax purposes only, not for trade tax. Ignoring the solidarity surcharge, the tax benefit will be DM120,000 pa at the rate for distributed earnings of 30 per cent.

The conversion model outlined in Figure 25.4 would not have given rise to a step up if the shares had been held at any time in the ten years prior to the conversion by non-residents or residents who were not taxable on the disposal of the shares.

Under the new structure, Foxtrot Holdings GmbH will be able to offset its entire interest expense against Oskar's operating profits for corporation tax purposes, subject to thin capitalisation rules. For trade tax purposes, 50 per cent of the interest expense will be deductible and offset against Oskar operating profits automatically, with the rest being disallowable.

One consequence of the step up is that Foxtrot Holdings GmbH will not qualify as a holding company for thin capitalisation purposes. Therefore, in calculating the safe haven for Foxtrot Holdings GmbH, first, the book value of participations will have to be deducted from shareholders' equity and, second, the maximum debt to equity ratio will be 3 to 1 instead of 9 to 1.

In order to maximise the deduction for interest in Germany, the finance for the acquisition of the Oskar shares will have to be injected into Foxtrot Holdings GmbH in the ratio of three parts debt to one part equity, ie DM7.5 million debt and DM2.5 million equity. The safe haven calculation will be as shown in Table 25.2.

Table 25.2 *Safe haven calculation*

	DM (million)
Investment in Romeo SpA	5
Assets of Oskar trade (stepped up)	10
Loan from Foxtrot Ltd	(7.5)
Shareholders' equity	7.5
Less: Investment in Romeo SpA	(5)
Adjusted equity	2.5
Safe haven (3 × adjusted equity)	7.5

The tax benefit of the goodwill amortisation will therefore be offset to a certain extent by the lower interest expense of DM300,000 pa (DM7.5 million × 4 per cent), as opposed to DM400,000 previously. Foxtrot Ltd will, however, still obtain a tax deduction for the DM100,000 difference in the UK, albeit at a lower effective tax rate.

In order to obtain a tax deduction in Germany for DM300,000 interest with immediate effect from 1 July 1999, it is vital that the step up is carried out retroactively with effect from 30 June 1999.

DISTRIBUTION STRATEGY

Given the difference between the corporation tax rates for retained and distributed earnings, Foxtrot Holdings GmbH should be aiming to pursue a maximum distribution policy in respect of its taxed earnings. This can be achieved without depriving the Oskar business of cash funds by reinvesting the dividend in the business as shown in Figure 25.5.

The immediate reinvestment of the dividend would not prejudice the corporation tax refund that the distribution would achieve.

DISPOSAL OF SHARES IN ROMEO SPA

Three years after the acquisition of Oskar GmbH, the Foxtrot group decides to dispose of its investment in Romeo SpA for DM15 million.

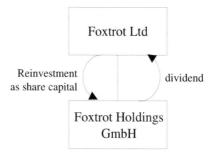

Figure 25.5   *Dividend reinvestment*

Foxtrot Holdings GmbH will realise a gain on this disposal for German tax purposes of DM10 million, being the DM15 million consideration less DM5 million base cost. This gain would be exempt from German corporation and trade tax under the participation exemption on capital gains and exempt from Italian tax under the Germany–Italy double tax treaty.

Foxtrot decides to retain the disposal proceeds in Foxtrot Holdings GmbH, as it is considering acquiring a loss-making company in Germany in the near future (described below).

UTILISATION OF TAX LOSSES FOLLOWING THE CHANGE OF OWNERSHIP OF A COMPANY

Shortly after the sale of Romeo SpA, Foxtrot Holdings GmbH acquires the entire share capital of Kanzler GmbH, another German company, for DM13 million. Kanzler GmbH has net assets of DM10 million. Although Kanzler GmbH is currently loss making, the Foxtrot directors are confident that they will be able to turn the business around in the short to medium term. Oskar GmbH & Co KG now makes an annual operating profit of DM2.5 million pa and has a net asset value of DM15 million.

The Foxtrot directors would like to know what options are available for utilising the significant corporation and trade tax losses carried forward in Kanzler GmbH of DM10 million.

Under Germany's anti-loss trading rules, a company can offset losses brought forward for corporation and trade tax purposes if it is economically identical with the company that incurred the loss. A company is *not* economically identical with the company that incurred the loss if:

- there has been a transfer of more than 50 per cent of the shares in the company; and
- there has been a significant contribution of business assets to the company, which is deemed to be the case where the total assets of the company more than double as a result of the contribution. Contributions aimed specifically at turning around a loss-making business are not treated as harmful.

Under the above rules, Kanzler GmbH will be able to offset its losses brought forward against future profits of the Kanzler trade, although it may be a number of years before the losses are fully utilised. Contributions by Foxtrot in the meantime to support the Kanzler business should not jeopardise the availability of the losses.

The above rules may, however, prevent the Foxtrot group from contributing, for example, the Oskar trade and assets to Kanzler GmbH in order to utilise the Kanzler losses against Oskar profits. Calculations would need to be done to confirm whether the contribution of the Oskar trade and assets would constitute a significant contribution (see above).

GENERAL ANTI-AVOIDANCE RULE

One final point that needs to be highlighted is Germany's general anti-avoidance provision. Under this provision the tax consequences are deemed to follow the substance of a transaction where there are no valid economic reasons for the legal form adopted. The provision is very widely drawn and, given a lack of relevant case law, it is often very difficult to eliminate the risk of it applying, particularly where aggressive tax planning is involved.

TO BE CONTINUED . . . ?

At this point we leave the story of the Foxtrot group. Planning of the type described above can deliver significant savings in the amount of tax payable on German profits. However, at the time of going to press, Germany is poised to embark on a major reform of the taxation of business and rules in some of the key planning areas will come under review. So we can expect the story to continue. In the meantime investors should make sure they consult their advisers at an early stage to maximise the tax efficiency of planned investments.

26

Group Accounting and Developments in Public Financial Reporting

Morag McLean, PwC Deutsche Revision AG, Hamburg

GROUP ACCOUNTING

Consolidation requirements and rules

All groups of companies headed by a stock corporation (*Aktiengesellschaft* or AG), a limited partnership with shares (*Kommanditgesellschaft auf Aktien* or KGaA) or a limited liability company (*Gesellschaft mit beschränkter Haftung* or GmbH) are required to prepare, within the first five months of the end of the group´s financial year, consolidated financial statements and a group management report for the preceding group financial year if:

1. the parent company and its subsidiaries together meet two of the following three criteria on the reporting and the preceding balance sheet date:

	Total assets in excess of DM million	Total net sales in excess of DM million	Total number of employees (annual average)
Before consolidation entries	63.72	127.44	500
or			
After consolidation entries	53.1	106.2	500

2. or, regardless of size, if securities of the parent or any of the subsidiary companies are traded on a stock exchange within the European Union.

Under the provisions of the the German Commercial Code (*Handelsgesetzbuch* or HGB) in general all domestic and foreign subsidiary companies (ie companies over which the parent company can exercise control) must be consolidated. Such control is usually indicated if one of the following conditions is satisfied:

- ownership of the majority of voting rights;
- capacity to control the composition of the investee's management or supervisory board by virtue of being a shareholder;
- capacity to exercise a controlling influence based on a contract of domination concluded with the investee company, or based on its articles of association.

A subsidiary may be excluded from consolidation if it is not significant in relation to the group's net worth, financial position and results, or if exercise of the parent company's rights concerning the subsidiary's assets or management is seriously impaired, or the information required for consolidation purposes cannot be obtained without unreasonable expense or delay, or if the investment in the subsidiary is held solely for purpose of resale.

The consolidated financial statements comprise the consolidated balance sheet, the consolidated profit and loss account and the notes. They must, in compliance with generally accepted accounting principles, present a true and fair view of the net worth, financial position and results of the group.

In the consolidated financial statements the net worth, financial position and results of the consolidated companies must be shown as if they all formed a single business entity. This therefore requires the following consolidation entries:

- equity consolidation;
- elimination of receivables from and liabilities to consolidated companies;
- elimination of intra-group profits;
- elimination of income/expenses from services rendered/received to/from consolidated companies.

The assets and liabilities of the companies included have to be valued uniformly in accordance with the valuation policies of the parent company. Any deviations have to be disclosed in the notes to the financial statements along with the justification for the deviation.

Consolidated financial statements must include a set of notes that are an integral part of the financial statements. The HGB prescribes minimum disclosures, including:

- disclosure of material changes in the companies included in the consolidated financial statements in order to allow a comparison of the various years;
- the accounting and valuation methods applied, inconsistencies with these methods and the justification for same, along with a quantification of their effects on the net worth, financial position and results of the group;
- the basis for translation of foreign currency financial statements;
- the names and the registered offices of the consolidated and associated entities, along with the percentage shareholding in the capital of each entity held by the parent either directly or indirectly;
- reasons for excluding from consolidation or equity accounting companies that would normally have been required to be included.

In Germany, consolidated financial statements are never used as a basis for taxation or determination of dividends.

Goodwill

The calculation of goodwill is performed either at the time of the acquisition of the subsidiary company or on first inclusion of the subsidiary in the consolidated financial statements. Two methods of goodwill calculation are permitted by the HGB.

1. Book value method

The book value method is the more commonly used method in Germany. The fair value of the consideration is compared with the book value of the net assets acquired and any excess of the consideration given is allocated to the individual items up to their fair value. Any remaining excess would be recorded as goodwill. Negative goodwill cannot arise under this method, as long as the purchase consideration exceeds the acquired book values. The minority interest component of the goodwill calculation is valued at the book value.

2. Revaluation method

This is the method commonly used in the UK and the United States. In this case, the book values are replaced by market values so that hidden reserves are fully reflected, also in respect of the shares held by minority interests. The revalued net equity of the subsidiary attributable to the parent may however not exceed the historical cost of the investment in that subsidiary. The general opinion is that the value of the minority interest component is also subject to the same restriction, ie the maximum value is determined by reference to the purchase price paid for the remainder of the company. There are varying opinions as to whether negative goodwill can only result from the purchase consideration being lower than the acquired book values or whether the full revalued net equity is reduced to the cost of the investment by a corresponding amount of negative goodwill shown under equity. The former is the more prevalent opinion.

Capitalisation of goodwill on consolidation is in both cases optional. If goodwill is capitalised, it may be amortised over four years starting with the year following the initial capitalisation, or systematically over the years that the company is likely to benefit from it. However, for income tax purposes, the amortisation period is fixed at 15 years starting with the year of initial capitalisation, so many companies also adopt the 15-year amortisation period for their consolidated financial statements. If goodwill is not capitalised, it is deducted from reserves on the face of the balance sheet.

Negative goodwill is shown under equity and can only be released to income at a later date if one of the following conditions is met:

- a deterioration in the future income position of the company expected at the time it was acquired or consolidated for the first time actually takes place, or expenses expected at that time have to be accounted for; or
- it is clear at the balance sheet date that the release corresponds to a realised profit.

Capitalised goodwill and material changes from the preceding year have to be explained in the notes to the consolidated financial statements.

Foreign exchange

The legal obligation to present consolidated financial statements in deutschmarks necessitates the translation of all foreign currency financial statements. The HGB does not prescribe a specific method of foreign currency translation. However, in May 1998 the main technical committee of the Institute of German Public Accountants (HFA), published a draft statement on foreign currency translation in consolidated financial statements.

This statement distinguishes between two translation methods (the closing rate method and the temporal method) and their respective uses. It also covers specific problems in the case of hyperinflationary economies.

1. The (modified) closing rate method

The closing rate method has to be used when it is expected that exchange movements between the currency of the subsidiary and that of the parent will not have a significant impact on the income of the group. The balance sheets of subsidiaries are translated at the closing rate. The profit and loss statements are translated at an annual weighted average rate. Differences arising on translation are generally taken direct to reserves. *Note that this method should not be used for companies operating in highly inflationary economies as it may be misleading.*

2. Temporal method

If it is expected that exchange movements between the currency of the subsidiary and that of the parent will have a significant impact on the income of the group because of the financial relationship between the two entities, the temporal method has to be applied. Under the temporal method, non-monetary assets and liabilities are in principle translated at historical rates and monetary assets and liabilities are translated at closing rates. This complies with the international definition of the temporal method. However, in Germany, a lowering of cost and market value test also has to be performed, ie assets are stated at the lower of the historical and closing rate, liabilities are stated at the higher of the historical and closing rate. The exception to this is long-term assets where a lower closing rate only has to be applied if the drop is assumed to be permanent. Profit and loss account items are translated at the rates corresponding to the underlying transactions, ie depreciation and cost of materials are translated at the same rates as the related assets and all other items of income and expenditure are translated at average rates.

The idea behind the temporal method is that gains and losses are recorded in the profit and loss statement. However, as a result of the German imparity and realisation principles, gains can only be recorded if they are due to a reduction in a loss. Gains from a positive translation difference have to be equalised by, for example, setting up a provision for currency risks. The reduction of a positive translation difference leads to the utilisation of the aforementioned provision.

Hyperinflationary economies

In principle, the fact that an economy is hyperinflationary or not has no relevance on which of the above two methods should be adopted. However, if the closing rate method is adopted, the values used as a basis for the conversion should be adjusted for inflation, preferably in accordance with International Accounting Standard 29. This is not necessary where the temporal method is applied.

The method applied has to be disclosed in the notes to the financial statements along with the reasoning behind the choice. Other disclosures include the method of calculating average rates and the value of translation gains and losses taken to the profit and loss account.

Associates and joint ventures

Associated companies

If a consolidated company can exercise a significant influence on the operating and financial policies of a company that is not consolidated, and in which the company has a participating interest, then this participation has to be shown in the consolidated balance sheet under a separate heading with an appropriate description. A significant influence will be assumed if one company holds at least a fifth of the voting rights in another company (associate).

A participation in an associated company is initially recorded in the consolidated balance sheet either at book value or at the amount corresponding to the group's share of the associated company's net equity valued on the basis of fair value accounting. In the latter case, the historical cost of the investment is the ceiling.

After the initial recording, the investment in the associated company must be accounted for in accordance with the equity method, ie the carrying value of the investment is adjusted each year to correspond with the development in the investee's equity. When accounting for associated companies for the first time it is therefore necessary to compare the book value of the investment with the corresponding share of equity; the resulting difference must be allocated to individual assets and liabilities or goodwill in the same way as in the case of a full consolidation, with the exception that the differences are carried forward and developed in a memorandum calculation. The effect of the annual movements on these differences is taken into account when determining the annual movements in the investee's equity.

The associate does not need to be accounted for using the equity method if the participation is not significant for the presentation of a true and fair view of net worth, financial position and results of the group.

The name, registered office and the group's share of the capital of each associated company must be included in the notes. Disclosure must also be made if the provisions concerning associates are not applied on the grounds of immateriality.

Joint ventures

The term joint venture is not legally defined. A joint venture is usually a combination under uniform control of two or more legally and economically independent companies in order to pursue the same purposes.

If a consolidated company manages another company jointly with one or more companies not included in the consolidation, then that other company may be proportionately consolidated. The principle of joint management must be exercised in relation to all important areas such as planning, performance and supervision and relates to day-to-day management and not simply to the shareholder/supervisory board role.

The name, registered office and the group's share of the capital of each joint venture must be included in the notes. Disclosure must also be made of the basis of consolidation.

DEVELOPMENTS IN PUBLIC FINANCIAL REPORTING

Use of IAS

At present, only quoted companies are allowed to present financial statements prepared using international accounting standards (IAS) as an alternative to financial statements prepared applying the HGB (see also below, *Kapitalaufnahmeerleichterungsgesetz*). At present roughly 70 German companies of varying sizes and industries have either published or made reference to IAS in external publications, saying that they will adopt IAS for their consolidated financial statements within the next one or two years. The use of IAS has been promoted by the fact that the alternative German stock markets prescribe that entrants must prepare financial statements under IAS or US GAAP. To date, the majority of entrants have opted to apply IAS, whether because of increased flexibility *vis-à-vis* US GAAP, the fact that they do not actually wish to pursue a US listing or national pride.

Use of US GAAP

Daimler Benz was the first large German corporation to prepare US GAAP financial statements for the years 1991 and 1992. A number of other companies have since followed suit. Many have however opted to meet the New York Stock Exchange's requirements by preparing US GAAP reconciliations, either from IAS or directly from their German GAAP statements. For the reasons already mentioned above, IAS is however still preferred by entities in the process of internationalising their financial statements, particularly by smaller entities less attracted by the US capital markets.

Kapitalaufnahmeerleichterungsgesetz (KapAEG)

To date it has not proved possible for a German corporation to obtain a listing on the New York Stock Exchange (NYSE) by filing its consolidated financial statements prepared using the provisions of the HGB. This is at least partly due to the fact that there are basic differences in accounting philosophy between Germany and the Anglo-Saxon countries. For historical reasons, German financial statements are oriented very much to the protection of creditors. The balance sheet is therefore seen as the most important primary financial statement. This contrasts strongly with the Anglo-Saxon approach, where the balance sheet is generally considered less important than the income and cash flow statements. With the exception of the financial statements of publicly quoted companies for years beginning after 31 December 1998, a cash flow statement is indeed not a mandatory part of a set of German financial statements.

To obtain a listing on the NYSE, and latterly also on the alternative domestic exchanges, German corporations had therefore to prepare two sets of consolidated financial statements, one to meet the requirements of the HGB and one to comply with US GAAP or IAS. To simplify matters for these corporations and to remove the disadvantages *vis-à-vis* their foreign competitors, new legislation (*Kapitalaufnahmeerleichterungsgesetz*) became effective on 24 April 1998.

By taking advantage of this change in the legislation, it is possible for a company quoted on the main Frankfurt exchange to prepare consolidated financial statements using international accounting principles, in particular IAS or US GAAP, instead of German accounting principles. These consolidated financial statements and the group management report have to be published in the German language and in either deutschmarks or euros (although the use of the euro is mandatory for financial years ending after 31 December 2001). A description of the accounting principles applied and the differences between these policies and German accounting principles have to be disclosed in the notes. This legislation is valid until 31 December 2004.

The new legislation also introduced changes for parent companies that do not prepare consolidated financial statements on the grounds that they are exempt because their ultimate parent companies are resident in a member state of either the European Union or the European Economic Area *and* prepare consolidated financial statements which are published in the German language in the *Federal Gazette*. These companies now also have to explain the differences between the accounting principles applied and German accounting principles in the notes to the financial statements.

Other recent developments and forces for change

The globalisation of business and business practices is still the strongest force for change within Germany. As a nation that is used to being at the fore in technological innovation, business leaders are pressurising the German accountancy bodies to modify German accounting principles so that businesses can compete with their foreign counterparts in the global capital markets as well as in technical and marketing excellence.

At present only quoted companies can take advantage of the changes mentioned above. The next step, which is already being discussed, is to extend this to all consolidated financial statements. Once this has happened it would seem to be only a matter of time before the umbilical cord between tax and statutory accounting principles is broken.

New standard setting body (DRSC)

The goal of the KapAEG was to align German accounting principles with those that are internationally recognised by the end of 2004. KonTraG (see below) also included provisions to create a German standard setting body (*Deutsches Rechnungslegungs Standards Committee*, or German Accounting Standards Committee) whose task it is to make recommendations in relation to consolidation accounting, to advise government on legislation in relation to accounting matters and to represent Germany in international standard setting committees.

The DRSC is made up as follows:

- representatives of the following federal ministries: Justice (Chairman), Finance and Economics;
- four representatives of industry;
- four representatives of the accounting profession;
- two academics.

KONTRAG AND CORPORATE GOVERNANCE

The legislation on control and transparency in public companies (*Gesetz zur Kontrolle und Transparenz im Unternehmensbereich*, KonTraG) became effective on 1 May 1998. The majority of the changes, now included in the HGB, have to be applied at the latest for business years beginning after 31 December 1998. The changes relate inter alia to the installation and assessment of risk management systems, to the extension of the information to be provided to supervisory boards, shareholders and other users of financial statements, to restrictions on persons who can hold office as members of supervisory boards and to the extension of the duties of supervisory boards and auditors. Some of the detailed changes are as follows:

- Quoted companies must include a consolidated cash flow statement and segmental reporting as part of the notes to their consolidated financial statements;
- Quoted companies must disclose investments of over 5 per cent in large incorporated firms in the notes to their consolidated financial statements;
- The executive board of directors must set up a system of risk management and of internal accounting control;
- The executive board of directors must inform the supervisory board of the company's future plans;
- The minimum number of supervisory board meetings has been increased to four meetings per year for quoted companies;
- The auditor must be appointed by the supervisory board and the auditor has to report directly to the supervisory board (applies already for 1998);
- The Group Directors' Report has to describe future risks to the company.

Part Six

Legal Issues

Introduction

Eversheds

Germany has a well-established and proven system of law. In fact, the legal structures developed in Germany in the 19th century have become one of the important backbones for the success of the German economy. Anglo-American business people can expect to familiarise themselves reasonably quickly with legal concepts that are practice orientated, have been modernised over the years and are backed up by a considerable amount of case law. German law, like many other continental European legal systems, is based on codification. The main statutes represent a systematic and interrelated body of laws. Legal information can be relatively easily obtained in the form of commentaries and legal journals. Case law is electronically accessible.

Statutes are efficiently organised and apply always in their most recently amended form. Amendments are immediately integrated. When interpreting statutes, German judges look at the intentions of parliament and the purpose of the relevant provision. German judges are called upon to give all legislation a meaning that complies with the principle of fairness (the so-called 'doctrine of good faith'), which can be compared with the Anglo-American concept of equity.

The law is subdivided into specific branches, each of which has its own separate jurisdiction and hierarchy of courts. Thus, separate jurisdictions exist for civil law (including criminal law), administrative law, labour law, tax law, social security law and constitutional law. Each of these branches of the court system provides for two appeal stages, the second appeal being sometimes restricted to legal questions of general importance.

The main codes with which the business community will come into contact are:

- Civil Code *(Bürgerliches Gesetzbuch / BGB)*
- Commercial Code *(Handelsgesetzbuch / HGB)*
- Code Regulating Private Limited Companies *(GmbH-Gesetz / GmbHG)*
- Code Regulating Public Limited Companies *(Aktiengesetz / AktG)*
- Act on General Business Conditions *(AGBG)*
- Act Against Restrictions on Competition *(Gesetz gegen Wettbewerbsbeschränkungen / GWB)*
- Act Against Unfair Competition *(Gesetz gegen unlauteren Wettbewerb / UWG)*

Labour law is largely part of the general civil law but also comprises special statutes dealing with restrictions on dismissals, the establishment and operation of works councils and co-determination. The main body of tax law consists of the General Taxes Act (AO) and the Income and Corporation Taxes Act (EStG and KStG). Tax statutes will be interpreted in Germany by looking at the commercial realities and the intended commercial effect rather than the literal meaning.

Germany, being a founder member of the EEC and thus having the longest possible connection with European law, has had an important impact on all European legislation and has itself been influenced by it. Many concepts contained in EU Directives have their origin in German law. It is for that reason that many east European countries decided to adopt German legal principles in order to stay as close as possible to mainstream Europe.

Germany has an undivided legal profession in that all attorneys *(Rechtsanwälte)* are qualified to do both advisory work and appear in court. However, for civil litigation there is still a system of local admission that may require the appointment of a locally admitted lawyer. The legal profession has recently become more specialised and it is important to make a careful search for a suitable candidate. The average size of law firms has grown substantially since unification and there are now many large, supra-regional firms fielding lawyers in most of the major commercial centres in Germany. Nevertheless, one still finds excellent small 'boutiques' with specialists offering particular skills and experience.

The traditional method of charging fees was based on the statutory fee scale for attorneys, which took account of the value of a particular claim or matter and disregarded time. This is now often replaced by individual agreements providing for fees to be calculated by reference to the time spent. Such arrangements can be made both in relation to advisory work and court work. However, the courts will only award recovery of fees and costs on the basis of the statutory fee scale.

German lawyers are generally allowed to practise both as lawyers and as accountants and tax advisers, provided they hold the necessary qualifications. The debate about multidisciplinary practices is still undecided.

Many transactions in company law as well as property transactions require the involvement of a notary. Such transactions will not be valid and will not be entered in the respective register unless they are contained in a notarial deed *(Urkunde)*. For historical reasons notaries in some parts of Germany are civil servants, whereas in others they can practise both as attorneys and notaries and, in yet other parts of Germany, they will be private practitioners but restricted to purely notarial work. Notaries charge on the basis of their own statutory fee scale, which is based on the value of the transaction.

27

Methods of Doing Business

Eversheds

INTRODUCTION

When considering an investment in Germany, a number of opportunities and approaches present themselves to the foreign investor. Depending on such factors as capital available for investment, marketing objectives and tax considerations, foreign businesses can choose between various forms of sales and distribution strategies on the one hand and the establishment of their own German operation on the other hand.

AGENCY, DISTRIBUTORSHIP AND FRANCHISE OPERATION

The terms agent and distributor are often thought to be synonymous. However, there is a legal difference between the sale of products or services through an agent and their sale using a distributor.

The commercial agent (*Handelsvertreter*)

A commercial agent is an independent entrepreneur (ie not an employee) who works on a commission basis. He brings about a contract between the principal (or manufacturer) and the customer. The agent himself is not a party to that contract and accordingly the risk that the customer fails to pay is normally borne by the principal. Agency is a cheap method of introducing a product to a new market. Given that the agent will not get paid his commission unless he is able to sell the product, the principal loses little if sales figures are low. An investment will, of course, have to be made in sales promotion and advertising and an agent will look to his principal to support his sales and marketing efforts. German law sets out the basic framework of an agency agreement in the Commercial Code *(HGB)*. The Code imposes certain duties and obligations on the parties to the agency agreement. It seeks to protect the agent, who is often regarded as the weaker party, against unfair contractual terms. It prescribes minimum notice periods and payment terms.

In addition, it protects the successful agent against the loss of the generated value of the goodwill and the customer base created by him in the event that the contract comes to an end and the agent is not himself at fault (Section 89b *HGB*). Complex calculation guidelines exist in German case law determining the value of an agency business. Following the implementation of the European Directive on Commercial Agents in all other EU member states, similar compensation is now payable to all agents based within the EU. However, German law has the distinct advantage of providing clear calculation guidelines that are still absent in the laws of other EU countries. It is therefore often considered desirable – in the interests of certainty – that a contract between an English principal and a German sales agent be governed by German law; if the agent performs his duties essentially in Germany, German law is mandatory in any event. Business organisations generally recommend a standard form of agreement to their members. These should be used with care and checked against the particular terms intended by the parties and any development in the law.

The distributor *(Vertriebshändler)*

The distributor (as opposed to the agent) purchases a product in his own name and for his own account – often exclusively – from a manufacturer, usually at wholesale or discount prices. His profit is the mark up which he is able to charge. In particular, brand name products are often sold through highly sophisticated, centrally controlled, exclusive distribution networks.

Distributors often do their own marketing with the support of the manufacturer. They set their own prices and bear the risk is bad debts themselves. In fact, any attempts by the manufacturer to influence prices charged by his distributor are illegal and competition authorities (including the EU Commission) will impose fines to prevent this happening. (In contrast, in an agency network price fixing is permitted and this may be one of the reasons why certain businesses prefer agents to distributors.) The German Commercial Code does not contain express provisions that govern a distributorship agreement. A professionally drafted distribution agreement is therefore essential. In addition, a large body of case law exists applying certain statutory provisions to certain types of distributorship.

One particular aspect of German law that is often relied on by disappointed distributors should also be mentioned. In certain cases the compensation rules of German agency law are applied to distribution and franchise agreements. In order for these provisions to apply to distribution agreements there must be more than a mere seller–purchaser relationship. The distributor must be integrated into the organisation of the manufacturer and have obligations similar to an agent. In particular, the supplier must be able to use the customer base of the distributor after termination of the agreement. To meet this condition, it is not necessary that the distributor is contractually obliged to pass customer lists or other information to the supplier. It is sufficient if the supplier is in practice able to continue to use the customer base acquired by the distributor. Compensation claims can be substantial. To avoid the risk of exposure it is possible to agree with a German distributor that the rights and obligations of the parties will be governed by English law. Under English law the compensation rules for agents are presently not applied to distributorships and there is no law preventing the parties from choosing English law as the law of their contract.

Another area where the choice of the applicable law is of great relevance regards restrictive covenants. In German law restrictive covenants are easy to enforce provided that they are not excessive. However, statute requires that the agreement provides in advance that reasonable compensation is paid to the party observing the restrictions to compensate it for its loss of income. This can be expensive, as the compensation payable will rarely be less than 50 per cent of the previous income from the restricted activity. On the other hand there are situations where the restriction itself has a much higher value to the manufacturer. It allows him to prevent his previous distributor from acting for a direct competitor. In a highly competitive market it may therefore be preferable to bite this particular bullet. In English law, on the other hand, restrictive covenants are cheap but often difficult to enforce. Careful thought needs therefore to be given to the choice of the applicable law.

Franchising

Franchising is yet another method of expanding one's business abroad that is less capital intensive than the operation of a subsidiary or branch office. When compared with agency and distribution systems, however, it should be borne in mind that substantially more support and advice will be expected from a franchiser. People who franchise in their home country will have a support system prepared and can thus limit themselves to adjusting their system to the market of the target country. Those who have not franchised before are looking at a substantial initial investment in terms of manpower, marketing and the creation of a handbook and training facilities. Would-be franchisers are also well advised to use the services of a franchising consultant when seeking to convert their business concept into a franchise.

Once a decision has been made that franchising is the way forward several choices present themselves. A master franchisee can be appointed who will develop the entire country. Alternatively, it is possible to franchise directly to individual local franchisees who may not have the resources or capacity to service a larger region. Finally, it is possible to work with regional development plans, allocating regions or countries to a developer. The choice depends on numerous factors and advice should be sought from franchising specialists.

Whatever the choice, a professionally drafted franchise agreement will be required to implement the franchising concept. When franchising internationally it is usually prudent to have this agreement checked by local lawyers. German law imposes a number of restrictions on franchisers and franchisees that restrict their freedom of contract.

Unlike agency or distribution agreements, franchise agreements must be in writing. This written form requirement exists to enable the German Cartel Office to investigate the franchise system and ensure that it does not illegally restrict competition. If several documents are used, the main franchise agreement containing the provisions restricting competition will affect all other relevant documents.

Franchise agreements operating in Germany are generally subject to the provisions of the German equivalent of the Unfair Contract Terms Act (AGBG) because the franchiser will want to use the same standard agreement with all franchisees. The AGBG applies to all pre-formulated contracts that are to be used for more than one contractual relationship. If the franchisee can be classified as a 'merchant' in the sense of the Commercial Code before entering into the franchise agreement, the application of the Act is restricted to the more general clauses; but if the franchisee starts his first business with the franchise all provisions of the Act apply. The consequence of the applicability of this Act is that many provisions that are disadvantageous to the franchisee may be invalid and unenforceable. Also, jurisdiction clauses agreed in advance with a non-business person are void. It is therefore not advisable to simply use the wording of franchise agreements drafted for other countries without having them thoroughly checked against the implications of German law.

As with distribution agreements, many statutory provisions regarding commercial agents may be applicable by way of analogy to the franchise relationship. Again, this applies in particular to the entitlement to compensation after termination. The conditions for such a vicarious application are the same as in the case of a distribution agreement. In the case of a franchise agreement it will usually be easy for the franchisee to prove that he was integrated into the franchiser's business, as this is the nature of a franchise system. The decisive question will be if the franchiser is able to use the customers acquired by the franchisee after the termination of the franchise agreement. Recently, the courts have become more and more willing to accept this condition as given and grant the franchisee compensation.

Franchise agreements will also have to comply with competition law. Apart from the European Block Exemption Regulations, German national competition rules apply. They stipulate (*inter alia*) that the franchiser must lay down binding rules as to prices and terms of trade that the franchisee must use *vis-à-vis* his customers. Rules containing restrictions on who the franchisee may contract with are in principle permitted but subject to supervision by the Cartel Office. Such restrictions will only be prohibited if the Cartel Offices is of the opinion that they restrict competition unfairly.

BRANCH OR SUBSIDIARY

Agents, distributors and franchisees are all, by law, independent entrepreneurs. In some cases they may well be substantial companies. These relationships can be difficult to manage from abroad and many foreign investors prefer the simple and direct route of setting up their own local structures instead. German law provides a variety of legal entities, starting with the branch of the foreign company and leading to the commercial partnership (*Offene Handelsgesellschaft* – OHG), the limited partnership (*Kommanditgesellschaft* – KG), the limited partnership with a limited company as general partner (GmbH & Co KG) and the private limited company (*Gesellschaft mit beschränkter Haftung* – GmbH).

Branch

Any foreign partnership or company can act in Germany through a branch. This will involve registration with the local Commercial Register (*Handelsregister*) as well as with the local tax authorities. Depending on the trade in question it may be necessary to obtain a licence and/or become a member of the local trade association. The branch will not be a separate legal entity; ie local management will have to be authorised to bind the foreign company or partnership contractually as well as *vis-à-vis* the German authorities. If the German branch is responsible for any turnover arising in the German business, it will, as a permanent establishment, be liable to German tax thereon.

Trading partnership (OHG) and limited partnerships (KG)

If it is intended to involve a German partner in the conduct of the business in Germany, it is possible to do this by forming a trading partnership (*Offene Handelsgesellschaft*) or, if liability is to be restricted, a limited partnership (*Kommanditgesellschaft*). Even though the German language uses the word *Gesellschaft*, these entities have the character of partnerships and do not rank as corporations. They are capable of entering into contracts in their partnership names and can sue and be sued under those names. However, they are not entirely separate legal entities, a fact that has important consequences in tax law. Even the GmbH & Co KG, a limited partnership with a private limited company as general partner, which thus achieves total limitation of liability to the combined capital of the partnership and the general partner, is still classified as a partnership and not as a corporate entity. These partnerships are of particular attraction to family businesses as they provide great flexibility for tax planning while keeping the control in the hands of the dominant partners.

GmbH *(Gesellschaft mit beschränkter Haftung)*

The most popular investment vehicle chosen by foreign investors is the GmbH, which is the German equivalent of the English private limited company. Its formation and management are governed by the rules of the Act on Private Limited Companies (GmbG). A minimum share capital of €25,000 (DM50,000) is required, of which €12,500 (DM25,000) must be paid up by the shareholder(s) before the company can be incorporated. As a result, there are generally no shelf companies available for purchase. Shelf companies or pre-incorporated GmbHs, with €12,500 (DM25,000) already paid up, come at a premium because of the costs involved. Also, great care must be taken to ensure that these companies do not have a trading history or debts that may have to be discharged by the shareholders. Usually, foreign investors incorporate their own tailor-made subsidiaries for these reasons.

AG *(Aktiengesellschaft)*

The German equivalent to a public limited company or a joint-stock company is the *Aktiengesellschaft*. There is a separate act regulating this type of corporation (*Aktiengesetz* – AktG) that not only deals with the requirements as to formation and the regulation of the company's internal organisation but also deals with the formation and management of groups (*Konzernrecht*). Only *Aktiengesellschaften* and *Kommandit-gesellschaften auf Aktien* (a rare and dying breed in German partnership law) can apply for listing on any stock exchange.

CHECKLIST FOR THE FORMATION OF A GERMAN LIMITED LIABILITY COMPANY (GMBH)

1.   COMPANY NAME

The name of the company must contain the words '*Gesellschaft mit beschränkter Haftung*' or common and understandable abbreviations thereof, eg 'GmbH'. The choice of the name is restricted by the following rules:

a.   The name must be capable of identifying the company and must be distinguishable, ie it must not be so vague that it has no character-istics of its own, eg 'the Bank';

b.   The name must not be misleading, eg a company only operating in a part of Germany may not call itself 'European' or a company producing textiles may not call itself 'software centre';

c.   The name must not be the same as or confusingly similar to the name of an existing company at the place of registration (*Note: the German registration system operates locally, not nationwide*).

2.   NAME(S) AND ADDRESS(ES) OF MEMBER(S)

There is no minimum or maximum number of members (shareholders). The names, dates of birth and addresses and details of the respective participation shares (see 5 and 6 below) of the members must be listed and the list must be signed by the members.

3.   MAIN OBJECTS (*GESELLSCHAFTSGEGENSTAND*)

The Articles of Association (*Satzung*) must briefly state the main areas of activity of the company. German law does not operate an 'ultra vires' doctrine, ie the Company will be contractually bound even if the transaction is outside its objects.

4.   SEAT OF THE COMPANY (*SITZ*)

Instead of a registered office, the company must have a seat, ie state in its Articles of Association (*Satzung*), the city, town or village where its management and administrative centre is located. The seat need not be specified by an exact postal address, but it must be the place where the company's actual centre of management is situated rather than, for example, a solicitor's office.

5. SHARE CAPITAL (*STAMMKAPITAL*)

The minimum share capital for a GmbH is €25,000 of which at least half (€12,500) must be paid up, and a quarter (€6,250) must even be paid up before the application for registration is submitted.

If there is only one shareholder, half must be paid up before the application for registration is submitted and a security must be granted for the remaining contributions in cash.

The share capital must be capable of being divided by €50.

6. CONTRIBUTIONS (*STAMMEINLAGEN*)

The Articles of Association (*Satzung*) must state the amount of each shareholder's contribution, the minimum contribution amounting to €100. The contributions of the different shareholders may vary in amount but each shareholder may only make one contribution and thus obtain one shareholding, the different shareholdings varying in amount.

Each shareholder has one vote per €50 shareholding.

The Articles of Association (*Satzung*) must state whether the contributions are to be in cash or in kind. Special rules apply to contributions in kind.

7. ARTICLES OF ASSOCIATION (*SATZUNG*)

In addition to containing the main details on the company's name, seat, objects and share capital, the Articles of Association also regulate the internal life of the company, such as:

a. whether the sale or other disposition of participation shares is possible only with the consent of all shareholders (without a provision to this effect participation share can be transferred freely);
b. the number of directors (*Geschäftsführer*) and whether they require the consent of the shareholders for certain transactions (which may be set out in a separate shareholders' resolution);
c. whether directors may act on behalf of the company alone or only in conjunction with another director or a plenipotentiary (*Prokurist*);
d. whether when acting on behalf of the company a director may contract with himself/herself in a different capacity (eg personally or as attorney for another party);

e. provisions regulating the calling and holding of shareholders' meetings;
f. provisions regarding the requirements for valid shareholders' resolutions;
g. whether participation shares may be revoked, and if so, whether and under which circumstances this may be done without the consent of the affected shareholder.

8. DIRECTORS (*GESCHÄFTSFÜHRER*)

There must be at least one director. Directors are appointed by shareholders' resolution (unless the company chooses to have a supervisory board and the appointment of directors is delegated to that board) and must visit a German notary or German consular officer to sign their application for registration. There is no requirement for German nationality; however, as the management must be conducted mainly in Germany, there must never arise a situation where all directors live abroad and do not or cannot (eg in case of non-EU citizens because no visa will be granted) travel to Germany to conduct business.

9. FINANCIAL YEAR (*GESCHÄFTSJAHR*)

The Articles must define the financial year of the company. Commonly the calendar year is chosen.

10. PUBLIC NOTICES (*BEKANNTMACHUNGEN*)

Notices of any changes (eg change of director, name, seat etc) must be published and the appropriate publication must be chosen. Commonly such notices are published in the *Federal Gazette* (*Bundesanzeiger*).

11. COST OF FORMATION (*GRÜNDUNGSAUFWAND*)

Notary costs must be borne by the shareholders unless the Articles of Association provide for them to be borne by the company up to a stated maximum amount.

12. TRANSFER OF PARTICIPATION SHARES

Shares are freely transferable subject to pre-emption rights and any securities created over them. Any contract for a transfer has to be in notarial form by way of assignment. The notary will charge on the basis of a statutory fee scale. There is also Capital Transfer Tax (*Kapitalverkehrsteuer*) payable at the rate of 1 per cent based on the purchase price.

28

Corporate Governance

Eversheds

The two most popular types of corporation for foreign investors are: firstly, the private limited company (GmbH), which is the preferred form of corporation for small and medium-sized businesses. Approximately 500,000 in number, the GmbH dominates the German economy. Secondly, the public limited company (AG), which is the appropriate form of corporation for large businesses. Numbering only approximately 2500, the AG is far less common than the GmbH, which shows that the German economy is still dominated by small and medium-sized businesses.

GMBH (*GESELLSCHAFT MIT BESCHRÄNKTER HAFTUNG*)

A GmbH usually has two governing bodies, the *shareholders* and one or more managing director (*Geschäftsführer*). Furthermore, a GmbH employing more than 500 employees is obliged to form a supervisory board (*Aufsichtsrat*), which must consist, as a matter of co-determination, of members appointed by the shareholders and members appointed by the employees.

The most powerful entity within a GmbH are the shareholders. They appoint and dismiss the *Geschäftsführer*. Moreover, the shareholders as a body have the right to control the activities of the *Geschäftsführer* and are entitled to give him general directions. Because of the influence that the shareholders have in a GmbH, this form of corporation is often chosen for subsidiaries. The great advantage for a parent company as single or majority shareholder in a GmbH is that it has ultimate control of the activities of its subsidiaries.

The governing entity in charge of managing the company internally and representing it externally is the *Geschäftsführer*. Often, particularly in larger businesses, two or even more *Geschäftsführer* are appointed by the shareholders. Under German law, any individual person with unrestricted business capacity can serve as a *Geschäftsführer;* accordingly shareholders as well as third persons, regardless of their nationality or residence, may be appointed.

Without a special provision in the Articles of Association or a specific shareholders' resolution, several *Geschäftsführer* are only entitled to represent the company jointly. A single *Geschäftsführer* is always entitled to represent the company alone. In companies with several *Geschäftsführer*, some are often authorised to represent the GmbH alone.

Such an authorisation, as well as any other modification of the statutory form of representation, has to be filed with the Commercial Register (*Handelsregister*). In addition to the *Geschäftsführer*, senior employees in a position of trust are often made plenipotentiary (*Prokurist*) with the authority to represent the company *vis-à-vis* third parties, normally jointly with a *Geschäftsführer*. German business relies on the so-called 'four-eyes-principle'.

As explained above, the Co-Determination Act requires companies with more than 500 employees to establish an *Aufsichtsrat*, one-third of whose members must be elected by the employee. In companies with more than 2000 employees, half of the members of the *Aufsichtsrat* must be elected by the employees. To protect the interests of the shareholders in companies having more than 2000 employees, the chairman of the *Aufsichtsrat*, who in practice is a member appointed by the shareholders, has a casting vote.

In companies with more than 500 employees, the aim of the *Aufsichtsrat* is to control the management. In companies with more than 2000 employees, the *Aufsichtsrat* also has the power to appoint and dismiss the *Geschäftsführer*.

AG (*AKTIENGESELLSCHAFT*)

In general, an AG has three governing entities: the shareholders' general meeting (*Hauptversammlung*), the supervisory board (*Aufsichtsrat*) and the management board (*Vorstand*).

In contrast to a GmbH, where the shareholders are very powerful, their direct influence on the conduct of the business in an AG is more limited.

Under German law, the shareholders of an AG have the right to pass shareholders' resolutions on fundamental corporate matters, such as the distribution of profits, the formal approval of the record of activities of the *Vorstand* during a given period, the nomination of the auditors, amendments of the Articles of Association, any change in the share capital, as well as the dissolution of the company. Questions of management do not fall within their ambit, unless the *Vorstand* expressly requests a particular management decision to be made by the shareholders during the *Hauptversammlung*. The shareholders of an AG, in contrast to a GmbH, are not empowered to issue directions to the *Vorstand*. In order to properly exercise their rights, ie to pass resolutions regarding the above-mentioned matters with sufficient knowledge of the respective facts, the shareholders have a right to be informed by the *Vorstand*, a right that can be exercised during the *Hauptversammlung*. Last but not least, the shareholders have the right to appoint the members of the *Aufsichtsrat* (which in turn appoints and dismisses members of the *Vorstand*).

The *Aufsichtsrat*, which is appointed by the *Hauptversammlung* for a period of up to four years, consists of at least three members. The Articles of Association may provide for a larger number, depending on the size of the company. The number of members of the *Aufsichtsrat* must always be divisible by three. The Co-Determination Act requires that in companies with more than 500 employees, one-third of the members of the *Aufsichtsrat* must be elected by the employees. In companies having more than 2000 employees, the portion of the members of *Aufsichtsrat* elected by the employees increases to one-half. To protect the interests of the shareholders in companies with more than 2000 employees, the chairman of the *Aufsichtsrat,* who is always one of the members appointed by the shareholders, has a casting a vote.

Under German law, any natural person with unrestricted general business capacity may serve as a member of the *Aufsichtsrat*. Restrictions only apply to those persons holding more than ten other mandates in the *Aufsichtsräte* of other German companies. The mandate is strictly personal and no representation by proxy is permitted. There is no restriction on reappointment.

Basic rights and obligations of the *Aufsichtsrat* are the overall control of the management, the appointment and dismissal of the *Vorstand* as well as the representation of the company *vis-à-vis* the *Vorstand*. To be able to fulfil its obligations, the *Aufsichtsrat* has the right to detailed information and is entitled to inspect all corporate books and records.

Moreover, the Articles of Association may require the approval by the *Aufsichtsrat* of particular corporate transactions or transactions of a certain type or size.

The *Vorstand*, which is appointed by the *Aufsichtsrat* for a maximum of five years, has to manage and represent the company. In contrast to the *Geschäftsführer* of a GmbH, the *Vorstand* has to exercise its duties under its own responsibility and is not subject to directives of the *Aufsichtsrat* or the *Hauptversammlung*. However, there is often an active process of consultation. Moreover, members of the *Vorstand* can only be dismissed by the *Aufsichtsrat* and only for cause, for example gross misconduct or flagrant violation of duties. As a result, the *Vorstand* plays the most important role in the day-to-day corporate governance of an AG.

The *Vorstand* of an AG may consist of one or more members. If there is more than one, a chairman is usually chosen.

Under German law, any individual with unrestricted business capacity can serve as *Vorstand*, so that the shareholders as well as third persons, regardless of their nationality or residence, can be appointed. A renewal of the appointment is usually allowed but may only be agreed during the 12 months prior to the expiry of the current term.

29

Corporate Combinations, Mergers and Acquisitions

Eversheds

Germany has been busy with small, medium and large-scale corporate transactions. The market in companies ranges from the small family enterprise to the large, German-based international concern. The former will typically involve a limited partnership or a private limited company being sold or merged.

PRIOR REORGANISATION

For tax or corporate reasons it is often advisable to first conduct a reorganisation in order to change the corporate status prior to the transaction. This can be done under special German laws (*Umwand-lungsgesetz*) allowing for the change from one corporate status to another without loss of identity (thereby minimising the tax consequences), or even a genuine merger of two legal entities into one (again, whilst retaining the corporate identity of both participants with the consequent tax benefits). Thus, German law allows for a genuine merger of two or more entities, whereas most other legal systems require a full-scale acquisition involving the loss of identity of at least one of the participants.

It is thus possible not only to transform a limited partnership into a private or public limited company (or vice versa) but also to hive down businesses into new legal entities, without producing incidents which previously gave rise to certain tax charges. German law therefore provides for a new alternative to the previous choice between a share deal and an asset deal.

Under the Act it is possible not only to split the assets and then transfer all of them into new legal entities (*Aufspaltung*); the same advantages also apply if only part of the assets are transferred to a new entity, owned by the shareholders of the transferring unit, whilst the remaining assets are retained by the latter (*Abspaltung*). If the transferee is owned by the shareholders of the transferor, the same principles apply (*Ausgliederung*).

In all these cases, the important consequence of the maintenance of corporate identity consists in the continuing effect of contracts without the need for assignments or novations in addition to the avoidance of taxable incidents. The documentation required for such transactions has to meet the requirements set out in the Transformation Act, must be notarised and eventually entered in the Commercial Register.

SALES DOCUMENTATION

The documentation of share purchase agreements differs from that normally found in common law systems. If the target is a private limited company (GmbH), the contract must be in notarial form which, if the German transaction is only a side-show of a global deal, may need prior consideration if the closing has to coincide with the completion of the main transaction.

Notaries charge their fees on the basis of a fee scale that relates to the value of the transaction. Notaries in a limited number of cantons of Switzerland, whose fees are sometimes more competitive, are also recognised under German law.

Warranties in German acquisition agreements are often more general, less specific and shorter compared to their Anglo-American equivalent. This can be explained by the greater reliance on statutory obligations, extensive case law and due diligence.

ORGANISATION OF GROUPS

The relationship between associated companies can, subject to any merger control restrictions, be regulated by contract. In particular, it is possible to enter into subordination agreements (*Beherrschungs- und Gewinnabführungsvertrag*) in which the subordinated company agrees to accept and observe directions given by the dominating company and/ or deliver up all of its profits. Detailed provisions exist for the protection of minority shareholders and creditors. If such an agreement is entered into, the dominating company will be deemed to have assumed all liabilities of the subordinate company, ie the corporate veil has been lifted.

FRIENDLY TAKEOVERS

The German corporate culture has not yet been subjected to the upheavals of hostile takeovers. All acquisitions of companies, large and small, have been agreed and, an essential element in Germany, supported by the main providers of working capital. One important reason for the absence of hostile takeovers from the German scene is the multiple role the banks play as lenders to the parties to the transaction, lenders to the target and very often holders of general proxies or shareholders of invested pension funds. A voluntary code of conduct (*Übernahmekode*) is in place to serve as a guideline to the regular players in corporate deals.

MERGER CONTROL

Competition issues play a major part in every corporate takeover or joint venture in Germany and it is important to check in advance whether the transaction requires prior clearance by the *Bundeskartellamt*, the German anti-trust authority. With the EU Commission concentrating on the control of very large corporate groups, most medium-sized transactions are still under the scrutiny of the *Bundeskartellamt* in Berlin (Bonn from autumn 1999). A merger will be investigated by the *Bundeskartellamt* if the parties to the transaction together have a world-wide group turnover in excess of DM1 billion (€500 million) or if one of the companies involved had a domestic turnover of more than DM50 million (€25 million).

Transactions need not be notified if the world-wide turnover of at least one of the parties was below DM20 million (€10 million) and if the turnover of the relevant market was below DM30 million (€15 million).

30

Typical Contractual Issues

Eversheds

INTRODUCTION

There are certain aspects of contract law where German law differs from common law, thus when entering into contracts the requirements and prescription of German law represent potential pitfalls for individuals and companies accustomed to the common law. In addition, certain issues have to be kept in mind when entering into cross-border agreements. This chapter cannot claim to give a comprehensive overview of all issues that can arise when entering into such contracts; however, the five issues dealt with are particularly important and may help to avoid unpleasant surprises.

WHICH COURT WILL BE COMPETENT TO DEAL WITH ANY DISPUTE?

For all transactions with an international element and which do not provide for arbitration, it must be first decided which court should resolve a dispute. This question is resolved in civil and commercial matters for the countries of the European Union (EU) and the European Free Trade Association (EFTA) by the provisions contained in the Brussels and Lugano Conventions respectively. These rules have all been implemented in Germany.

Where at least one of the parties is situated in an EU or EFTA country the rules of the Conventions apply. This means that the parties' choice as to which court will be competent will be respected. For the sake of certainty it is advisable to make an express choice at the outset in the contract. The choice might depend on the parties' location, potential language barriers, costs of litigation, the law applicable to the contract and the location of the parties' assets. However, as to the latter point, even if the defendant's assets are located in a different EU or EFTA country, this is not a bar to enforcement. A judgment obtained in one of the EU or EFTA states will generally be recognised and enforced by the courts of another EU or EFTA state.

If no express choice has been made, the competent court will be the court having local jurisdiction in the country where the defendant resides. In addition, depending on the situation, the court in the place where the contract should have been performed or where a branch or agency of the defendant is located, might have concurrent jurisdiction.

In certain insurance and consumer contracts, policy holders or consumers, as the case may be, have a right to sue in their own country. Special rules also exist for disputes concerning rights in immovable property, company law and intellectual property rights. The court with jurisdiction over the matter will apply its law of procedure. Only lawyers admitted to that court may represent the parties.

WHICH LAW APPLIES?

For all transactions with an international element it must then be decided which country's substantive laws should apply. If a German court is called upon to decide this question it will apply the German conflict of law rules. These are mainly contained in the Introductory Law to the Civil Code and are based on the Rome Convention, which has also been ratified by the UK.

CHOICE OF LAW CLAUSES

In order to avoid uncertainties, a contract with an international element should include an express choice of law clause and this choice will normally govern the contract. This choice depends on the familiarity of the parties with the legal system and which of the possible substantive provisions are more favourable. In this context it should be noted that certain so-called mandatory rules cannot be excluded (see below). Another factor is jurisdiction. It is usually preferable if a court applies its own law since, for example, a German court applying English law will have a more complex task. This will involve academic experts and may make the result less predictable and more expensive.

Mandatory provisions of German law

As mentioned above, certain mandatory rules cannot be avoided by a choice of law clause. These are usually rules that protect one of the parties on public policy grounds. For example, certain jurisdictions and laws protecting consumers or employees in their country of residence cannot be excluded.

Proper law of the contract in the absence of a choice of law

If no choice of law is expressed in the contract, the court will look at all circumstances to see whether the parties presumed that a particular law should apply to the contract. For this the court will take into account such factors as the legal structure of the contract, its concepts, its language etc. If such a presumed choice of law cannot be established with certainty, the law of the country where the party is located that carries out the characteristic performance will be the law applicable to the contract. In a contract for the supply of goods or services payment is not regarded as a characteristic performance. In a sale of goods contract, the seller and in an agency/distribution agreement the agent/distributor will carry out the characteristic performance and the contract will be governed by the law of the place where the seller/agent/distributor is located.

The legal capacity of natural persons follows the law of nationality. The capacity of companies is determined by the law of the actual centre of administration and not by the law of the country where the company is incorporated. Non-resident companies are therefore not recognised as legal entities although a recent judgment of the European Court of Justice is likely to change that.

Corporate officers are governed by the laws of the country in which the actual centre of administration of the company is located.

The transfer of title to property is governed by the law of the place where the property is situated.

Public policy and renvoi

However, there are two situations where German law applies to the contract despite the fact that the German conflict of law rules point to foreign law:

1. In rare instances where the foreign law would be contrary to German public policy.

2. If the foreign law that applies as a consequence of German conflict of law rules refers back to German law.

As will be seen below, the application of German law may also include the application of international conventions that have been signed and ratified by Germany. Some of those are not also part of English law.

STANDARD CONTRACT TERMS

In Germany the incorporation of standard contract terms and their validity are governed by the *Gesetz zur Regelung des Rechts der Allgemeinen Geschäftsbedingungen* (AGBG) (Regulations governing the law of standard contract terms – comparable to the English Unfair Contract Terms Act).

Incorporation

As under English law, care must be taken to ensure that the standard contract terms are properly incorporated into the contract. The rules in this respect are similar (see Sections 2 and 3 of the AGBG). According to Section 2, standard contract terms can only be incorporated into a contract if the party purporting to introduce those terms explicitly informed the other party of those terms and if the other party agreed to those terms when the contract was made.

To the extent that the two competing sets of standard terms are identical they both apply, and insofar as there is a conflict between them they are both disregarded. Any gaps caused thereby are filled by the statutory provisions of German law. This is different from the English rule of the 'last shot' (whereby the last communication regarding the applicable standard terms decides which set of terms applies).

Surprise clauses

According to Section 3 of the AGBG, so-called 'unexpected terms' will not become part of a contract if under the circumstances the other party could not expect such a term to be included in the standard contract terms. Whether a term is unexpected or not has to be decided in the context of the circumstances of every single case.

Any ambiguities in the terms will be construed against the party that introduced those terms.

Once it is decided that a term is incorporated in a contract, the content of this term is then subject to the substantive control provided for by the AGBG.

Generally speaking, a standard contract term is only valid if the term is fair and reasonable. The court has general discretion to strike out any term that does not fulfil this requirement (Section 9).

Reasonableness

Section 10 contains a list of clauses where the court has discretion to decide whether such clauses are valid or not. By way of example, the following clauses might be invalid under this section:

- Unreasonably long or unspecific time limits for acceptance of an offer or for the performance of the contract.
- A clause that allows a party to rescind the contract without a substantial reason. This does not apply to long-term or framework contracts.
- A clause that gives one party a unilateral right to render a different performance or to vary the contract.

Generally unacceptable clauses

Section 11 contains a list of clauses that are automatically invalid. In these cases, the court has no discretion to rule such a clause valid. For example:

- A clause that restricts a party's right to set off an undisputed claim or a claim on which judgment has been entered is invalid.
- Liability for damage caused intentionally or by gross negligence cannot be excluded.
- A clause that provides for a contractual penalty in the case of late or non-acceptance of goods or services, late payment or rescission is invalid.
- A clause containing certain restrictions of the other party's remedies is invalid.
- There are restrictions on clauses excluding the statutory conditions as to satisfactory quality of goods.
- A clause allowing one party to transfer the contract to an unnamed party is invalid unless the other party can terminate the contract.
- Certain clauses rendering the proof of facts or the giving of notice to the other party more difficult are invalid.

Special rules for 'merchants'

The above rules apply to consumers as well as non-consumers (unlike the English Unfair Contract Terms Act 1977, which provides significant reduced protection of non-consumers). However, persons qualifying for the German definition of 'merchants' as set out in the Commercial Code are less protected than persons acting in a private capacity.

LIABILITY FOR BREACH OF PRE-CONTRACTUAL DUTIES (*CULPA IN CONTRAHENDO*)

When entering into negotiations with a prospective German business partner it is important to be aware of the concept of *culpa in contrahendo* (CIC) under German law. The concept is based on the general duty to act in good faith (Section 242 BGB). If there is a breach, remedies may already be available with regard to misrepresentations during the pre-contractual phase of negotiations. German law in this respect differs from English law, where the dominant view is that prior to final commitment the parties are entitled to withdraw from negotiations at any time and that agreements have to be expressly agreed.

The liability under CIC is based on a pre-contractual duty to act during negotiations in a fair manner and not to abuse a party's reliance on the other party's stated intentions.

One example for this duty is not to make misrepresentations. This is vaguely similar to the English tort of misrepresentation. However the concept is much wider and can include the situation where one party unreasonably causes a breakdown of negotiations. The party that caused the breakdown may be liable for damages to the other party, which relied on that party's demonstrated intention to conclude the agreement. Such damages might include costs incurred in negotiating the contract. These claims are not easy to substantiate as the burden of proof is high. However, unsuspecting parties should beware.

If the conditions are met, a plaintiff may prefer a contractual claim in CIC to a claim under German tort law since in contract law an employer/principal is variously liable for the acts of an employee and there is a longer limitation period.

As can be seen, liability can be far reaching and it is important to keep this potential liability in mind when conducting contractual negotiations.

APPLICABILITY OF THE UN CONVENTION ON CONTRACTS FOR THE INTERNATIONAL SALE OF GOODS (CISG)

The United Nations Convention, also called the Vienna Convention, which provides for uniform rules for contracts dealing with the international sale of goods, is part of German national law. This Convention, amongst others, has been ratified by a large number of countries, including the United States and Germany, but not the UK. The UK has only ratified the old Hague Convention which, however, only applies to UK parties if it has been expressly incorporated by the parties into the contract. This is almost never done.

The Vienna Convention (Article 1 CISG) applies automatically to contracts for the sale of goods between parties situated in two different countries if either: both these countries have ratified the Vienna Convention; or the law that governs the contract is the law of a country that has ratified the Vienna Convention.

As a result, the rules of the Vienna Convention will automatically apply to an international contract for the sale of goods that is governed by German law. In order to avoid the automatic application of the CISG rules, they have to be specifically excluded.

This is an important point to remember, since this might catch the unaware: any unqualified choice of German law has the effect that the CISG rules apply.

In some cases the CISG rules are substantially different from German contract law. For example, Article 39 CISG gives the buyer under an international sale of goods contract a period of two years after the handing over of the goods in which to notify the seller of any lack of conformity of the goods with the agreed standard of quality (unless the time limit is inconsistent with an expressly agreed contractual period). In contrast, the German Civil Code provides for a six-month period, which begins to run once a lack of conformity of the goods has been discovered.

Therefore it should be carefully considered whether the parties wish the CISG rules to apply to their contract or whether they prefer to exclude them.

31

Employment Law

Eversheds

INTRODUCTION

It is well known internationally that German law provides considerable protection for employees. The extent of these rights may sometimes surprise foreign employers.

Whilst there have recently been some changes to German employment law that were intended to ease the position of employers, the law is still very much driven by the general objective of employee protection. The relationship between employers and employees is largely based on what is known as 'social partnership', where the aim of consensus is emphasised. The present government, elected in September 1998, has in some instances reversed the position.

Parties involved in employment law relationships

Depending on the circumstances, there can be up to four parties involved in an employment relationship. The primary parties are, of course, the employer and the employee. In this context *a distinction is drawn between employees on the one hand and* (independent) *consultants and freelances on the other.* A further complication has recently arisen with regard to so-called 'part-timers'. Only employees receive statutory protection and are subject to compulsory social security contributions (*Sozialversicherung*) and PAYE (*Lohnsteuerabzugsverfahren*). The distinction does not depend on the title chosen by the parties but on the actual circumstances of the relationship. A court will investigate how the relationship is structured in practice and on how independent the alleged consultant is. Since 1 January 1999 there exist statutory presumptions on when someone is an employee rather than a consultant.

In addition to these main parties there are trade unions, which are organised on an industry or trade basis. The determining factor in deciding which union will be competent to deal with a particular employer usually depends on the nature of the employer's business. German trade unions are organised nationally and regionally by reference to large trade sectors, eg metalworkers or chemical workers. Closed shops are not allowed.

Lastly, there are the works councils (*Betriebsräte*). A works council can be formed in any undertaking (*Betrieb*) with five or more employees. There is no obligation on the employer to assist in any way with the formation of a works council, which can be left to the initiative of the employees (who normally avail themselves of this right). *Betriebsräte* are often regarded as a useful channel of communication between management and workforce.

Applicable law and other rules

There is a large volume of legislation and agreements with quasi-statutory effect.

Statutes

The current law is largely contained in statutes. Important specific aspects are regulated in separate Acts that are often difficult to reconcile. The codification of employment legislation in one single code is planned but has not yet materialised. German employment law is also an area where case law is particularly important.

Furthermore, European law, mainly in the form of directives and rulings of the European Court of Justice, has a fast-growing influence on German employment law.

Collective agreements (*Tarifverträge*)

Agreements between employers' associations and trade unions are binding on the parties to a dispute if:

- both the employer and the employee are members of the respective employers' organisation or union;
- the employer agrees directly with the trade union a house or company 'tariff';
- the employer is a member of the respective employers' organisation and matters concerning the undertaking or works council matters are regulated, eg employee protection or behaviour rules for the employees;

- a trade union agreement has been given force of law by the Federal Ministry of Employment or by a State Ministry for Employment. In such a case the trade union agreement is binding irrespective of trade union recognition. Such trade union agreements are often regional rather than being applicable to the whole of Germany. Accordingly, an employer operating in different parts of Germany will have to consider different trade union agreements.

Trade union agreements prevail over works council agreements and employment contracts unless these are more advantageous to the employee.

Works council agreements (*Betriebsvereinbarungen*)

An agreement between the employer and the works council can regulate questions that fall within the scope of authority of the works council (eg duration of the lunch break, when it is to be taken, creation of a common room, allocating of shifts, redundancy schemes). The works council, however, cannot agree matters that are agreed in a tariff (eg wages, number of working hours per week). This is so even where the works council is able to negotiate a package that is perceived as beneficial by the relevant employees.

Custom and practice (*Betriebliche Übung*)

Occasionally, custom and practice within the employer organisation can create rights in favour of employees even if the employer did not intend to create any such rights; eg if an employer repeatedly pays a Christmas bonus for a number of years (in general, three years suffice) without stating that the bonus is discretionary, the employees may well acquire an enforceable right to such a bonus in future years.

INDIVIDUAL EMPLOYMENT AGREEMENTS

Formation of an employment contract

Form

The employment contract is entered into like any other contract and generally does not require any particular form. The employer must provide written particulars of employment to the employee within one month of the employee starting work.

Rules for the selection of employees

Germany has similar anti-discrimination rules to England and a job applicant may not be rejected on grounds of sex, race or any such discriminatory reasons. Certain questions should not be asked in an interview as they are considered to be discriminatory, eg a female applicant cannot be asked if she is pregnant. Nor may an applicant be asked if he is member of a trade union. An applicant may even answer such questions untruthfully without having to fear any adverse consequences.

Obligations of the employer to notify

The employer has an obligation to notify the competent collection body for social security contributions (*Einzugsstelle*) of the start of the employment relationship. The identity of that body depends on which insurance organisation the employee is insured with. Also, the relevant professional body for the compulsory accident insurance and the tax authorities must be notified.

TERMS AND CONDITIONS OF EMPLOYMENT

Duration

Usually an employment contract will be for an indefinite term. German law only allows fixed-term agreements in certain circumstances. Originally fixed-term contracts were prohibited unless there were certain compelling reasons recognised by the courts.

Parliament created new exceptions by statute which, however, apply only until 31 December 2000 unless extended. Under these rules fixed-term contract may be entered into for a period of up to two years without giving any reasons. If the fixed-term contract was initially for less than two years it can be extended up to three times, as long as the total term does not exceed two years. If an employee is over 60 years old, there are no restrictions on fixed contractors. However, in any of the above situations a fixed-term contract is prohibited if there is a close connection with a previous employment contract with the same employer. Such a connection is deemed to exist if the previous employment ended less than four months previously.

If a fixed term is invalid the employment contract continues for an indefinite term.

Remuneration

At the moment there is no statutory minimum wage in Germany, with the exception of the construction industry. However, the current lack of a statutory minimum wage does not mean that employers are free to set wage levels at will.

If there is a relevant trade union agreement in place and applicable that specifies wage levels, these will constitute minimum wages that must be adhered to. Also, there is a prohibition on 'wage dumping'. There are no hard and fast rules on when wage dumping occurs but there are judgments that give guidance. Some of these judgments state that a wage is usurious if it is only two-thirds of the wage agreed in the tariff for the particular sector of industry. In any event, wage dumping is seen to exist if, despite full-time work, the wage is less than the existing minimum (currently DM1209 per month for a single person without maintenance obligations, and more if there are such obligations).

On setting remuneration the employer will also have to bear in mind the following points:

- Part-time staff must not be treated less favourably than full-time staff.
- Wages must not be discriminatory, eg because of gender.
- In the undertaking (*Betrieb*) the rule of equal treatment applies.

Holiday

The Holiday Act (*Bundesurlaubsgesetz* – BUrlG) gives a statutory right to a minimum paid holiday of 24 working days based on a six-day week (the equivalent of 20 days on a five-day week). The right to full holiday entitlement is acquired after six months' service. If the employment is terminated and the employee has less than six months' service, he will be entitled to a pro-rated period of paid holiday. The same applies if the employee leaves before the year end. If holiday cannot be taken because of termination of the employment, the employee must be paid for the unused holiday.

Sickness

Under the Sick Pay Act (*Entgeltfortzahlungsgesetz*) every employee is entitled to sick pay amounting to 100 per cent of his wages for the first six weeks of sickness, provided he has completed one moth's service with the employer.

The six-week period will start to run on each separate occasion of sickness absence, unless the sickness is due to the same continued illness and less than six months have passed since the occasion of the last sick leave due to this illness, or less than 12 months since the beginning of the last sick leave due to this illness.

Working time

There are statutory provisions on maximum working hours in the Working Time Act (*Arbeitszeitgesetz*). These apply to most employees, the most notable exception being managers and other 'leading employees' (*Leitende Angestellte*). Special rules exist for employees in the aviation and shipping sectors.

Regular working time should by law not exceed eight hours per working day; however, this may be increased to up to ten hours, provided that within six calendar months or 24 weeks the average of eight hours per working day is not exceeded. Working days are Monday to Saturday so that the maximum is a 48-hour week.

Exceptions may be permitted by trade union agreement or in cases where there are unforeseeable circumstances or urgency, but usually an equalisation has to be reached over a longer period. If these provisions are breached a fine of up to DM30,000 can be imposed on the employer.

There are compulsory breaks: at least 30 minutes when working between six and nine hours; at least 45 minutes when working over nine hours. Breaks may be split but must be at least 15 minutes long. There are also compulsory rest periods of at least 11 hours between work days.

Generally, work on Sundays and Bank Holidays is prohibited, but there are exceptions.

Confidentiality/non-compete obligations during the term of the agreement

During the employment relationship the employee is under an obligation not to harm the employer's business which includes the duty not to compete with it or to pass confidential information to competitors.

Restrictive covenants

A post-termination non-compete clause can be agreed for a period of up to two years if it is reasonable and necessary to protect the employer's interests. However, it is only valid if the employer agrees in advance to pay compensation. Such compensation must be paid monthly for the duration of the non-compete provision and amount to at least

50 per cent of the employee's salary as at the date of termination. Other remunerations of the employee (eg bonuses) will only be taken into account if they amount to more than eleven-tenths of the salary as at the date of termination (or five-fourths if the employee had to relocate).

DISCRIMINATION

German law prohibits any discrimination based on gender, race, background etc.

Rulings of the European Court of Justice have extended the prohibition of sex discrimination to cover indirect discrimination. If, for example, part timers are treated less favourably than full-time employees and a larger proportion of part-time employees are women compared with equivalent full-time employees, the less favourable treatment of part timers may amount to indirect discrimination based on gender.

TERMINATION

Termination by mutual agreement

It is possible to terminate the employment relationship by agreement between the parties, thus avoiding any statutory dismissal protection. However, an employee will only agree to this if there is some benefit in it for him, and accordingly reasonable compensation will normally have to be paid in order to secure the employee's agreement. Another factor that has to be borne in mind is that if the statutory notice period is not adhered to, the employee will be barred from receiving unemployment benefit until such time as the notice period would have ended.

Termination by giving notice

The employment relationship can be terminated by either party giving the agreed notice. Notice periods can be specified in the employment contract, but must comply with minimum statutory notice periods. All employees have a minimum statutory notice period of four weeks, either with effect to the 15th day or the end of a calendar month. The period of notice by the employer increases with length of service as follows:

more than 2 years' service	–	1 month with effect to the end of a calendar month
more than 5 years' service	–	2 months with effect to the end of a calendar month
more than 8 years' service	–	3 months with effect to the end of a calendar month

more than 10 years' service	–	4 months with effect to the end of a calendar month
more than 12 years' service	–	5 months with effect to the end of a calendar month
more than 15 years' service	–	6 months with effect to the end of a calendar month
more than 20 years' service	–	7 months with effect to the end of a calendar month

The employment contract may stipulate that the extended notice period shall also apply to notice given by the employee. Exceptionally, a two-week notice period can be agreed for the duration of a probationary period, such a period not to exceed six months.

After six months' service the statutory dismissal protection under the *Kündigungsschutzgesetz* (KschG) (Protection Against Dismissal Act) applies to all employees, with the exception of directors of private limited liability companies, if the business has more than five employees.

If dismissal protection applies, ordinary notice may only be given if the dismissal is justified by one of the following reasons:

- Reasons having their foundation in the person of the employee (*Personenbedingte Gründe*), constant illness or regular short sickness leaves that interrupt the business to such an extent that the employer can no longer be expected to tolerate it.
- Reasons having their foundation in the behaviour of the employee, (*Verhaltensbedingte Gründe*), eg regular late arrival at work or other persistent breaches of duty; a prior warning is almost always required.
- Company reasons (*Betriebsbedingte Gründe*), eg redundancy. In a redundancy situation the employer must select from all relevant employees, ensuring that employees dismissed are those least affected socially (so-called *Sozialauswahl*), and basing the selection on length of service, age, existing maintenance obligations and 'other social criteria' (eg single parent). The selection process must be thorough and can be reviewed by the courts in unfair dismissal proceedings.

German law does not allow payments in lieu of notice so notice periods must always be observed. The employer can inform the employee that his services are not required any more during the notice period if – and only if – this has been provided for in the contract or otherwise agreed, but the employee will remain an employee until the expiry of the notice period and all other obligations remain, eg regular payment of wages and social security contributions (garden leave).

Summary dismissal

Each party may terminate the contract with immediate effect without notice for an 'important reason'. Termination with cause should be used as a last resort and can only be given in such circumstances where it is unreasonable for the party terminating to be expected to continue the employment relationship. The decision factor is that the relationship of trust that must exist between employer and employee has been fundamentally destroyed.

Summary dismissal must take place within two weeks of acquiring knowledge of the circumstances giving grounds for termination.

Formalities of notice

Notice must be given either by:

- an officer of the employing company in his capacity as such and in accordance with company law rules/the employer personally; or
- the personnel manager; or
- a person who produces a written power of attorney signed by either of the above.

Failure to have the correct person given notice entitles the employee to reject the dismissal provided he does so without undue delay, ie usually within a few days.

Unfair dismissal proceedings

If statutory dismissal protection applies, an employee can apply to the employment courts and claim that the dismissal was unfair. This must be done within three weeks of receipt of notice of termination. If the employee is successful the court will declare the termination void and the normal remedy is reinstatement. Compensation rather than rein-statement will only be granted if either party applies for it, and can show that reinstatement would not be tolerable. An exception applies in the case of 'leading employees' (*Leitende Angestellte*) such as managers, where the employer can apply for compensation to be fixed by the court instead of reinstatement without giving reasons.

Special dismissal protection

No dismissal is possible during pregnancy, maternity leave or national service except in very special circumstances and with the permission of the health and safety authorities. Special permission is also required for dismissal of handicapped employees, and there are restrictions on the dismissal of members of a works council.

Participation of the works council

If a works council exists it must be informed and its opinion sought on each dismissal. Failure to comply with the consultation requirements will lead to the dismissal being declared void. If the works council objects to a dismissal and the employee commences unfair dismissal proceedings, the employee is entitled to be kept in employment until the proceedings have been decided. In the case of mass dismissals, a so-called social packet plan (*Sozialplan*) will have to be worked out with the works council and the locally competent Labour Court. This plan will decide on priorities between and within classes of employees, redeployment and compensation.

COLLECTIVE AGREEMENTS

Trade union agreements *(Tarifverträge)*

Trade union rights are recognised in the constitution and trade unions play an important role in German employment law. Relationships between employers and trade unions are generally less confrontational and more co-operative than in many other countries.

There are strict rules on when industrial action is permitted and when it is not. In particular a strike is only permitted in order to reach agreement on items that can be regulated by a trade union agreement. Therefore, a political strike to put pressure on government or other bodies is illegal, and the same applies in principle to 'sympathy strikes', ie strikes in support of another union. Certain procedures must be followed in order for a strike to be legal, eg a ballot. A strike is not permitted during the term of a trade union agreement as the agreement implies a 'peace obligation'.

If a strike is legal the employees may not in any way be punished for participating, for example by being dismissed. The employer has a limited right of lock-out but only under strict conditions.

See above for rules on when a trade union agreement is binding. Individual employment contracts or works council agreements may also make specific reference to trade union agreements.

Issues regulated by trade union agreements vary, but usually include wages, holiday, extra payments (such as overtime or bonuses on special occasions like anniversary of service), safety at work and exclusion clauses. Closed shop agreements are illegal in Germany.

As most trade union agreements are regional rules may vary from one federal state to another.

Works council agreements (*Betriebsvereinbarungen*)

An agreement between an employer and a works council can regulate issues covered by the works council's authority, but must generally not deal with subjects that are provided for in a trade union agreement. Such an agreement can, for example, regulate the system for awarding bonuses, promotions, beginning and end of daily working hours etc. They are particularly important when major changes to the business occur (eg merger, closure of plant) that affect staff.

In such a case an agreement with the works council may state the principles that will apply when deciding who should be made redundant and how compensation should be calculated. Redundancies based on selection criteria in a works council agreement are usually more readily accepted by the courts than the employer's choice based on the application of the 'social criteria' (see above).

EMPLOYEE CO-DETERMINATION

Co-determination is effected in a number of different ways, as outlined below.

Works councils

The most basic right of employees is to form a works council, provided the undertaking has more than five employees. The works council has rights in three areas: social, personnel and economic matters. In the first two areas the rights are more extensive, going so far as a real right of co-decision making or veto in some instances, whereas in economic matters they are generally limited to rights of information. Of particular importance is the right to be heard before any dismissal is effected. The works council may only object to a dismissal on certain grounds, eg if the social selection criteria were incorrectly applied or if the employer discriminated, and the employer can then apply to the court to overrule this veto. However, failure to hear the works council will render the dismissal void.

Corporate governance

Co-determination in larger companies by employee representatives on the supervisory board

Large private limited companies (in excess of 500 employees) and all public limited companies are required to operate a co-determined supervisory board (see Chapter 28). Employee representatives on a company level and on a national trade union level are thus involved in strategic decision making. The ultimate control, however, rests with the shareholders. It can be said that, over time, the system has worked reasonably well and provided for a consensus-orientated culture.

IMMIGRATION

Every foreign national wishing to reside in Germany must apply for a residence permit. However, the rules differentiate between citizens of EU member states and those of other states.

EU nationals

EU nationals must apply for a residence permit, but the process is a formality as they are entitled to a permit. The first permit will be granted for five years, after which EU nationals can apply for a permit with unlimited duration provided they satisfy the authorities that they fulfil certain conditions, eg that they are in employment and they have a place to live. If these conditions are met the residence permit will be extended for five years. EU nationals do not require a work permit. Restrictions will only apply if the EU national wants to work in a profession where special qualifications are required. However, increasingly obstacles, such as the non-recognition of diplomas from other member states, are being removed by EU legislation.

Other nationals

Individuals not from EU member states will require both a residence permit and a work permit. Usually application for these permits must be made before entering the country and will only be granted if the individual already has a fixed job offer.

Special rules apply to citizens of certain states, often based on bilateral agreements. In some cases the citizens of certain states, for example those of the United States, Canada and Australia can travel to Germany without a visa and apply for a residence and work permit after arrival. Swiss citizens are treated similarly to EU citizens.

Employers who employ foreign nationals without the requisite work permits commit a criminal offence. The construction industry is under particular scrutiny in this respect.

TAX AND INSURANCE ISSUES

Social security *(Sozialversicherung)*

There is an obligation on the employer to pay contributions to three compulsory special security insurance schemes: health and care, pension and unemployment. The employer will have to pay half of the total contributions himself and is under an obligation to deduct the other half from the employee's wages and pay it to the administrative body (*Einzugsstelle*).

Contributions represent a relatively high percentage of gross wages. Currently total contributions are approximately 19.5 per cent for pension insurance, 13 per cent for health and care insurance and 6.5 per cent for unemployment insurance, these being split equally between employer and employee.

The employer must notify the employer's health insurance (*Einzugsstelle*) of the start of the employment, of any change in remuneration or benefits, of termination, and in any case regularly once a year.

Accident Insurance (*Unfallversicherung*)

The employer alone must pay contributions to the statutory accident insurance for each employee. The contributions are collected by the professional corporation relevant to the sector of industry (*Berufsgenossenschaft*). These contributions are not nearly as high as social security contributions and vary depending on the risks involved in jobs in the industry.

The rules on the statutory accident insurance provide that in case of a work accident the employee cannot sue the employer but has to rely on the insurance.

PAYE (*Lohnsteuerabzugsverfahren*)

There is a PAYE system in Germany and the employer is under an obligation to deduct tax from the gross wages and pay it to the tax authorities (*Finanzamt*). Accordingly, the employer must notify the *Finanzamt* of any employment commenced or terminated.

Exceptions apply if the employer is not a 'domestic' employer but a foreign employer. However, a foreign company employing staff in Germany will be considered to be a 'domestic' employer if it has a place of business or a permanent representative in Germany. There can therefore be only very little visible activity in Germany if PAYE is to be avoided.

CROSS-BORDER SECONDMENTS

There are two main issues to be considered when an employee gets sent to work abroad for a limited period of time: tax and social security.

Social Security

In general, there are rules allowing an employee to remain part of his own national security system despite working abroad, provided he is sent abroad for a fixed term. Conversely, the state to which the employee is seconded will usually provide that the employee is exempted from contributing to its social security system whilst he is still covered by the system of his own state. This is subject to any bilateral agreements.

Tax

Anyone earning a salary in Germany will be liable to German income tax on that salary. If the salary is not paid in Germany the tax liability will still arise if the employee is domiciled or usually resident in Germany. A person is usually resident in Germany for tax purposes if he has spent more than six months in Germany, either consecutively or interrupted only by short breaks. In most cases the Double Taxation Agreement will provide the details on where tax will have to be paid, and when.

32

Unfair Competition

Eversheds

INTRODUCTION

The term 'competition law' usually brings to mind cartels, mergers and other such structures in which companies come together, thereby restricting the number of competitors in a particular field (Act against Restraints of Competition – GWB).

In Germany, however, competition law also covers a second, different area. The Act against Unfair Competition (*Gesetz gegen den unlauteren Wettbewerb* – UWG), regulates the behaviour of business people who are trying to attract customers by methods that are regarded as unfair and against public policy. In addition to this Act there are further specialist statutes, such as the Act Governing Discounts (*Rabattgesetz*) and the Ordinance on Bonuses (*Zugabeverordnung*). Clearly, one main area where this becomes relevant is advertising, where these rules draw a thin, not always clear, line. Another area of concern exists when unrelated incentives are used to try to persuade customers to buy goods/ services, eg with the promise of a free gift, a discount etc.

The UWG is widely phrased, and in particular sections 1 and 3 are very general provisions aiming to cover a wide spectrum of activities. The Act not only deals with the behaviour of a business in relation to its customers or prospective customers but also in relation to other businesses. For example, it deals with the problem of inciting employees of one business to breach their contracts of employment and join another business. The nature of these general clauses means that the categories of unfair competition are never closed and case law plays a major role. In this context, it is impossible to give a detailed picture of the applicable rules. What is intended, however, is to point out some problematic issues in the areas of advertising and the use of incentives as they are common to all businesses; and the differences in rules, for example in the UK, which can be surprising. The areas of advertising and external incentives are very strictly regulated in Germany and it is important for a foreign business expanding into Germany to be aware of some of the pitfalls. Failure to comply with the rules against unfair competition can lead to an injunction with costs being imposed against the business, and may also lead to the award of damages.

ADVERTISING

There are two main general clauses that are relevant to advertising, namely sections 1 and 3 UWG. Section 1 stipulates that anyone who is in business, and for the purpose of competition, performs acts against *bonos mores*, can be prevented from further acts by an injunction or be sued for damages. Section 3 prohibits all kinds of misleading statements, an injunction once again being the appropriate remedy.

Both sections are very general and it was left to the courts to build on them by means of case law. In some cases the two sections and their areas of application overlap, therefore it is easier to list certain groups of cases that cause problems.

Comparative advertising

Traditionally, German courts considered all comparative advertise-ments, with some exceptions, to be unfair and therefore illegal. This situation has changed considerably and in a judgment on 5 February 1998 the Federal Supreme Court adopted a much more liberal approach. The judgment declared that, in principle, comparative advertisements are legal provided they comply with the conditions set out in Article 3, paragraph 1, letters a–h of European Directive 97/55/EC. This Directive amended the prior Directive 84/450/EEC regarding misleading advert-isements. Although Directive 97/55/EC has not yet been implemented in Germany, the Federal Supreme Court took the view that German law must be interpreted in light of this Directive and must therefore give up its previous, more restrictive attitude towards advertising. However, the exact state of the law at the moment is difficult to determine as there is a transition from the old, more restrictive law to a new, more liberal approach that is more in line with the one adopted by other member states.

The Federal Supreme Court has formulated the principle that an advertisement is legal if it fulfils the conditions set out in Article 3, paragraph 1, letters a–h of Directive 97/55/EC. These conditions are:

- The advertisement must not be misleading.
- The advertisement must compare goods or services that meet the same needs or are intended for the same purpose.
- The comparison must be objective and relate to a material, relevant and representative feature of the goods/services. The price is one such feature.
- The advertisement must not create confusion between the advertiser and a competitor or their trade marks.
- The creditor, its goods/services or its marks of origin must not be discredited.
- If the advertisement is for products with a designation of origin, it must relate in each case to products with the same origin.
- The advertisement must not take unfair advantage of the reputation of a competitor's mark of origin.
- The advertisement must not present goods or services as imitations or replicas of goods/services bearing a protected trade mark or trade name.

The main impact of these new rules on German law is that a direct comparison of a competitor's product is now legal provided that it is, generally speaking, objective, not misleading and not discrediting.

Sole position advertisements

Adverts that try to make the public believe that the advertiser has an outstanding or dominant position in the market are only permitted if they are true. In this context it is important to note that a small advantage over competitors is not sufficient to allow for this kind of advertisement. Also, it is essential that the advert is not connected with any form of aggressive reference to competitors. This is a very restrictive provision. For example, adverts like 'The best cigarette', 'Bielefeld's big newspaper' have already been considered degrading to competitors.

Misleading advertisements

There is a general rule that adverts must not be misleading. This includes the obvious cases of adverts giving misleading information, but it also covers cases where the information was correct but created the wrong impression with the public, as for example in the case where 'Oldest distillery for corn schnapps in Steinhagen' was considered misleading, despite the fact that the company was actually the oldest distillery. The argument was that the public would think that this sentence meant that the company distilled the oldest corn schnapps in Steinhagen, which was not true.

If any word or phrase in an advert is ambiguous each possible interpretation must be true and correct.

Another kind of misleading advert is one that is incomplete, thereby creating the wrong impression with the public. For example, if a furniture shop advertises in newspapers that it offers rental apartments to newly weds it must be made clear in the advert that such a rental contract is dependent on the purchase of furniture.

An advert can also be considered misleading even where self-evident facts are stated, as this puts the emphasis on a certain aspect of the product that all other products have as well. This is the case, for example, when certain requirements set down by law are emphasised, eg a product that calls itself whisky must conform to the rules on what whisky is, contain the right ingredients and have gone through the right production process. The producer is then not permitted to advertise in a way that emphasises the fact that the prescribed production process has been used.

It is therefore necessary to read every advert carefully and make sure that the impression that is created with the public corresponds with the facts.

Aggressive advertising

Advertising can be unfair if it is too pushy and aggressive. This is the case if the advertising is of such a character that the customer feels put under pressure and gets the impression that the only way to relieve that pressure is to give in and buy the product/service. The customer would then not buy the product/service for its own sake, but merely in order to be left in peace. One typical example of this is telephone sales. The practice of calling people at home, without any prior contact or request on their part, is unfair and thus illegal in Germany. Other examples are the sending of unsolicited goods or aggressive sales talk in public places that give the person the impression they cannot say 'no'.

These examples of the wide area of advertising are given in order to highlight the fact that careful consideration is required before any advertising is done, to ensure that it is legal.

Unrelated Incentives

This area of the law, apart from being subject to the general rules of the Act against Unfair Competition, is governed mainly by the Act Governing Discounts (*Rabattgesetz*) and the Ordinance on Bonuses (*Zugabeverordnung*). The general principle is that external incentives are prohibited.

Bonuses and gifts

Under the *Zugabeverordnung* virtually any gratuitous advantage, be it a free gift, a chance to win something or another similar incentive, is prohibited. Limited exceptions exist in the case of very small, virtually valueless, advertising gifts (eg a cheap pen with the company's name on it), additional quantities of the same goods/services (eg buy one, get one free) or customary extras or additional services (eg discount on production of a public transport ticket). However, even in cases where such advertising is permitted, the business must not advertise the extra as a free gift and under no circumstances is it legal to make the extra dependent on a prize draw or lottery.

Discounts

The *Rabattgesetz* governs any discounts granted to consumers that are, in principle, prohibited. The same applies to special discounted prices. The Act then provides exceptions to this general prohibition. For example, discounts for immediate cash payment are permitted provided they do not exceed 3 per cent. Discounts for bulk purchases are legal provided they are customary. This will depend on the particular area of business and no hard and fast rules exist. Staff discounts are permitted provided that they are restricted to the personal use of staff and their families.

The issue of discounts and incentives becomes relevant, for example, where a business wants to use loyalty cards, and any such scheme needs to be examined carefully to ensure it remains within the narrow legal exceptions to the general prohibition placed on such incentives.

SPECIAL PROCEDURAL ISSUES

There are two special procedural characteristics to observe in the field of unfair competition.

Special court panels

Cases that fall under the unfair competition legislation must be brought before the commercial chambers of the District Courts (*Landgericht*) unless a consumer brings a claim, in which case an ordinary civil chamber will decide. The UWG empowers the justice ministries of the federal states to order that cases should be heard before specialist competition chambers at certain *Landgerichte*. The aim of this is to reach more consistent rulings in an area particularly dependent on case law.

Proceedings by associations

Section 13 UWG allows consumer associations, trade associations and the Chamber of Industry and Commerce to issue proceedings if they think a business is using unfair competition methods. This means that not only the competitors or individual consumers affected by a certain measure can apply to the courts but powerful associations can become involved. In practice, a number of associations have been formed to monitor competition practices and a large number of cases are brought by them. Their existence makes it dangerous for any business to engage in 'borderline' activities as these associations are in a better financial position than ordinary businesses to issue proceedings in unclear, borderline cases, in order to clarify the legal position.

33

Intellectual Property Rights

Eversheds

In Germany, intellectual property in its various forms is protected by a number of different sets of rules, contained in separate Acts, which depend on the nature of the particular intellectual property right in question.

All intellectual property rights have a common feature, in that they are protected only for a certain limited period of time, such period being prescribed under the relevant Act. They also (in principle) exist independently of the time and place of their use, and they are independent of the form in which they are expressed, such that copying without the owner's consent will be a breach, even if the copier had prior knowledge of the pattern/model. A further common characteristic of intellectual property law is the principle of priority: the first person to create the intellectual 'product' and, in the case of rights capable of registration, generally the first person to register it, will be entitled to protection.

PATENTS

Currently three versions of the Patent Act (*Patentgesetz* – PatG) exist:

1. The PatG 1981 came into force on 1 January 1981 and applies to all patent applications from that date together with the patents that were registered based on such applications.
2. The PatG 1978 came into force on 1 January 1978 and applies to all granted patents that were based on applications made between 1 January 1978 and 31 December 1981.

3. The PatG 1968, which is the oldest version of the Patent Act, applies to all granted patents based on applications made before 31 December 1977.

The two later versions of the Act were passed in order to harmonise German patent law with European law. Apart from introducing some new provisions, the main purpose of the 1981 Act was to reorganise and restructure the provisions of the 1978 Act.

Requirements for a patent

In order for the PatG to be applicable, there must be a patentable invention. This requires in particular technical invention, novelty, inventive creativity and commercial applicability.

Technical invention

The invention must be based on a technical problem that cannot be solved by applying the current state of technical knowledge and its solution by technical means. The invention must create a new technical way of solving the problem and it is essential that technical means are used for the solution. Mere scientific theories do not qualify as a patentable technical invention, since natural forces beyond human reasoning alone must be applied.

The invention must be both capable of being executed and be repeatable, so that it can be successfully reworked. An exception to this exclusion has been recognised by the courts in relation to micro-organisms.

Novelty

The invention must be new from an objective point of view, ie it must not yet be generally known. The PatG provides that an invention is new if it goes beyond the current state of technology at the date when the patent application is submitted to the German Patent and Trade Mark Office (*Deutsches Patent- und Markenamt*) in Munich. At that date the invention must not have been publicly described (in writing or orally) or used anywhere in the world. Even the inventor's own public description or use of the invention can destroy the novelty of the invention, but the Act provides that such use or description is to be disregarded, provided that the inventor submits a patent application within six months of the first public description or use.

Inventive creativity

There must also be some inventive creativity involved, ie the invention must be of such a nature that an average specialist in the field would not automatically think of it, having regard for the current state of technology in the field in question. However, a less important invention that could have been achieved by an average specialist may be capable of protection as a utility model under a different Act (see below).

Commercial applicability

In order to be patentable, an invention must be capable of commercial/ industrial application (being used commercially in some way). The Act provides that methods of surgical or therapeutic treatment, or diagnostics, are deemed not to be capable of commercial application.

Exclusion from patentability

The Act treats certain inventions as not being technical in nature and this excludes them from its protective scope – examples include scientific theories and mathematical methods. The reasons behind this are that the subject matter of such 'inventions' always existed and that the 'inventor' does not actually create anything new but merely describes something that is already in existence.

Further, any aesthetic creations are excluded from the scope of the Act. However, they may be capable of protection under the Design Act (*Geschmacksmustergesetz*).

Lastly, plans, rules and methods for mental activities, games or business activities as well as programmes for data processing are excluded from the scope of the Act, but may be capable of protection under the Copyright Act (*Urheberrechtsgesetz* – UrhG). In addition to the rules defining the scope of what is to be regarded as a technical invention, a patent may also be refused grant on the grounds of public policy. Broadly speaking, such refusal covers patents relating to the issue of biological inventions.

Procedures

Anyone wishing to protect a technical invention with a patent must submit an application to the *Patent- und Markenamt* in the prescribed form. The applicant must state that the invention is technical in nature, new, creative and commercially applicable. The application must also explain and describe the invention, using drawings and plans if necessary, in order to fully disclose the invention sufficiently for a specialist to execute it.

Upon receipt of the application, the *Patent- und Markenamt* will examine whether it contains obvious faults and obstacles to patentability. Within seven years of the submission of the application, the applicant must submit an examination request. Failure to do so will lead to the application being deemed to be withdrawn. Once an examination request has been submitted the *Patent- und Markenamt* will proceed with a substantial examination of the invention based on the above-mentioned criteria. If the application survives the examination procedure the patent will be granted and will be published in the Patent List.

Within three months of this publication, anyone can raise objections to the granting of the patent. Any objections will be examined by the *Patent- und Markenamt,* which may either uphold the patent fully or in part, or withdraw it.

Anyone receiving an adverse decision from the *Patent- und Markenamt* may appeal against that decision, upon making the relevant application, to the Federal Patent Court *(Bundespatentgericht).* Any further appeal may be made to the Federal Supreme Court *(Bundesgerichtshof)* on questions of law only.

Effects of a patent

The duration of patent protection is 20 years from the date of registration, and full protection is enjoyed provided the annual patent renewal fee is paid. Prior to registration, and following disclosure of the invention in the patent application, the applicant will benefit from limited protection in that third parties using the invention must pay reasonable compensation to the *Patent- und Markenamt*, any such compensation being paid to the applicant. Once the patent is registered, the patentee has the exclusive right to use the invention and can prevent unauthorised use by way of injunction, and may also claim damages. Damages can be calculated by three methods at the choice of the patentee: damage suffered, delivery up and an account of the profits made from unauthorised use and payment of an equitable licence fee. The limitation period for any damages claim is three years. This protection also extends to indirect infringement, eg where a person supplies to another the means to use the patented invention in an unauthorised manner. There are, however, limits to this exclusivity provided for in the PatG. For example, private non-commercial use is not an infringement of the patent. The same applies to testing and research.

A more limited restriction of the owner's exclusive rights lies in the recognition of prior use: if another party was already using or about to use the invention at the time of the patent application, the other party remains entitled to use the invention in his own business without having to pay compensation, provided he acquired the invention without fraud or any other dishonest means. This protects 'parallel' inventions, where someone had the same idea but did not get to the patenting stage fast enough.

Patent procedures

Patent infringements

Claims based on patent infringement must be brought to the higher local courts (*Landgerichte*), some of which have special Patent Chambers. A claim can be brought in any court in the area in which an infringement occurred. Proceedings must be suspended if the infringer has instituted invalidity proceedings in the *Bundespatentgericht*.

Nullity

Once the three-month period for raising objections against a patent has expired, the only way an attack on the validity of a patent may be brought is by instituting proceedings in the *Bundespatentgericht* to have the patent declared invalid. Anyone can institute such proceedings, provided they submit that one of the grounds for revocation set out in the Patents Act exists. These grounds are lack of patentability (no invention, no novelty, no creativity, no commercial applicability), lack of disclosure of invention (insufficiency), inadmissible extension of patent, fraudulent abstraction or extension of the scope of protection beyond that of the application. If the proceedings are successful, the patent will be revoked with retrospective effect.

TRADE MARKS

The Trade Mark Act (*Markengesetz* – MarkenG) came into force on 1 January 1995 with the object of harmonising German law in this field with the laws of other EU member states.

Objects of trade mark protection

Before the existence of the MarkenG, only two-dimensional representations were capable of trade mark protection. Now, apart from words and pictures, letters, numbers, sound signs, three-dimensional designs (including the shape of the product of its packaging), as well as other designs, including colours and combinations of colours, can be given trade mark protection.

Obstacles to trade mark registration

A mark of origin cannot be registered as a trade mark if it has insufficient distinguishing characteristics, if it consists exclusively of a description of the product, if it misleads the consumer with regard to the product or service, if it affects public policy or morals or if it is a public sign (eg flag of a state, public examination stamps etc).

Procedure to obtain trade mark protection

There are two way to obtain trade mark protection: formally by registration and informally by usage. The first method is the more common.

Registration

Anyone wishing to register a trade mark must submit an application, together with the prescribed fee, to the *Patent- und Markenamt*. The application must contain a representation of the trade mark and a list of goods and/or services to which the trade mark is to be applied. The *Patent- und Markenamt* will only examine whether any of the abovementioned absolute obstacles to trade mark protection are present. If this examination is successful, the applicant has a right to have his trade mark registered. The *Patent- und Markenamt* will not and must not investigate whether there is another, prior registration that would be infringed by the applicant's trade mark.

The registration is published in the *Trade Mark Gazette (Markenblatt)*. Within three months of the date of publication of the registration, the owner of a registered trade mark or the owner of a well-known trade mark can raise objections to the registration by filing an objection to the *Patent- und Markenamt* in the standard form. The objection must be based on the claim that an older registered trade mark or a well-known trade mark with priority exists and is infringed by the registration, or that the trade mark was registered in the name of an agent or representative without the owner's consent. The owner of the new trade mark can raise the issue that the owner of the older trade mark be put to prove that the older trade mark was in use within the five years prior to the date of publication of the new trade mark (in substantially the same form as the one in which it is registered). If the owner of the older mark fails to prove this, the trade mark can be struck off the register. An appeal against the decision of the *Patent- und Markenamt* may be made to a special department (*Erinnerungsprüfer*), from there to the *Bundespatentgericht* and finally, on questions of law alone, to the *Bundesgerichtshot*. Owners of rights other than trade marks, eg rights to names, geographical designations of origin, commercial designations of origin, copyright etc, cannot use the objections procedure to protect their rights, but instead must issue cancellation proceedings against the new trade mark in the ordinary courts.

Obtaining trade mark protection by use

If the owner of a particular mark of origin can prove that the public believes all products or services bearing that mark come from one source alone, the mark can claim protection as 'get up'. As this depends solely on how the public perceives a mark of origin, the material protection enjoyed by 'get up' can be limited geographically. Proof of the public's view is usually adduced in the form of surveys organised by the Chamber of Commerce or polling institutes.

Independently of trade marks arising by national registration or use, the Trade Mark Act has introduced into German law the concept of the well-known trade mark, by which a foreign registered, well-known trade mark can claim protection. They can be used in objection procedures against the registration of the new trade mark, provided that the older mark is commonly known.

Scope of protection

Priority

All marks of origin, be they trade marks or others such as names or trade names, serve to document the origin of a product or service and thus enjoy the same protection. The question of which mark prevails is determined by the concept of priority, ie which right arose first in time. In the case of registration, the priority date is either the date of application, the date of a prior foreign registration or the date of first use, provided this date lies no earlier than six months before the submission of the application.

In the case of a mark arising by use, and in the case of all other non-registrable marks of origin, the priority date is the earliest date on which it can be proved that the public held the view that the mark was unique to one source.

Effect of protection

The owner of the trade mark has the exclusive right to use it and can prevent any other person from doing so by obtaining an injunction, irrespective of whether that other person acted intentionally, negligently or without fault. If there was intention or negligence there may be an additional claim for damages, provided actual loss was suffered. Like the owner of a patent, the owner of a trade mark has the choice between three methods of calculating damages: loss of profits, profit made by the infringer or a reasonable licence fee. Profits made by the infringer can be claimed, even if there was no fault, by a claim based on unjust enrichment.

Extent of protection

The trade mark owner is protected against the identical use of the mark, ie in the same form and for the same goods or services. In addition, the protection extends to use of a mark capable of confusing by being similar to the protected mark in respect of the goods or services to which the mark is applied. It is immaterial whether the infringer intended or even knew of this risk of confusion. The better known a trade mark is the more protection it enjoys, in that fewer similarities justify the view that the public would conclude that the infringer's goods or services bearing the mark originate from the same source. This can lead to the owner of such a well-known mark being able to stop others using a similar mark for totally different goods or services, if such use would exploit the reputation or interfere with the reputation of the well-known mark.

Defences available to the infringer

The trade mark infringer can raise only limited defences. He can claim a prior right, eg an earlier registration or an earlier mark that has arisen by use, or that the other trade mark has lapsed due to non-use, eg no use within the last five years. Furthermore, he can claim that the owner of the other mark is stopped from claiming protection because he knew of the infringer's mark for the last five years and only brought proceedings after that period had elapsed. Independently of the principle of estoppel, there is a limitation period for trade mark infringement claims of three years from the date of knowledge of the infringement.

Duration

The trade mark is protected for ten years from the date of the application and the protection can be extended as many times as desired, by a further ten years each time, upon payment of the appropriate renewal fee.

COPYRIGHT

Object of copyright

This area of law is governed by the Copyright Act (*Urheberrechtsgesetz* – UrhG). Copyright protects the creative work as an immaterial asset, independent of its embodiment. The work is a personal, mental creation by the author and can be literary, scientific or artistic. Thus, copyright can protect any written work such as a novel or a textbook, as well as computer programs, music, mime, dance, paintings, architectural designs, films etc. Adaptations, which in themselves are personal mental creations of the adapting person, are protected as works in their own right, eg translations. Even collections of works can be protected as works in their own right if the selection and combination of them is the result of a personal mental creation. So-called 'official' works, eg statutes, public orders, judgments, are excluded from copyright protection.

Conditions for copyright

In order for a work to be capable of copyright protection it must be the result of an individual mental creation. The author is the creator of the work and only an individual can be a creator. If several individuals have created the work together, they are co-authors. This is particularly relevant in relation to works created in the course of performing duties under a contract of employment. The creator will be the employee and, if the employer wants to use the creation without a licence for each individual use, there will usually have to be contractual provision providing for use by the employer. In the case of computer software, the UrhG stipulates that, even without a contractual provision, the employer has an exclusive right to use the software without paying for it.

Effect of copyright

Copyright gives the author an exclusive right to use the work, for example to reproduce, sell, exhibit, publish and present it, as well as to adapt and change it. In addition to these rights, the author has personal rights that are a separate and characteristic aspect of copyright, unique to this form of intellectual property right. The extent of this personal right is such that it is for the author alone to decide if, and in what form, the work is to be published, including whether a copyright sign is to be attached to it.

Exceptions to copyright

Copyright is restricted to a certain extent in cases where it is considered to be in the public interest. Thus, the use of a work in court proceedings, arbitration proceedings or administration procedures, and possible publication in connection with such proceedings, is permitted. Furthermore, the reproduction and publication of parts of works in collections for use in churches, schools or other educational establishments is allowed. Speeches on current issues held by public personae may be published in papers or other media. Similar exceptions apply for film, TV and radio reporting on current issues. Reproductions for private use are permitted. However, as with many of these restrictions, the author must still be paid a reasonable fee for the use.

Duration of copyright

Copyright lasts for 70 years after the death of the author, after which the work is free for use by anyone. In the case of co-authors, the death of the last co-author is the decisive date from which the 70 years period runs.

Dealing with copyright

Copyright cannot be assigned *inter vivos* but it can pass by way of succession. However, the author may enter into user agreements, granting to the other party certain (or all) of the economic rights that subsist in his copyright. The author can defend this right by obtaining an injunction and/or damages against an infringer. He can further demand the destruction or delivery up of any unauthorised copies.

Copyright arises through an act of creativity and there is no registration or other administrative procedure.

OTHER RIGHTS

Apart from the main areas of intellectual property outlined above, there are further specialised subjects that are regulated by special statutes. The protection of such rights is similar to that afforded to trade mark protection, ie by registration at the *Patent- und Markenamt*.

Utility models

The Utility Model Act (*Gebrauchsmustergesetz* – GebrmG) protects minor inventions that are not required to fulfil the stringent requirements as to a 'creative invention' of the PatG. Its provisions are, in general, parallel to those of the PatG with the following exceptions.

Upon submission of an application, only an examination that the formalities have been complied with takes place, and if the formalities have been complied with correctly the utility model is registered without examination of the subject matter itself. Protection starts from the registration, which creates the utility model right. The material issues of whether the invention complies with the conditions for protection as a utility model pursuant to the Act are only examined, either if infringement proceedings have been instituted and the non-fulfilment of these conditions has been raised as a defence, or in cancellation proceedings before the *Patent- und Markenamt*.

The protection of a utility model lasts for a maximum of ten years from registration. The initial period is three years and can be extended by payment of a renewal fee for a further three-year period and two two-year periods.

The fact that a utility model registration can be obtained very quickly without examination of the subject matter often makes it advisable to make a simultaneous application for a utility model when making a patent application, to take advantage of the earlier protection afforded to a utility model whilst the patent application is being processed.

Designs

Two-dimensional patterns and three-dimensional models are aesthetic creations and can be protected under the Design Act (*Geschmacksmustergesetz*) provided they are the result of an above-average creative idea and the design is new, ie previously unknown. In order to obtain protection, the design must be registered at the *Deutsches Patent- und Markenamt*. As with utility models, the application is only examined for errors in formalities and obvious obstacles, and there is no examination of the substantive subject matter (eg whether it is new). Protection lasts five years initially but can, upon payment of the appropriate renewal fee, be extended to a maximum 20 years.

Other Acts

There is a Plant Variety Protection Act (*Sortenschutzgesetz*) and a Semiconductor Protection Act (*Halbleiterschutzgesetz*) protecting intellectual property in these special areas.

Droit de suite – right of the artist to part of the proceedings on resale

Unlike Britain, Germany has given artists and their heirs a limited right to participate in the accretion of their work after the original sale. This claim amounts to 5 per cent of the consideration paid on any resale of the work during the lifetime of the artist and 50 years after his death.

34

Insolvency

Eversheds

With effect from 1 January 1999 the Bankruptcy Act (*Konkursordnung*), the Composition Code (*Vergleichsordnung*) and the Co-ordinated Enforcement Act (*Gesamtvollstreckungsordnung*) have been replaced by the new Insolvency Act (*Insolvenzordnung*). According to Section 1 of the Insolvency Act, a corporate insolvency can either be dealt with by way of liquidation or by reorganisation procedures. Insolvency proceedings can be initiated in respect of the assets of corporations as well as individuals. For the purpose of this book only corporate insolvencies will be dealt with.

INSOLVENCY PROCEEDINGS

Commencement of proceedings

The insolvency petition must be sent to the local County Court (*Amtsgericht*) nearest to the District Court (*Landgericht*) that is competent for the area where the legal entity's general place of jurisdiction is located. A petition for an insolvency order may be filed by one of the creditors or the debtor. However, in case of a creditor being the applicant, the insolvency proceedings will only be instituted by the competent court if he or she has a legal interest in the institution of the insolvency proceedings (this will for example not be the case if the insolvency is being pursued only in order to eliminate a competitor or to terminate a contractual relationship), and if he or she is in a position to furnish prima facie evidence for the existence of the claim and the existence of suitable grounds for the institution.

Reasons for the institution of insolvency proceedings

There are three reasons available to an applicant filing for insolvency proceedings:

1. The debtor is unable to meet his debts as they fall due (*Zahlungsunfähigkeit*). According to the Insolvency Act this will usually be the case if the debtor has ceased to make payments.
2. In addition *the debtor* is entitled to apply for the institution of insolvency proceedings if it has become clear that he is unable to meet his debts as they fall due (*drohende Zahlungsunfähigkeit*).
3. In case of a legal entity, *Überschuldung* provides for an additional reason to institute insolvency proceedings. A legal entity is *überschuldet* if it has a deficiency of assets ascertained by comparing the assets and liabilities of the legal entity. In verifying the assets of the legal entity the assets will be valued on a going concern basis rather than a liquidation basis, if it is more likely than not that the business will be continued.

It has to be noted that the representatives of a legal entity, eg the managing director (*Geschäftsführer*) of a private limited company (GmbH), is under an obligation to file an insolvency petition in the case that the legal entity is in financial difficulties (ie in case of *Zahlungsunfähigkeit* or *Überschuldung*). Failing to do so may result in criminal proceedings and a claim for damages against the *Geschäftsführer*.

Provisional measures to secure the debtor's assets for the benefit of all creditors

The court will decide which provisional measures are necessary to secure the position of the creditors. If the court chooses to do so, a provisional insolvency administrator (*voräufiger Insolvenzverwalter*) can be appointed. Furthermore, the court can deprive the debtor of his right to deal with and to dispose of any of his assets. The court will usually vest this right in the provisional insolvency administrator, since he will otherwise be just an adviser to the debtor. Until the court decides on the institution of the insolvency proceedings the provisional insolvency administrator will continue the debtor's business. The provisional insolvency administrator has to secure, trace and evaluate the debtor's assets. Based on his findings, the provisional insolvency receiver will also evaluate the possibility of reconstruction measures.

The court can also order that any enforcement measures against the debtor be suspended. This order can be made in order to prevent individual creditors from satisfying their claims with the possible result that the business cannot be continued. However, enforcement measures concerning the debtor's real estate are not covered by such an order.

In addition, the court can order any other measures it considers appropriate in order to secure the debtor's estate for the benefit of all creditors.

Rejection of the petition/insolvency order

The court will then decide whether or not the insolvency proceedings will be instituted.

If the court is not satisfied with the evidence furnished in relation to the claim, or the grounds for the institution of the proceedings, the petition will be rejected. The same is true if the costs of the court and the (provisional) insolvency administrator exceed the debtor's assets.

If sufficient assets are available to cover the costs of insolvency proceedings, they are instituted by the court by means of an insolvency order (*Eröffnungsbeschluss*). With the insolvency order, the court appoints the insolvency administrator (however the creditors have the right to replace the court-appointed insolvency administrator), and states the date and the hour of the institution of the proceedings. At the same time the creditors are asked to register their claims with the insolvency administrator before a given date.

The insolvency administrator and the debtor's assets

The insolvency administrator has the authority to deal with and dispose of the debtor's assets. The insolvency administrator's main task is to gather in and secure as many of the assets of the insolvent company as possible for the benefit of the creditors. In addition, the insolvency administrator will produce a list of all creditors.

The creditors, the creditors' meeting and the creditors' committee

A creditor is anyone who has a pecuniary claim against the debtor at the time of the institution of the proceedings. There are four different types of creditors:

1. Creditors entitled to the costs of the insolvency proceedings (costs of the court, the provisional insolvency receiver, the insolvency administrator and the members of the creditor's committee – see below). Any claims that result from the insolvency administrator's actions will be satisfied ahead of any other claims.
2. Creditors who are directly entitled to property that does not belong to the debtor's estate (for example, goods that have been delivered under a retention of title clause) and that has to be segregated from the debtor's estate.

3. Claims of preferential creditors (eg holders of charges over property of the debtor). These creditors are entitled to satisfaction of their claims ahead of all unsecured creditors.
4. Claims of unsecured creditors.

Once the insolvency proceedings have been instituted the so-called creditors' meeting (*Gläubigerversammlung*) will be convened by the court. The creditors' meeting will decide whether the insolvent company will be wound up or whether the company business is to be continued. For the creditors to be able to decide this question the insolvency administrator will advise the creditors' meeting on the financial situation of the company. The creditors' meeting may decide to appoint a so-called creditors' committee (*Gläubigerausschuss*). The creditors' committee consists of representatives of the preferential creditors, the major creditors and the smaller creditors. The creditors' committee assists and supervises the insolvency administrator.

British readers will note that German law does not recognise the concept of the floating charge or the appointment of a receiver by the debenture holder. This type of preferential security has been held to be too oppressive on the debtor and on other creditors, and against public policy.

Distribution and proceeds

Ahead of the distribution of the proceeds, the court will have to decide in a special hearing (*Prüfungstermin*) which of the claims that have been registered in time are valid and which are being contested. A creditor whose claim has been contested can bring proceedings in order to assert his claim. If the claim is not contested, it will be registered by the court in a list of creditors' claims. During the *Prüfungstermin* it will also be decided which sort of creditors will receive any of the proceeds from the realisation of the assets. In particular, it will be decided whether the unsecured creditors will receive a dividend or whether the assets of the company are not sufficient to allow payments to the unsecured creditors.

Following this procedure the assets will be distributed between the creditors. Once all assets have been distributed the insolvency proceedings will be closed.

INSOLVENCY PLAN (*INSOLVENZPLAN*)

One of the main objectives of the new Insolvency Act was to encourage reconstruction measures. The old Composition Code was considered unsuitable to achieve this objective.

To make up for the deficiency, the new Act provides for the possibility of a so-called insolvency plan. This plan can be agreed between the creditors and the debtor irrespective of the usual insolvency proceedings as described above. This insolvency plan can either be used in order to reconstruct the company or to liquidate its assets.

The plan consists of two parts:

1. a descriptive part describing the measures that have been taken since the institution of the insolvency proceedings, and the measures that ought to be taken in order to achieve the proposed objectives (which may either be the reconstruction or the liquidation of the company);
2. the second part describes in what way the legal position of the interested parties is meant to be changed by the insolvency plan.

The insolvency plan can be drawn up either by the debtor (who can submit it to the court together with the insolvency petition if he considers the reconstruction of the company to be a feasible objective) or by the insolvency receiver. The creditors have to approve the insolvency plan. Once this has been achieved the court will confirm the insolvency plan. Once this confirmation has been given by the court the insolvency proceedings described above will be terminated. The company will be reconstructed/liquidated according to the insolvency plan.

35

Disputes and Arbitration

Eversheds

INTRODUCTION

There are five different branches of courts in Germany, each of which has jurisdiction over a certain area of law. These five are made up of the Ordinary Courts (dealing with all civil as well as criminal matters), the Labour Courts, the Administrative Courts, the Social Security Courts and the Tax Courts. For the purposes of this book, only the area of civil litigation will be dealt with in more detail. Each of these branches has its own appeal court up to a highest federal court.

CIVIL COURTS

As far as civil law is concerned, the court hierarchy starts at the bottom with the *Amtsgericht,* equivalent to the English County Court. It deals with civil claims with a value of up to DM10,000. The court of first instance for all other civil cases is the *Landgericht,* with a jurisdiction similar to that of the English High Court. It is before this court that the vast majority of commercial cases are brought. Appeals from decisions of the *Landgericht* go to the competent local Court of Appeal (*Oberlandesgericht*), from which there is a possibility of further appeal on points of law to the Federal Supreme Court (*Bundesgerichtshof*). At each *Landgericht* there is at least one panel of judges (*Kammer*) that deals exclusively with commercial cases. These panels are called *Kammer für Handelssachen.* If the plaintiff so applies, it is the competent court for a defined number of commercial matters, which includes disputes arising from commercial agreements, disputes between shareholders or partners, disputes concerning trade marks, copyright and passing off, as well as disputes concerning unfair competition.

DETERMINATION OF VENUE

Questions of international jurisdiction are regulated by the provisions of the 1968 Brussels Convention on Jurisdiction and Enforcement of Judgments, as amended in 1982. Once German jurisdiction has been established by means of the Brussels Convention, the local venue is established by applying the rules of the German Code of Civil Procedure (*Zivilprozessordnung* or ZPO) in the following way.

The proper venue in a tort case (including infringement of patents) is alternatively the place where the act was committed, the place where the damage occurred or the place where the defendant resides. In a contract matter, the proper ordinary venue is the place where the defendant has his residence or place of business; concurrent local jurisdictions may exist in the place where the contract has to be performed or where the defendant has assets. In disputes over property, the local court where the property is situated has jurisdiction. As it is possible for several local courts to have jurisdiction, the plaintiff often has a choice and this may require careful tactical consideration.

Jurisdiction may also be agreed between the parties. It is very common to include a jurisdiction clause in contracts or standard contract terms. However, clauses that commit all employees to bring proceedings against their employer only at the employer's place of business may be held invalid.

CERTAIN CHARACTERISTICS OF GERMAN CIVIL PROCEDURE

Compared with the English courts, judges in Germany take a more active and investigative role. Procedural rules are less flexible, eg in respect of time limits for the serving of proceedings. However, following the reform of civil procedure in England, these differences may lessen over the years.

Pleadings and oral hearing

German litigation is mainly based on written submissions, which take the form of correspondence with the court rather than the opposing side. The pleadings contain the assertions made by the parties and how these assertions can be shown in evidence. The rules of the *Zivilprozessordnung* encourage the judiciary to reduce the oral proceedings to only one hearing, as opposed to a long drawn-out series of hearings. However, pre-trial hearings are possible where special applications are made for specific issues, such as jurisdiction, security for costs, securing evidence, or other interlocutory matters. Having received the statement of claim and the defence (and, if applicable, further pleadings), the court will set a date for an oral hearing.

Discovery

German procedural law differs fundamentally from the common law systems so far as pre-trial discovery is concerned. This goes back to the historical differences in the development of continental European law and common law. In Germany, the autonomy of the parties is comparatively restricted, as the court takes a more prominent role in the taking of evidence. Thus, there is no procedure comparable to English-style discovery. On the contrary, an application to the court to allow discovery would generally be dismissed as being oppressive on the other party. This is compensated for by a much wider discretion of the judge in the evaluation of the available evidence.

Expert reports

Expert reports that have been commissioned by the parties must be distinguished from reports that are being ordered by the court. Expert reports can be offered by a party in support of a particular statement of fact (including the questions of foreign law) and are annexed to the respective pleadings. If the court feels it necessary to call for an independent expert it will normally ask the parties whether they can agree on a name. The parties are free to comment on any expert report that has been introduced to the proceedings. However, there is a presumption that the expert report commissioned by the court has a higher degree of independence.

Witnesses

No witness statements are generally prepared. The court has very wide discretion as to how the evidence is taken. Witnesses will only be heard by the court if the court decides by order that the witness shall give oral evidence at the hearing. The order to hear oral evidence will specify on what issues it is to be taken. At the hearing the court will put questions to the witness. Only after the judges have completed their interrogation may the parties' representative ask additional questions.

Fee and costs

As outlined above, German procedural rules are more streamlined than, for example, in England. Therefore, in general, litigation in Germany is much cheaper than in England.

Unlike in England, the legal basis for lawyers' fees, court fees and additional costs are extremely transparent, and one can easily obtain very precise forecasts of the total cost risk in any litigation. There are statutory scales for lawyers' fees and court fees that are based on the value of the claim. Both scales are adjusted from time to time and will, in due course, be expressed in euro. In the majority of cases lawyers increasingly ask for higher fees, often based on an hourly rate. However, compared to English court fees, German court fees can be quite substantial. These court fees will have to be advanced by the plaintiff.

Unlike in England, the successful party in Germany is awarded all his costs (based on the statutory fee scale) and any advanced court fees and other incidental disbursements.

In the context it should be noted that foreign plaintiffs may be asked to provide security for costs, unless there is an arrangement between both countries providing for exemption, or the plaintiff is a national of a member state of the European Union.

INJUNCTIVE RELIEF

In cases where evidence is likely to be destroyed or to perish during proceedings, or where the funds claimed by the plaintiff are likely to be removed from the jurisdiction of the court so as to avoid enforcement, injunctive relief is available to assist the plaintiff. On the other hand, such injunctive relief stops short of 'search and seek orders' (eg Anton Piller Order in England) as they are regarded as unfair 'fishing expeditions' and oppressive on the defendant.

REMINDER PROCEEDINGS

If it is unlikely that the defendant can or will put up a valid defence, in particular where money claims are concerned, the plaintiff may start by issuing so-called reminder proceedings in the *Amtsgericht* (*Mahnverfahren*). This is a highly formalised procedure specifically suited to simple debt collection cases involving documentary evidence only. Following the application for a payment order of the court, this will generally be issued by the court official and will become enforceable unless a statement of willingness to defend is received within two weeks from service. Generally, these reminder proceedings are considered cheaper, easier and quicker in appropriate cases. Only if a defence is lodged will the case proceed to trial.

THE CONCEPT OF PRECEDENT

The English doctrine of precedent does not apply in German law. All decisions of the higher courts, including the Federal Supreme Court, are of persuasive force only. However, in practice, high regard is given to all judgments of the Federal Supreme Court and its predecessor, the *Reichsgericht*, as well as a selection of judgments of the Courts of Appeal.

ARBITRATION

The Code of Civil Procedure provides for detailed rules concerning domestic arbitration proceedings. However, arbitration agreements are not very common in Germany, the reason being that German state courts generally work rather cost effectively and quickly. In an international context, German parties often choose dispute resolutions by arbitration when the ICC (International Chamber of Commerce) Rules or other respected arbitration rules and venues are determined. Germany has signed the New York Convention and will enforce awards accordingly.

JUDGES AND LAWYERS

In contrast to England, Germany has professional judges who follow separate careers that usually commence directly after the Second State Examination. While this examination is the common prerequisite for almost all legal professions, academic courses and practical training are aimed at producing career judges. It is therefore possible to find relatively young judges sitting on the bench. However, only judges of some seniority are appointed to the *Kammer für Handelssachen,* and the panel of judges dealing exclusively with commercial matters.

In common with more European countries, but contrary to most common law countries, Germany has an undivided legal profession. A lawyer in Germany (*Rechtsanwalt*) will deal with all legal matters, be they of an advisory nature or involving advocacy, apart from those reserved for notaries. They are restricted to practising civil litigation only in the local court to which they have been admitted. Over the past few years there has been a discussion of a reform of the system of local admission but the issue is as yet unresolved. Most German law firms have several members who speak English reasonably well. As one would expect in a country with an export-dominated economy, one finds throughout Germany widespread experience in dealing with international commercial legal matters and in conducting cases involving foreign parties.

Appendices

Appendix 1

Business Agencies

Compiled by Catherine McDowell,
The New German Länder Industrial
Investment Council (IIC), Berlin

FEDERAL (BUND) AND EU LEVELS

General information and orientation on the whole of Germany

Special Envoy for Foreign Investment in Germany
Markgrafenstraße 34
10117 Berlin
Germany
Tel: +49 30 2065 70
Fax: +49 30 2065 7111
E-mail: sekretariat-blofai@snafu.de

Federal Centre for Foreign Investment in Germany
Federal Ministry of Economics and Technology
(Bundesministerium für Wirtschaft und Technologie (BMWi)
Scharnhorststraße 36
10115 Berlin
Germany
Tel: +49 30 20 14 77 50
Fax: +49 30 20 14 70 36
E-mail: zfa@bmwi.bund.de
Website: www.business-in-germany.de

Business Location Germany
(BMWi office in the USA)
401 N. Michigan Ave, Suite 2525
Chicago, IL 60611-4212
USA
Tel: +1 312 494 21 67
Fax: +1 312 644 39 88
E-mail: info@blg.org

Specific project assistance in the new eastern states of Germany

The New German Länder Industrial Investment Council GmbH (IIC)

Head Office:
Charlottenstrasse 57
10117 Berlin
Germany
Tel: +49 30 2094 5660
Fax: +49 30 2094 5666
E-mail: info@iic.de
Website: www.iic.de

New York Office:
500 Fifth Avenue, Suite 4220
New York, NY 10110
USA
Tel: +1 212 391 9390
Fax: +1 212 391 9391
E-mail: LKarnath@iic.de

London Office:
Mecklenburg House
16 Buckingham Gate
London SW1E 6LB
Tel: +44 20 7976 4164
Fax: +44 20 7630 9019
E-mail: symes@iic.de

Favourable credit and bank guarantee programmes

Deutsche Ausgleichsbank (DtA)
(Bank for Equalisation)
Ludwig-Erhard-Platz 3
53170 Bonn
Germany
Tel: +49 228 831 24 00
Fax: +49 228 831 22 55
E-mail: dtabonn@t-online.de

Sarrazinstraße 11–15
12159 Berlin
Germany
Tel: +49 30 850 85 0
Fax: +49 30 850 85 299
E-mail: dtaberlin@t-online.de

Kreditanstalt für Wiederaufbau (KfW)
(Bank for Reconstruction)
Palmengartenstraße 5–9
60325 Frankfurt am Main
Germany
Tel: +49 69 7431 0
Fax: +49 69 7431 2944
E-mail: KfW.vs@kfw.de
Website: www.kfw.de

Charlottenstraße 33/33a
10117 Berlin
Germany
Tel: +49 30 20 264 16
Fax: +49 30 20264 192

European Investment Bank (EIB)
100 Boulevard Konrad Adenauer
2950 Luxembourg
Luxembourg
Tel: +352 437 91
Fax: +352 437 704
E-mail: EIB@-innet.lu

Federal Bank Guarantee Programme
PWC PricewaterhouseCoopers
Auf'm Hennekamp 47
40225 Düsseldorf
Germany
Tel: +49 211 9810
Fax: +49 0211 9812644

R&D/Innovation support programmes

Research Centre Jülich
(Forschungszentrum Jülich GmbH)
(for biotech, energy & environment)
Breiterstraße 3
10178 Berlin
Germany
Tel: +49 30 201993
Fax: +49 30 23199 479

VDI/VDE-Technologiezentrum Informationstechnik GmbH
Rheinstraße 10B
14513 Teltow
Germany
Tel: +49 3328 435 0
Fax: +49 3328 435 141
E-mail: vdivde-it@vdivde-it.de
Website: www.vdivde-it.de

Working Group of Industrial Research Associations 'Otto von Gueriche'
(Arbeitsgemeinschaft Industrieller Forschungsvereinigungen eV (AIF))
Tschaikowskistraße 49
13156 Berlin
Germany
Tel: +49 30 481 633
Fax: +49 30 483 34 401
E-mail: afb@aif.de
Website: www.aif.de

Grant programmes supporting trade fair participation

Confederation of German Trade Fair and Exhibition Industries
(Ausstellungs- und Messe-Ausschuß der Deutschen Wirtschaft eV (AUMA)
Lindenstraße 8
50674 Cologne
Germany
Tel: +49 221 20 90 70
Fax: +49 221 20 90 7 12
E-mail: info@auma.de
Website: www.auma.de

Grants supporting certification of quality management systems

German Management and Productivity Centre
(Rationalisierungs-Kuratorium der Deutschen Wirtschaft eV (RKW)
Düsseldorferstraße 40
65760 Eschborn
Germany
Tel: +49 6196 4951
Fax: +49 6196 495 303
E-mail: rkw@rkw.de
Website: www.rkw.de

Employment support programmes

Federal Institute for Employment
(Bundesanstalt für Arbeit)
90327 Nuremberg
Germany
Tel: +49 911 179 0
Fax: +49 911 179 21 23

STATE (*LAND*) LEVEL

Initial contacts for grant, credit, bank guarantee and other programmes administered by state governments

New federal states and Berlin

Berlin Economic Development Corporation
(Wirtschaftsförderung Berlin GmbH)
Ludwig Erhard Haus,
Fasanenstraße 85
10623 Berlin
Germany
Tel: +49 30 399 80 213
Fax: +49 30 399 80 239
E-mail: info@wf-berlin.de
Website: www.berlin.de

Brandenburg Economic Development Corporation
(Wirtschaftsförderung Brandenburg GmbH)
Am Lehnitzsee 7
14476 Neu Fahrland
Germany
Tel: +49 33208 55 220
Fax: +49 33208 55 100
E-mail: info@wfb.brandenburg.de
Website: www.brandenburg.de

Economic Development Corporation **Mecklenburg-Vorpommern**
(Gesellschaft für Wirtschaftsförderung Mecklenburg-Vorpommern mbH)
Schlossgartenallee 15
19061 Schwerin
Germany
Tel: +49 385 59 22 50
Fax: +49 385 59 22 5 22
E-mail: connect@gfw-mv.de
Website: www.gfw.mv.de

Saxony Economic Development Corporation
(Wirtschaftsförderung Sachsen GmbH)
Bertolt-Brecht-Allee 22
01309 Dresden
Germany
Tel: +49 351 31 99 11 28
Fax: +49 351 31 99 10 99
E-mail: info@wfs.saxony.de
Website: www.sachsen.de

Business Promotion and Development Company **Saxony-Anhalt**
(Wirtschaftsförderungsgesellschaft für das Land Sachsen Anhalt)
Association for the Promotion of Economic Development for the Land
of Saxony-Anhalt
Schleinufer 16
39104 Magdeburg
Germany
Tel: +49 391 568 99 30
Fax: +49 391 568 99 99
E-mail: welcome@wisa.de
Website: www.wisa.sachsen-anhalt.de

State Development Agency **Thuringia**
(Landesentwicklungsgesellschaft (LEG) Thüringen mbH)
Mainzerhofstraße 12
99084 Erfurt
Germany
Tel: +49 361 560 3443
Fax: +49 361 560 3 333
E-mail: leg-thueringen@t-online.de
Website: www.leg.th-online.de

Old federal states

Baden-Württemberg Agency for International Economic Co-operation
(Gesellschaft für internationale wirtschaftliche Zusammenarbeit (GWZ)
Baden-Württemberg mbH)
Willi-Bleicher-Straße 19
70174 Stuttgart
Germany
Tel: +49 711 227 870
Fax: +49 711 227 8722
E-mail: gwz@gwz.de
Website: www.business.germany-southwest.de

Bavarian Ministry for Economic Affairs, Transport and Technology
(Bayerisches Staatsministerium für Wirtschaft, Verkehr und
Technologie)
Prinzregentenstraße 28
80538 Munich
Germany
Tel: +49 89 21 62 26 42
Fax: +49 89 21 62 28 03
E-mail: locate-in-bavaria@t-online.de
Website: www.stmwvt.bayern.de

Bremen Business International GmbH
World Trade Centre Bremen
Birkenstraße 15
28195 Bremen
Germany
Tel: +49 421 1746613
Fax: +49 421 1746622
E-mail: bbi@bremen-business.de
Website: www.bremen-business.de

Economic Development Corporation **Bremen**
BBI Bremen Business International GmbH
(Wirtschaftsförderungsgesellschaft der Freien Hansestadt Bremen
GmbH)
Hanseatenhof 8
28195 Bremen
Germany
Tel: +49 421 30 88 50
Fax: +49 421 30 88 5 44
E-mail: bbi@bremen-business.de
Website: www.bremen-business.de

Hamburg Business Development Corporation
(Hamburgische Gesellschaft für Wirtschaftsförderung (HWZ) mbH)
Hamburger Straße 11
22083 Hamburg
Germany
Tel: +49 40 2270190
Fax: +49 40 22701929
E-mail: hwz@t-online.de
Website: www.hamburg.de

Economic Development Agency and Investment Bank of **Hessen**
(HLT Wirtschaftsförderung Hessen Investitionsbank AG)
Abraham-Lincoln-Straße 38-42
65189 Wiesbaden
Germany
Tel: +49 611 774 357
Fax: +49 611 774 265
E-mail: info@hlt.de
Website: htpp://www.hlt.de

Investment Promotion Agency (IPA) **Lower Saxony**
Hamburger Allee 4
30161 Hanover
Germany
Tel: +49 0511 343 466
Fax: +49 511 361 5909
E-mail: 73360.2071@compuserve.com

Economic Development Corporation **North Rhine-Westphalia**
(Gesellschaft für Wirtschaftsförderung Nordrhein-Westfalen mbH)
Kavalleriestraße 8–10
40213 Düsseldorf
Germany
Tel: +49 211 130000
Fax: +49 211 1300054
E-mail: gfw@gfw.nrw.de
Website: htpp://www.gfw.nrw.de

Investment and Economic Structure Bank of **Rhineland Palatinate**
(Investitions- und Strukturbank (ISB) Rheinland-Pfalz GmbH
Wilhelm-Theodor-Römheld-Straße 22
55130 Mainz
Germany
Tel: +49 6131 985200
Fax: +49 6131 985299
E-mail: isb-standortinfo@isb.rlp.de
Website: www.isb.rlp.de

Economic Development Corporation **Saarland**
(Gesellschaft für Wirtschaftsförderung Saarland mbH)
Trierer Straße 8
66111 Saarbrücken
Germany
Tel: +49 681 948550
Fax: +49 681 9485511
E-mail: gwsaar@t-online.de
Website: www.gwsaar.com

Business Development Corporation of **Schleswig-Holstein**
(Wirtschaftsförderung Schleswig-Holstein GmbH)
Lorentzendamm 43
24103 Kiel
Germany
Tel: +49 431-593390
Fax: +49 431 5933930
E-mail: info@wsh.de
Website: www.wsh.de

Official German institutions providing information on business with eastern Europe

Bureau for East–West Co-operation
(Kooperationsbüro der Deutschen Wirtschaft)
Uhlandstraße 28
10719 Berlin
Germany
Tel: +49 30 882 65 96
Fax: +49 30 882 51 93
E-mail: kooperationsbuero@compuserve.com
Website: ourworld.compuserve.com/homepages//kooperationsbuero1

Eastern Committee of the German Economy
(Ost-Ausschuß der Deutschen Wirtschaft)
Gustav-Heinemann-Ufer 84-88
50968 Cologne
Germany
Tel: +49 221 37 08 45 2
Fax: +49 221 3708540
E-mail: initial.nwname@bdi-online.de

Federal Office of Foreign Trade Information
(Bundesstelle für Außenhandelsinformation (BfAi))
Scharnhorststraße 36
10115 Berlin
Germany
Tel: +49 30 20 14 52 63
Fax: +49 30 20 14 52 04

Agrippastraße 87-93
50676 Cologne
Germany
Tel: +49 221 20 57 0
Fax: +49 221 20 57 212-, 275
Website: www.bfai.com

Technology transfer: principal agents and intermediaries

ZENIT
Dohne 54
4330 Mülheim/Ruhr 1
Germany
Tel: +49 208 3000 421
Fax: +49 208 3000 429
E-mail: info@www.zenit.de
Website: www.zenit.de

Technology Transfer Agency (TVA) Berlin
(Technologie Vermittlungs Agentur)
Wattstraße 11–13
13355 Berlin
Germany
Tel: +49 30 46 30 23
Fax: +49 30 46 30 24 44
E-mail: webmaster@tva.de
Website: www.tva.de

Centre of Innovation for Northern Germany
(Erfinderzentrum Norddeutschland GmbH)
Hindenburgstraße 27
30175 Hanover
Germany
Tel: +49 511 813051
Fax: +49 511 283 40 75
Website: www.ezn.hanover.de

UK Partner
The Technology Exchange Ltd
Wrest Park
Silsoe
Bedford MK45 4HS
Tel: +44 1525 860 333
Fax: +44 1525 860 664
E-mail: info@uktech.net
Website: www.uktech.net

Research organisations

Max Planck Society for the Advancement of Science
(Max Planck Gesellschaft für Förderung der Wissenschaften eV)
Hofgartenstraße 2
80539 Munich
Germany
Tel: +49 89 21080
Fax: +49 89 2108 1111
E-mail: surname@mpg-gv.mpg.de
Website: www.mpg.de

Fraunhöfer Society for the Promotion of Applied Research
(Fraunhöfer Gesellschaft zur Forderung der Angewandten Forschung eV)
Leonrodstraße 54
80636 Munich
Germany
Tel: +49 89 120501
Fax: +49 89 120537

Steinbeis Foundation for Economic Development
(Steinbeis Stiftung für Wirtschaftsförderung)
Willi-Bleicher-Straße 19
70174 Stuttgart
Germany
Tel: +49 711 18395
Fax: +49 711 226 1076
E-mail: stw@stw.de
Website: www.stw.de

Patent agents

Address list of over 900 patent agents from:

Patent Legal Chamber
(Patentanwaltkammer)
Molassistraße 2
Munich
Germany
Tel: +49 89 24 22 78 0
Fax: +49 89 2998

Appendix 2

Economic Incentives

Federal Center for Foreign Investment,
Federal Ministry of Economics and
Technology, Berlin

Below is a brief description of the economic incentives most interesting to a foreign investor, followed by a list of additional financial assistance programmes offered in Germany. This information is taken from the brochure, 'Economic Support: Help for Investments and Innovations' (*Wirtschaftliche Förderung: Hilfen für Investitionen und Innovationen*), recently published by the German Federal Ministry of Economics and Technology. At present it is currently available in German only, although an English version of the publication will be completed in the near future.

FINANCIAL ASSISTANCE FOR STARTING YOUR OWN BUSINESS

- **The European Recovery Programme's (ERP) Equity Capital Assistance Programme**
  This programme provides loans without collateral for investments in the old and new federal states by small and medium-sized enterprises (SMEs). Those starting a business must personally finance at least 15 per cent of their capital needs. The difference between the capital financed by the business's founder (at least 15 per cent) and 40 per cent of the needed capital can be financed under this programme. The maximum amount provided by the ERP is €500,000 per business. In the cases of privatisation or re-privatisation in the new federal states, the maximum sum is up to €1 million.

- **ERP Business Start-up Programme**
  People starting their own businesses can receive loans for investments in their new companies up to three years after its establishment. A prerequisite is that the business is the main source of income for the person applying for assistance under this programme. Only natural persons can apply. The maximum amount of the loan can be up to €1 million for businesses started in the new states or Berlin, and €500,000 for investments in the old states.

- **Deutsche Ausgleichsbank (DtA)[1] Business Start-up Programme**
  Up to eight years after the founding of a new business, the businessman can receive a loan to finance investments necessary to the founding of his company. This programme is available to natural persons founding a company, and SMEs. The maximum amount for such a loan is €2 million.

- **DtA Start-up Money**
  This programme provides loans for people starting businesses whose financing needs do not exceed €50,000, and is only available to natural persons.

FINANCIAL ASSISTANCE FOR INVESTMENTS

- **Tax benefits**
  - *Investment allowance*
    The investment allowance is given for new movable capital goods, ie fixed assets, and new immovable goods, eg buildings, and can only be claimed when an investment has been made in one of the new federal states before 2005. The allowance is up to 10 per cent or 20 per cent of the sum of the investment depending on the industry and the type of investment. More information about this programme can be received from the Municipal Finance Office where the business is located.
  - *Special depreciation*
    In addition to the 'straight-line' method there is a possibility to claim a special depreciation rate for the production or acquisition of new movable capital assets of up to 20 per cent of their costs. In addition to this special depreciation, SMEs are permitted to create a reserve of up to 50 per cent of the future production or acquisition costs for movable goods that

[1]The Deutsche Ausgleichsbank (German Equity Fund) and the Kreditanstalt für Wiederaufbau (German Development Bank) are both financial support agencies of the German federal government.

are depreciable. The maximum amount of the reserve is DM300,000 (DM600,000 for start-ups) which can be held for 2 years (five for start-ups).

- **Regional Assistance**
  - *Improvement of the regional economic structures*
    The aim of this programme is to balance out the disadvantages of structurally weak areas with regional subsidies. Under this programme grants are available for investments in both the new and old federal states under certain conditions. The state in which the investment takes place decides for which projects it will provide the grants.

    The regions that fall under this programme, and the maximum amount of the grants available are as follows:

Table A3.1 *Regions and maximum grants available*

Area		Maximum grant for SMEs	Maximum grant for other companies
Region A[*]	structurally weakest areas in the new states	up to 50% of investment	up to 35% of investment
Region B[*]	Berlin and structurally stronger areas in the new states	up to 43% of investment	up to 28% of investment
Region C[*]	structurally weak areas in the old states	up to 28% of investment	up to 18% of investment

[*]see Map 2 (p. 147)

The Improvement of Regional Economic Structures Programme can also be combined with additional subsidies, for which the investment is eligible. In such cases, the combined total of the financial aid cannot exceed the maximum amounts listed above.

- *ERP Reconstruction Programme*
  The ERP Reconstruction Programme offers long-term loans at favourable fixed interest rates for investments in the new states and eastern Berlin. This programme can finance up to three quarters of the investment costs that meet the programme's criteria. The maximum amount of the loan is usually €1 million. With certain projects, however, this can be increased.

- *ERP Regional Programme*
  The ERP Regional Programme offers long-term loans at favour-able fixed interest rates for investments in the old states and western Berlin. Only investments made in the regions identified by the Improvement of the Regional Economic Structures Programme are eligible. Loans given under the ERP Programme cannot be used for a project receiving grants from the Improvement of the Regional Economic Structures Pro-gramme. The ERP Regional Programme is only available to companies whose yearly turnover does not exceed €50 million. The programme can finance up to 50 per cent of the investment costs that meet its criteria. The maximum amount of the loan is €500,000.

- **Further programmes for Small and Medium-sized Enter-prises (SMEs)**
  - *Kreditanstalt für Wiederaufbau (KfW) SME Programme*
    The KfW SME Programme offers long-term loans at favourable fixed interest rates for all types of investments. This pro-gramme is available to SMEs with an annual turnover not exceeding €500 million. Up to 75 per cent of the investment cost that meet the programme's criteria can be financed under this programme. The maximum amount of this type of loan is usually €5 million for companies with an annual turnover of more than €50 million. The maximum amount of the loan can be increased for companies with an annual turnover of less than €50 million.
  - *KfW SME Programme – Liquidity Assistance*
    Under this programme SMEs having temporary liquidity problems can receive long-term loans with favourable fixed interest rates. The programme can also be used to improve the financial structure or expand the business's existing activities. To receive this assistance a company must be com-petitive and have a promising future. Businesses applying for this loan must have an annual turnover of less than €500 million. The loan can be up to 30 per cent of the company's most recent financial balance, but normally cannot be more than €5 million.

LOAN GUARANTEES

- **Loan guarantees from guarantee banks**
  Guarantee banks are in all of the states and are prepared to provide guarantees for loans for investments granted to all SMEs and start-ups, which do not possess the typical collateral to

guarantee their loans. Guarantees cover up to 80 per cent of the defaulted loan. The maximum amount of the guarantee cannot exceed DM1.5 million. The loan repayment period must not exceed 15 years.

● **DtA Guarantee Programme**
Under this programme guarantees are provided for loans which finance certain types of investments in the new states and eastern Berlin by SMEs. The guarantees cover up to 80 per cent of the defaulted loan. The minimum amount of the guarantee is normally DM1.5 million. The maximum amount is DM20 million.

● **Guarantees from the Federal Government and the States**
In the new states, the federal government and the state government in which the investment is made will provide loan guarantees for projects requiring guarantees of at least DM20 million. These guarantees normally cover up to 80 per cent of the default risks.

In the old states, the state governments offer state loan guarantee programmes.

RESEARCH AND INNOVATION

● **Grants**
  – *Promotion of research, development, and innovation in SMEs*
    Under this programme financial assistance is available for both research personnel and project costs for SMEs in the new states and eastern Berlin. The main prerequisites for the aid are as follows:
    1. the company and the research and development activities are in one of the new states or eastern Berlin;
    2. the company has no more than 250 employees, its annual turnover does not exceed €40 million or its balance is less than €27 million;
    3. more than 20 per cent of its production is engaged in value-added activities;
    4. no more than 25 per cent of the capital or the voting shares of the company are owned by one or more large businesses.
    Up to 40 per cent of the personal costs can be funded through the programme. The grants cannot exceed DM300,000 per year per company.

    SMEs in the new states and eastern Berlin are provided with funding of research and development projects under this programme. The recipients of the grants must be innovative companies that are no more than three years old or industrial research institutes that meet the same requirements mentioned above. Under certain conditions, the grants can cover up to 45 per cent of the research and development costs for companies and up to 75 per cent of the research institutes' R&D costs.

- The federal government offers several additional financial assistance programmes for research and development, such as the Promotion of the Industrial Community Research, the INSTI SMEs Patent Action, and the PRO INNO Programme Innovations Competency. A wide range of programmes are also sponsored by the Federal Ministry for Education and Research.

- **Loans**
  - *ERP Innovation Programme (Loans)*
  Under this programme, loans with favourable fixed interest rates are granted to finance the research and development phase, which includes personal costs, trips, material, research and development advising, investments, further development and improvement of the innovation and quality control. Companies whose annual turnover does not exceed €125 million are eligible for this programme, as well as large companies whose innovative product is new to Germany. Certain marketing activities can also be financed by this type of loan, if the company involved has an annual turnover of less than €40 million, less than 250 employees, and less than 25 per cent of the company is held or owned by a large company.

- **Venture capital for innovative companies**
  - *BTU – Venture Capital for Small Technology Companies*
  Under this programme, the *Technologie-Beteiligungs-Gesellschaft* (TBG), a subsidiary of the DtA, goes into a silent partnership with the small technology company. In addition to the TBG, the technology company must have a lead investor who will provide at least the same amount of venture capital as that provided by the TBG. The programme also offers the lead investor refinancing loans through the *Kreditanstalt für Wiederaufbau* (KfW). To qualify for assistance under this programme, the company must be less than 10 years old and in possession of the required technical and business know-how. The following conditions also apply:
    1. 50 employees or less;
    2. maximum annual turnover of €7 million or maximum balance sheet total of €5 million;
    3. less than 25 per cent of the company can be held by a large company.
  - *DtA Venture Capital Programme (TBG)*
  Under this programme the TBG finances a company's activities

from the initial phase right up to the exit phase. Recipients of this assistance are technology-oriented companies with an annual turnover of less than DM250 million. The TBG partnership can either be open or silent.

– *FUTOUR*
  The aim of this programme is to promote technology in the new federal states through grants from the Federal Ministry for Economics and Technology and the TBG's silent participation in technology companies. This programme is available to people intending to establish a technology-oriented business and also new technology companies that are no more than three years old and have less than 10 employees.
– *ERP Innovation Programme (Venture Capital)*
  This programme offers companies providing venture capital to innovative SMEs refinancing credit under favourable terms. This programme is available to credit institutions, venture capital companies, businesses and private individuals with an annual turnover of less than €125 million.

INVESTMENT/VENTURE CAPITAL

- **ERP Venture Capital Programme**
  This programme offers venture capital companies refinancing credit at favourable rates when they participate in a small or medium-sized company.
- **KfW Venture Capital Funds (East)**
  Under this programme refinancing credit at favourable rates is provided to investors participating in middleclass companies with a plant in one of the new states. The venture capital provided to this company must finance projects or investments at the plant located in the new state.
- **Equity Capital Increase Programme (EKE)**
  This programme offers SMEs in the new states and eastern Berlin the opportunity to build up their capital base. Companies participating in this programme must have an annual turnover of 125 million Euro or less. Investments funded under this programme must meet certain criteria.
- **GBB Consolidation and Growth Funds (East)**
  The GBB *Beteiligungs Aktiengesellschaft*, a subsidiary of the DtA, offers this programme to SMEs in the new federal states that are suffering from liquidity problems or trying to regain competitiveness.
- **KfW Risk Capital Programme**
  This programme guarantees a business's participation in a small or medium-sized company. Risk capital provided to SMEs in the

old states under this programme can only be used for certain projects. Risk capital provided to SMEs in the new states can be used for almost any purpose. The company providing the risk capital must meet certain criteria.

ENVIRONMENTAL PROGRAMMES, ENERGY SAVING PROGRAMMES, AND RENEWABLE ENERGY PROJECTS

- **Environmental Programmes**
  - *ERP Environmental Programme*
  - *DtA Environmental Programme*
  - *KfW Environmental Programme*
- **Energy Savings Programmes**
  - *KfW-CO$_2$ Reduction Programme*
  - *Energy Savings Assistance*
- **Renewable Energy Projects**
  - *Promotion of Renewable Energy Programme*
  - *100,000 Roofs Solar Energy Programme*

TRADE FAIRS, FOREIGN TRADE ASSISTANCE

- **Trade Fair Promotion, Export Promotion**
  - *Domestic Trade Fair Promotion*
  - *Foreign Trade Fair Promotion*
  - *Marketing Assistance*
  - *ERP Export Financing Programme*
  - *Export Credit Guarantees (Hermes Coverage)*
- **Investment in Foreign Countries**

SCHOOLING, ADVISING

- **Advising for SMEs**
- **Promotion of Informative and Schooling Courses**

LABOUR ASSISTANCE

- **Grants for Integrating New Employees**
- **Promotion for Self-employment**
- **Grants for Employment at a New Company**
- **Assistance for Employing Long-term Unemployed**
- **Grants for Labor Costs for Companies in the East**

INFRASTRUCTURE AND LIVING QUARTERS

- KfW Infrastructure Programme
- KfW Housing Modernization Programme
- KfW Programme for the Promotion of Housing Ownership for Young Families

German Chambers of Industry & Commerce

ARGENTINA

Cámara de Industria y Comercio
Argentino-Alemana
Florida 547, Piso 19°
1005 Buenos Aires
Tel: +54 1 322 01 73, 393 90 06/7, 394
    00 98/9
Fax: +54 1 394 09 79, 393 51 51
E-mail: ahk@ahkar.com.ar
Contact: Daniel M Scheidel

AUSTRALIA

Sydney

German-Australian Chamber of
Industry and Commerce
PO Box A 980
Sydney South
NSW 1235
Tel: +61 2 92 65 22 00
Fax: +61 2 92 65 22 11
E-mail: ahkaust@magna.com.au
Contact: Heinrich E Zimmermann

Melbourne

German-Australian Chamber of
Industry and Commerce
Melbourne Office
Hoechst House, 5th Floor
606 St. Kilda Road
Melbourne VIC 3004
Tel: +61 3 95 10 58 26
Fax: +61 3 95 10 18 35
Contact: Knut Feddersen

AUSTRIA

Vienna

Deutsche Handelskammer in
Österreich
Postfach 107
A-1103 Wien
Tel: +43 1 545 14 17
Fax: +43 1 545 22 59
E-mail: ahkwien@mail.ahk-ermany.de
    106340.2461@compuserve.com
Website: www.ahk-germany.de/ahkwien/
    ahkwien.htm
Contact: Dr Rolf Schäfer

Salzburg

Getreidegasse 13
A-5020 Salzburg
Tel: +43 662 84 79 52-0
Fax: +43 662 84 05 89
E-mail: ahksalz@mail.ahk-germany.de
Contact: Paula Koppensteiner

BELARUS

Repräsentanz der IHK Bonn
Prospekt Gasety Prawda 11
220116 Minsk
Tel/Fax: +37 5172 703893
Contact: Dr Vladimir Avgoustinski
(Please direct questions to Herrn
Ulrich, IHK Bonn, *Tel:* +228 22 84166)

BELGIUM/ LUXEMBOURG

Brussels

debelux Handelskammer
Manhattan Office Tower
Bolwerklaan 21, Avenue du Boulevard
B-1210 Brussels
Tel: +32 2 203 50 40
Fax: +32 2 203 47 58
E-mail: debelux@arcadis.be
Contact: Dr Peter Toebelmann

**Deutscher Industrie- und
Handelstag Vertretung bei der
Europäischen Union**
49 A, Boulevard Clovis
B-1000 Brussels
Tel: +32 2 286 16 11
Fax: +32 2 286 16 05
E-mail: diht@bruessel.diht.ihk.de
Contact: Peter Korn

Cologne

debelux Handelskammer
Belgisches Haus
Cäcilienstraße 46
D-50667 Köln
Tel: +221 257 54 77, 257 54 85
Fax: +221 257 54 66
Contact: Gerd Marmann

Luxemburg

Chambre de Commerce DEBELUX
7, Rue Alcide de Gasperi
L-1615 Luxembourg-Kirchberg
Tel: +35 2 42 39 39-1
Fax: +35 2 43 83 26
Contact: Paul Hippbert

BOLIVIA

**Cámara de Comercio e Industria
Boliviano-Alemana**
Casilla 2722
La Paz
Tel: +591 2 41 17 74
Fax: +591 2 41 33 21
E-mail: cambolal@datacom-bo.net
Contact: Jörg Zehnle

BOSNIA-HERZEGOVINA

**Predstavnistvo njemacke privrede
u Bosni i Hercegovini**
c/o Privredna Komora Bosne i
Hercegovine
Branislava Djurdjeva broj 10
B i H-71000 Sarajevo
Tel: +387 71 21 21 67
Fax: +387 71 21 21 68
E-mail: delgbih@bih.net.ba
Contact: Dr Peter Presber

BRAZIL

Porto Alegre

Câmara de Comércio e Indústria Brasil-Alemanha do Porto Alegre
Caixa Postal 20 95
BR-90430-010 Porto Alegre RS
Tel: +55 51 222 57 66
Fax: +55 51 222 55 56
E-mail: ahkpoa@ez-poa.com.br
Contact: Gabriel A Brennauer

Rio de Janeiro

Câmara de Comércio e Indústria Brasil-Alemanha do Rio de Janeiro
Avenida Graça Aranha, 1/4° and.
BR-20030-002 Rio de Janeiro RJ
Tel: +55 21 224 21 23
Fax: + 55 21 252 77 58
E-mail: ahk-rio@rionet.com.br
Contact: Peter Klam

São Paulo

Câmara de Comércio e Indústria Brasil-Alemanha
Rua Verbo Divino 1488
BR-04719-904 São Paulo SP
Tel: +55 11 51 81 06 77
Fax: +55 11 51 81 70 13
E-mail: ahk-brasil@originet.com.br
Website: www.ahkbrasil.com
Contact: Dr Klaus-Wilhelm Lege

Curitiba

(subsidiary of São Paulo office)

Câmara de Comércio e Indústria Brasil-Alemanha
Rua Emiliano Perneta 424
BR-80420-080 Curitiba PR
Tel: +55 41 323 59 58
Fax: +55 41 222 03 22
Contact: Christina Mathias

Salvador

(subsidiary of São Paulo office)

Câmara de Comércio e Indústria Brasil-Alemanha
Av. da Franca 164
BR-40010-000 Salvador BA
Tel: +55 71 241 02 24
Fax: +55 71 243 66 75
E-mail: ahkssa@bahianet.com.br
Website: www.ahkbrasil.com
Contact: Monika Schülter

BULGARIA

Repräsentanz der Deutschen Wirtschaft
F.J. Curie Str. 25 A
BG-1113 Sofia
Tel: +359 2 963 30 71, 963 34 67,
963 43 01
Fax: +359 2 963 33 91, 963 44 97
E-mail: rdw_bg_mwassilew@ibm.net
Contact: Dr Mitko Vassilev

CANADA

Toronto

Canadian German Chamber of Industry and Commerce Inc (Head Office)
480 University Ave., Suite 1410
Toronto, ON M5G 1V2
Tel: +1 416 598 3355
Fax: +1 416 598 1840
E-mail: 106170.2643@compuserve.com
info.toronto@germanchamber.ca
Website: www.germanchamber.ca
Contact: Uwe Harnack

Montreal

Canadian German Chamber of Industry and Commerce Inc.
1010 Sherbrooke Street West,
Suite 1604
Montreal, PQ H3A 2R7
Tel: +1 514 844 30 51
Fax: +1 514 844 14 73
E-mail: 76443.2106@compuserve.com
    info.montreal@german
    chamber.ca
Website: www.germanchamber.ca
Contact: Harald Modis

Vancouver

Canadian German Chamber of Industry and Commerce Inc.
1030 West Georgia Street, Suite 617
Vancouver BC V6E 2Y3
Tel: +1 604 681 44 69
Fax: +1 604 681 44 89
E-mail: 102717.2241@compuserve.com
    info.vancouver@german
    chamber.ca
Website: www.germanchamber.ca
Contact: Thomas W Felber

CENTRAL AMERICA

for letters:
Cámara de Comercio e Industria Alemana
Regional para Centroamerica y el Caribe
Section 2969
PO Box 02-5339
Miami, FL 33102-5339
USA

for packages:
Cámara de Comercio e Industria Alemana
Regional para Centroamerica y el Caribe
Section 2969/GUA
7801 N.W. 37th St.
Miami, FL 33166-6559
Tel: +502 367 55 52/62/82
Fax: +502 333 70 44
E-mail: ahkzakk@quik.guate.com
Website: www.ahkzakk.com
Contact: Wolfgang Schilling

CHILE

Cámara Chileno-Alemana de Comercio e Industria
Casilla 19, correo 35
Santiago
Tel: +56 2 203 53 20
Fax: +56 2 203 53 25
E-mail: ahkchile@reuna.cl
Contact: José-Volker Rehnelt

CHINA (see also Hong Kong)

Canton/Guangzhou

Delegate of German Industry and Commerce in Guangzhou/Canton
Representative Office
2915 Metro Plaza
Tian He North Road
510620 Guangzhou
Tel: +86 20 87 55 23 53
Fax: +86 20 87 55 18 89
Contact: Ekkehard Goetting
(Please direct questions to Hong Kong office)

Peking/Beijing

Delegate of German Industry and Commerce in Beijing/Peking
Representative Office
Beijing Landmark Towers, 5/F
8 North Dongsanhuan Road
Chaoyang District
100004 Beijing
Tel: +86 10 65 01 19 26, 65 90 09 26
Fax: +86 10 65 08 63 13, 65 90 63 13
E-mail: ahkbeij@public.bta.net.cn
Contact: Dr Jörg-Meinhard Rudolph

Shanghai

Delegate of German Industry and Commerce in Shanghai
5/F Bund Center
555 Zhongshan Dong Er Road
200010 Shanghai
Tel: +86 21 63 26 97 91/2
Fax: +86 21 63 26 97 94, 63 26 92 05
E-mail: ahksha@stn.sh.cn
Contact: Dr Klaus Grimm

COLOMBIA

Cámara de Industria y Comercio Colombo-Alemana
Apartados Aéreos 91 527, 91 528
Santa Fe de Bogotá
Tel: +57 1 623 33 30
Fax: +57 1 623 33 08, 623 33 75
E-mail: 102213.2242@compuserve.com
Contact: Norbert Pudzich

COSTA RICA*

Cámara de Comercio e Industria Costarricense Alemana
Apartado Postal 2139 – 1000
San José
Tel: +506 222 47 89
Fax: +506 221 12 19
E-mail: cacoral@sol.racsa.co.cr
Contact: Carla De Abate

CZECH REPUBLIC

Cesko-nemecká obchodní a prumyslová komora
Masarykovo nábrezí 30
CZ-110 00 Praha 1
Tel: +420 2 24 91 52 16/7, 29 80 51
Fax: +420 2 24 91 38 27
E-mail: info@dtihk.cz
Contact: Dieter Mankowski

DENMARK

Det Tysk-Danske Handelskammer
Børsen
DK-1217 København K
Tel: +45 33 91 33 35
Fax: +45 33 91 31 16
E-mail: 106623.300@compuserve.com
Contact: Gerhard Glaser

DOMINICAN REPUBLIC*

Cámara de Comercio e Industria Dominico Alemana
Apartado Postal 8335
Santo Domingo
Tel: +1 809 683 25 97
Fax: +1 809 683 61 56
E-mail: camdomalemana@hotmail.com
          @ccdomalemana@codetel.net.com
Contact: Thomas Kirbach

ECUADOR

Cámara de Industrias y Comercio Ecuatoriano-Alemana
Casilla 17-16-083
Quito
Tel: +593 2 43 55 06/7
Fax: +593 2 43 60 57
E-mail: ahkecua1@ahkecuador.org.ec
Contact: Claus Hübener

EGYPT

Cairo

Deutsch-Arabische Handelskammer
POB 385
11511 Ataba
Cairo
Tel: +20 2 341 36 62, 341 36 64
Fax: +20 2 341 36 63
E-mail: info@gerarcham.com
Website: www.gerarcham.com
Contact: Dr Peter Göpfrich

Alexandria

2 Mohamed Masoud Street
Wabour El Maya – Alexandria
Tel/Fax: +20 3 422 84 78

EL SALVADOR*

Cámara de Comercio e Industria Salvadoreña Alemana
Apartado Postal 01-550
San Salvador
Tel: +503 222 26 86
Fax: +503 222 60 44
E-mail: camalem@cyt.net
Contact: Matthias Müller

ESTONIA

Saksa Majandusesindus Eestis
Suurtüki 4B
EE-10133 Tallinn
Tel: +372 6 44 67 26, 6 44 99 29
Fax: +372 6 46 02 48
E-mail: rdwe@koda.ee
Contact: Dr Ralph-Georg Tischer

FINLAND

Deutsch-Finnische Handelskammer
Postfach 83
FIN-00101 Helsinki
Tel: +358 9 61 22 12-0
Fax: +358 9 64 28 59
E-mail: info@dfhk.fi
Website: www.dfhk.fi
Contact: Hans-Joachim Maurer

FRANCE

La Chambre Franco-Allemande de Commerce et d'Industrie
18, rue Balard
F-75015 Paris
Tel: +33 1 40 58 35 35
Fax: +33 1 45 75 47 39
E-mail: ahk@ahk-ccifa.fr
Website: www.ahk-ccifa.fr
Contact: Ass. Joachim Wischermann

GREECE

Athens

Deutsch-Griechische Industrie- und Handelskammer
Doryleou 10-12/IV
GR-115 21 Athínai
Tel: +30 1 644 45 02/3, 644 45 24/5,
   644 45 46/7
Fax: +30 1 644 51 75
E-mail: ahkathen@mail.ahk-germany.de
Website: www.german-chamber.gr
Contact: Götz Funck

Thessaloníki

**Deutsch-Griechische Industrie-
und Handelskammer**
Geschäftsstelle Nordgriechenland
Voulgari Str. 50/V
GR-54249 Thessaloníki
Tel: +30 31 32 77 33
Fax: +30 31 32 77 37
E-mail: ahkthess@mail.ahk-
germany.de
Contact: Martin Knapp

HONG KONG

**German Industry and Commerce
Hong Kong, South China, Vietnam
German Business Association of
Hong Kong**
3601 Tower One, Lippo Centre
89 Queensway
Hong Kong
Tel: +852 25 26 54 81
Fax: +852 28 10 60 93
E-mail: info@ahk.org.hk
Website: www.ahk.org.hk
Contact: Ekkehard Goetting

GUATEMALA*

**Cámara de Comercio e Industria
Guatemalteco Alemana**
Apartado Postal 1163
09901 Guatemala
Guatemala/C.A.
Tel: +502 333 60 36/37/38
Fax: +502 368 29 71
E-mail: camalegu@quik.guate.com
Contact: Franz Ulrich Appel

HUNGARY

**Német-Magyar Ipari és
Kereskedelmi Kamara**
Lövöház u. 30
H-1024 Budapest
Tel: +36 1 3 45 76 00
Fax: +36 1 3 45 76 02
E-mail: ahkungarn@compuserve.com
Contact: Jürgen Illing

INDIA

Bombay

HONDURAS*

**Cámara de Comercio e Industria
Hondureño Alemana**
Apartado Postal No. 3811
Tegucigalpa
Tel: +504 236 53 63
Fax: +504 236 53 71
E-mail: ccha@david.intertel.hn
Contact: Doris Sohn de Maradiaga

**Indo-German Chamber of
Commerce (Head Office)**
PO Box 11092
(Bombay) Mumbai 400 020
Tel: +91 22 218 61 31
Fax: +91 22 218 05 23
E-mail: igcc.igccd@axcess.net.in
igcc.igccb@giasbm01.vsnl.net.in
106025.342@compuserve.com
Contact: Dr Günter Krüger

Bangalore

Indo-German Chamber of Commerce
P.O.Box 144
Bangalore 560 052
Tel: +91 80 226 56 50
Fax: +91 80 220 37 97
E-mail: igccbg@giasbg01.vsnl.net.in
Contact: Audrey D'Souza

Calcutta

**Indo-German Chamber of
Commerce**
P.O.Box 25 04
Calcutta 700 001
Tel: +91 33 247 41 47, 240 56 45
Fax: +91 33 247 61 65
E-mail: igcc@giascl01.vsnl.net.in
Contact: C Dasgupta

Chennai (Madras)

**Indo-German Chamber of
Commerce**
P.O.Box 8779
Chennai (Madras) 600017
Tel: +91 44 821 18 35, 821 18 36
Fax: +91 44 821 18 37
E-mail: igccmds@giasmd01.vsnl.net.in
Contact: TR Gopalan

Düsseldorf
(affiliated office)

Deutsch-Indische Handelskammer/
Deutsch-Indisches Wirtschaftsbüro e.V.
Oststraße 84/II
40210 Düsseldorf
Tel: +211 36 05 97, 36 27 49
Fax: +211 35 02 87
E-mail: dihk@compuserve.com
        106736.2564@compuserve.com
Contact: Dirk Matter

New Delhi

**Indo-German Chamber of
Commerce**
GPO Box 252
New Delhi 110 001
Tel: +91 11 687 87 21, 611 17 30
Fax: +91 11 611 86 64
E-mail: igcc@giasdl01.vsnl.net.in
        106112.465@compuserve.com
Contact: Ajay Singha

INDONESIA

**Gedung Perkumpulan Ekonomi
Indonesia-Jerman (EKONID)**
P.O. Box 3151
Jakarta 10031
Tel: +62 21 315 46 85
Fax: +62 21 315 52 76
E-mail: ekonid@io.com
        sys_dept@rad.net.id
        106007.101@compuserve.com
Website: www.io.com/ekonid
Contact: Dr Fritz Kleinsteuber

IRAN

**Official Irano-German Chamber of
Industry and Commerce**
P.O. Box 14155-3478
Tehran
Tel: +98 21 871 22 30, 871 52 10, 871
      92 50
Fax: +98 21 871 11 23
E-mail: diihk@dpi.net.ir
Contact: Matthias Boddenberg

IRELAND

German-Irish Chamber of Industry and Commerce
46 Fitzwilliam Square
IRL-Dublin 2
Tel: +353 1 676 29 34
Fax: +353 1 676 25 95
E-mail: info@german-irish.ie
Website: www.german-irish.ie
Contact: Dr Dieter Tscherning

ISRAEL

Israeli-German Chamber of Industry and Commerce
P.O. Box 34 88
IL-52134 Ramat Gan (Tel Aviv)
Tel: +972 3 613 35 15/6
Fax: +972 3 613 35 28
E-mail: ahkisger@inter.net.il
Contact: Yohanan Bi-Lev

ITALY

Camera di Commercio Italo-Germanica
Via Napo Torriani 29
I-20124 Milano
Tel: +39 02 67 91 31
Fax: +39 02 66 98 09 64
E-mail: 106030.3323@compuserve.com
Contact: Ass. Heinz Friese

JAPAN

Tokyo

Zainichi Doitsu Shoko Kaigisho
CPO Box 588
Tokyo 100-8692
Tel: +81 3 52 76 98 11
Fax: +81 3 52 76 87 33
E-mail: dihkjmd@twics.com
Contact: Manfred Dransfeld

Institut für Marktberatung der Deutschen Industrie- und Handelskammer in Japan
CPO Box 588
Tokyo 100-8692
Contact: Lutz-Bodo Müller-Seip

Osaka

Zainichi Doitsu Shoko Kaigisho
Umeda Sky Building, Tower East 35F
1-88-3502, Oyodo-naka 1-Chome
Kita-ku, Osaka 531-6035
Tel: +81 6 440 59 91
Fax: +81 6 440 59 92
Contact: Dr Hans Georg Mammitzsch

KAZAKSTAN

Repräsentanz der Deutschen Wirtschaft in Almaty
c/o KVES International Ltd.
Company for Foreign Economic Cooperation
Dostyk Straße 38 (Zi. 525-532)
480100 Almaty
Tel: +7 3272 61 72 33, 61 37 38
Fax: +7 3272 63 85 77, 65 16 69
Contact: Dr Galia S Shunusalijeva

KOREA

Korean-German Chamber of Commerce and Industry
CPO Box 49 63
Seoul 100-649
Tel: +82 2 37 80 46 00
Fax: +82 2 37 80 46 37
E-mail: 100053.1642@compuserve.com
Contact: Florian Schuffner

LATVIA

Repräsentanz der Deutschen
Wirtschaft
BüroanschVilandes iela 1
LV-1010 Riga
Tel: +371 7 32 07 18, 9 34 65 28
(mobile number)
Fax: +371 7 83 04 78
Contact: Dr Guntis Strazds

LEBANON

The Delegate of German
Industry and Trade in Lebanon
P.O. Box 13/6025
Beirut
Tel/Fax: +961 1 74 26 12
Mobil-Tel: +961 3 35 28 98
E-mail: dihtddwb@inco.com.lb
Contact: Dr Peter Göpfrich

LITHUANIA

Repräsentanz der Deutschen
Wirtschaft in Litauen
Vokietijos Ukio Atstovybé Lietuvoje
P.O. Box 387
LT-2004 Vilnius
Tel: +370 2 23 11 22
Fax: +370 2 23 10 13
E-mail: ahk_lit@post.omnitel.net
Contact: Aldas Kikutis

LUXEMBOURG
(see Belgium)

MALAYSIA

Malaysian-German Chamber of
Commerce and Industry
P.O. Box 11683
50754 Kuala Lumpur
Tel: +60 3 238 35 61/2
Fax: +60 3 232 11 98
E-mail: mgcc@po.jaring.my
Contact: Dr Rainer Herret

MEXICO

Cámara Mexicano-Alemana de
Comercio e Industria, A.C.
Apartado Postal 41-740
11000 Ciudad de México, D.F.
Tel: +525 251 40 22
Fax: +525 596 76 95
E-mail: ahkmexiko@compuserve.
com.mx
Website: www.camexa.com.mx
Contact: Manfred Hoffmann

MOROCCO

Chambre Allemande de Commerce
et d'Industrie au Maroc
8, Bd. de Khouribga
MA-20 000 Casablanca
Tel: +212 2 44 98 22/3
Fax: +212 2 44 96 93
E-mail: dihkcasa@open.net.ma
Contact: Gerd M Doepner

NETHERLANDS

Nederlands-Duitse Kamer van
Koophandel
Postbus 80533
NL-2508 GM Den Haag
Tel: +31 70 311 41 14
Fax: +31 70 363 22 18
E-mail: ndkvk@bart.nl
Contact: Axel Gerberding

Düsseldorf (affilliated office)
Deutsch-Niederländische
Handelskammer
Postfach 32 02 13
D-40417 Düsseldorf
Tel: +211 498 72 01
Fax: +211 498 72 22
E-mail: dnhk@dnhk.d.uunet.de
Contact: K van der Beek

NEW ZEALAND

New Zealand-German
Business Association Inc.
P.O. Box 95
Auckland 1
Tel: +64 9 307 10 66
Fax: +64 9 309 02 09
Contact: Emma Mawson

NICARAGUA*

Cámara de Comercio e Industria
Nicaraguense Alemana
Apartado Postal 1125
Managua
Tel: +505 2 68 10 66
Fax: +505 2 22 78 29
E-mail: cicna@munditel.com.ni
Contact: Alvaro Corea

NIGERIA

Representative Office of German
Industry and Commerce in Nigeria
P.O. Box 51 311
Falomo Ikoyi
Lagos
Tel: +234 1 261 97 51, 261 97 52, 262
39 84
Fax: +234 1 261 97 52, 262 39 85
E-mail: ahk_lagos_uschroeder@
   compuserve.com
   ahk_lagos_hgirkes@compuserve.
   com
   ngbcahk.nig@linkserve.com.ng
Contact: Ute Schröder

NORWAY

Norsk-Tysk Handelskammer
POB 2853 Solli
N-0230 Oslo
Tel: +47 22 12 82 10
Fax: +47 22 12 82 22
E-mail: 106025.355@compuserve.com
Contact: Ernst-Otto Gelfert

PALESTINIAN TERRITORIES

The Delegate of German Industry
and Trade in the Palestinian
Territories
P.O. Box 1562
Ramallah
Palestinian Territories, Via Israel
Tel: +972 2 298 47 51, 5 038 33 08
Fax: +972 2 298 47 50
E-mail: dgit@palnet.com
Contact: Dr Peter Göpfrich

PANAMA*

Cámara de Comercio e Industria
Panameña Alemana
Apartado Postal 55-2537
Paitilla
Tel: +507 263 11 18
Fax: +507 269 63 72
E-mail: ihkpanam@sinfo.net
Contact: Christine Göllner de Mejía

PARAGUAY

Cámara de Comercio e
Industria Paraguayo-Alemana
Casilla de Correo 919
1209 Asunción
Tel: +595 21 44 65 94, 45 05 57
Fax: +595 21 44 97 35
E-mail: ahkasu@mail.pla.net.py
Contact: Henning B Höltei

PERU

Cámara de Comercio e
Industria Peruano-Alemana
Casilla 27 – 0069
Lima 27
Tel: +51 1 441 86 16
Fax: +51 1 442 60 14
E-mail: postmast@camperal.org.pe
Contact: Oliver Jörk

PHILIPPINES

Makati

European Chamber of
Commerce of the Philippines
CPO Box 215
Makati
Tel: +63 2 759 66 80, 845 13 24
Fax: +63 2 759 66 90, 845 13 95
E-mail: eccpcom@globe.com.ph
        106005.3063@compuserve.com
Website: www.eccp.com
Contact: Henry J Schumacher

Cebu

European Chamber of Commerce of the
Philippines
Cebu Office
3/f HongKong Bank Building
14 Juana Osmena Street
Cebu City
Tel: +63 32 253 33 89, 254 37 67
Fax: +63 32 253 33 87
E-mail: rpaloma@eccp.com
        cecile@eccp.com
Contact: Roselu Paloma

POLAND

Polsko-Niemiecka Izba
Przemyslowo-Handlowa
PO Box 62
PL-00-952 Warszawa
Tel: +48 22 635 33 53, 635 80 34
    +4839 12 02 19 (via satellite)
Fax: +48 22 635 81 06, 831 99 09
E-mail: 106337.3371@compuserve.com
Contact: Dr Thomas Hardieck

PORTUGAL

Lisbon

Câmara de Comércio e
Indústria Luso-Alemã
Av. da Liberdade, 38-2°
P-1250 Lisboa
Tel: +351 1 321 12 00
Fax: +351 1 346 71 50
E-mail: ahklisboa@mail.telepac.pt
        106173.1615@compuserve.com
Website: www.ahk-germany.de/ahklis/
        ahklis.htm
Contact: Hans-Joachim Böhmer

Porto

Câmara de Comércio e
Indústria Luso-Alemã
Av. da Boavista, 3523, Sala 301
P-4100 Porto
Tel: +351 2 610 10 80, 619 76 60
Fax: +351 2 617 20 14
E-mail: ahkporto@mail.telepac.pt
        106173.1610@compuserve.com
Contact: Christine Malpricht

ROMANIA

Repräsentanz der Deutschen Wirtschaft
Str. Radu Cristian 4, App. 4
RO-70 336 Bucuresti
Tel: +40 1 3 13 31 41, 3 13 08 97, 3 12 59 90
Fax: +40 1 312 38 41
E-mail: 106004.2601@compuserve.com
Contact: Cristina Nitescu

RUSSIA

Delegierte der Deutschen Wirtschaft in der Russischen Föderation
c/o DIHT, Büro Berlin
An der Kolonnade 10
10117 Berlin
Tel: +7 095 234 49 50
   +7 503 234 49 50 (via satellite)
Fax: +7 095 234 49 51
   +7 503 234 49 51 (via satellite)
E-mail: diht@cityline.ru
   ahk@diht.msk.ru
Contact: Dr Andrea von Knoop

Kaliningrad

Delegation der Deutschen Wirtschaft in der Russischen Föderation
Außenstelle Kaliningrad
Postfach 32 64
D-2381 Lübeck
Germany
Tel: +7 0112 21 15 38, 55 55 44
Fax: +7 0112 55 42 36
E-mail: hkhamb.ahk@kaliningrad.ru
Contact: Stephan Stein

Novosibirsk

Delegation der deutschen Wirtschaft in der Russischen Föderation
Außenstelle Novosibirsk
c/o DIHT, Büro Berlin
An der Kolonnade 10
D-10117 Berlin
Germany
Tel: +7 3832 23 46 56
Fax: +7 3832 23 46 56
Contact: Hugo A Deis

Sankt-Peterburg

Delegation der Deutschen Wirtschaft in der Russischen Föderation
Außenstelle St. Petersburg
POBox 36
FIN-53501 Lappeenranta
Tel: +7 812 323 79 91/93
Fax: +7 812 323 04 70
E-mail: dihtspb@mail.wplus.net
Contact: Dr Dieter Schubert

SAUDI ARABIA

German-Saudi Arabian Liaison Office for Economic Affairs
P.O. Box 61695
Riyadh 11575
Tel: +966 1 403 15 00
Fax: +966 1 403 51 21
E-mail: +106005.3622@compuserve.com
Contact: Michael Tockuss

SINGAPORE

The Delegate of German Industry
and Commerce in Singapore
Asia Pacific Support Office
25 International Business Park
#04-65/77 German Centre
Singapore 609916
Tel: +65 562 90 00
Fax: +65 563 09 07
E-mail: ahksing@diht.com.sg
Website: www.diht.com.sg
Contact: Jürgen Franzen

SLOVAKIA

Delegát nemeckého hospodárstva
na Slovensku
Klariská 7
SK-816 45 Bratislava
Tel: +421 7 54 41 03 62/3
Fax: +421 7 54 41 03 64
E-mail: ahksvk@internet.sk
Contact: Dieter Mankowski

SLOVENIA

Repräsentanz der Deutschen
Wirtschaft
Trg republike 3 (TR 3)
SI-61000 Ljubljana
Tel: +386 61 126 25 67, 176 30 26/7/8
Fax: +386 61 126 47 80
E-mail: ahksi@ibm.net
Contact: Senka Andrijanic

SOUTH AFRICA

Southern African German
Chamber of Commerce and
Industry Ltd
P.O. Box 87078
Houghton 2041
Tel: +27 11 486 27 75
Fax: +27 11 486 36 25, 486 36 75
E-mail: sagc@jhb.lia.net
Website: www.sagc.co.za
Contact: Klaus Volker Schuurman

SPAIN

Madrid

Cámara de Comercio Alemana para
España
Apartado de Correos 61055
E-28080 Madrid
Tel: +349 1 359 70 10
Fax: +349 1 359 12 13
E-mail: ahk_spanien@compuserve.com
Contact: Ass. Peter Moser

Barcelona

Cámara de Comercio Alemana para
España
Calle Córcega 301–303
E-08008 Barcelona
Tel: +349 3 415 54 44
Fax:+ 349 3 415 27 17
E-mail: 101512.2537@compuserve.com
Contact: Ass. Peter Moser

SWEDEN

Tysk-Svenska Handelskammaren
Narvavägen 12
S-115 22 Stockholm
Tel: +46 8 665 18 00
Fax: +46 8 66518 04
E-mail: info@handelskammer.cci.se
Contact: Dr Jörn Gallwitz

SWITZERLAND

**Handelskammer Deutschland-
Schweiz**
Tödistrasse 60
CH-8002 Zürich
Tel: +41 1 283 61 61
Fax: +41 1 283 61 00
E-mail: 106523.3362@compuserve.com
     hk_d_ch@swissonline.ch
Contact: Martin Theurer

TAIWAN

German Trade Office Taipei
4F., No. 3, Sec. 3, Min-Sheng E. Road
Taipei 104
Tel: +886 2 25 06 90 28
Fax: +886 2 25 06 81 82
E-mail: ahktpe@ms7.hinet.net
Contact: Gunther Tetzner

THAILAND

**German-Thai Chamber of
Commerce**
GPO Box 1728
Bangkok 10501
Tel: +66 2 236 23 96, 235 35 10-13, 266
     49 24
Fax: +66 2 236 47 11
E-mail: ahkbkk@box1.a-net.net.th
     gtcc@box1.a-net.net.th
Contact: Dr Paul R. Strunk
Contact: Marc Landau

TUNISIA

**Chambre Tuniso-Allemande
de l'Industrie et du Commerce**
6, rue Didon
1002 Tunis-Notre Dame
Tel: +216 1 78 59 10, 78 52 38
Fax: +216 1 78 25 51
E-mail: ahktunis.recht@planet.tn
Website: www.ahk.net/de/tn
Contact: Herr Peter Höhne

TURKEY

**Alman-Türk Ticaret ve Sanayi
Odasi**
PK 22
TR-80840 Ortaköy-Istanbul
Tel: +90 212 259 11 95/6, 259 08 40
Fax: +90 212 259 19 39

UKRAINE

Kiev

**Delegierte der Deutschen
Wirtschaft**
ul. Puschkinska, 34
UA-252004 Kiev
Tel: +38 044 224 59 98; 224 55 95
Fax: +38 044 225 42 34; 224 59 77
E-mail: diht@gu.kiev.ua
     106025.374@compuserve.com
Contact: Karin Rau

Dnepropetrowsk

**Delegierte der Deutschen
Wirtschaft**
ul. Jermolowoj 35
UA-320122 Dnepropetrowsk
Tel: +38 0562 96 09 59
Fax: +38 0562 96 09 59
E-mail: diht@gu.kiev.ua
     106025.374@compuserve.com

UNITED ARAB EMIRATES

The German Industry and
Commerce Office (GIC)
P.O. Box 7480
Dubai
Tel: +971 4 59 91 99
Fax: +971 4 59 91 88
Contact: Gert W Adomeit

UNITED KINGDOM

**German-British Chamber of
Industry & Commerce**
Mecklenburg House
16 Buckingham Gate
GB-London SW1E 6LB
Tel: +44 171 976 41 00
Fax: +44 171 976 41 01
E-mail: mail@ahk-london.co.uk
Website: www.ahk-london.co.uk
Contact: Ulrich Hoppe

URUGUAY

**Cámara de Comercio Uruguayo-
Alemana**
Casilla de Correo 1499
11000 Montevideo
Tel: +598 2 917 03 07, 917 03 08
Fax: +598 2 916 32 81
E-mail: ahkurug@adinet.com.uy
Contact: Sven Heldt

USA

Atlanta

**German American Chamber of
Commerce of the Southern United
States, Inc.**
3340 Peachtree Road, NE Suite 500
Atlanta, GA 30326
Tel: +1 404 239 94 94
Fax: +1 404 264 17 61
E-mail: gaccsouth@mindspring.com
Contact: Thomas Beck

Chicago

**German American Chamber of
Commerce of the Midwest, Inc.**
401 North Michigan Ave., Suite 2525
Chicago IL 60611-4212
Tel: +1 312 644 26 62
Fax: +1 312 644 07 38
E-mail: gaccom@techinter.com
Website: www.gaccom.org
   www.christkindlmarket.com
   www.ihk.de/ahk/chicago
Contact: Christian Röhr

Los Angeles

**German American Chamber of
Commerce of the Western United
States, Inc.**
5220 Pacific Concourse Drive
Suite 280
Los Angeles, CA 90045
Tel: +1 310 297 79 79
Fax: +1 310 297 79 66
E-mail: gaccwest@compuserve.com
Website: www.GACCWEST.org
Contact: Michael Krieg

New York

German American Chamber of Commerce, Inc.
40 West 57th Street, 31st Floor
New York, NY 10019-4092
Tel: +1 212 974 88 30
Fax: +1 212 974 88 67
E-mail: gaccny@compuserve.com
Contact: Werner Walbröl

Houston

(subsidiary of Atlanta office)

German American Chamber of Commerce, Inc.
5599 San Felipe, Suite 510
Houston, TX 77056
Tel: +1 713 877 11 14
Fax: +1 713 877 16 02
E-mail: gacchou@mindspring.com
Website: www.gaccsouth.com
Contact: Friedrich W Kuhlmann

Philadelphia

(subsidiary of New York office)

German American Chamber of Commerce, Inc.
1515 Market Street, Suite 505
Philadelphia, PA 19102
Tel: +1 215 665 15 85
Fax: +1 215 665 03 75
E-mail: gaccphila@compuserve.com
Contact: Barbara Afanassiev

San Francisco

(subsidiary of Los Angeles office)

German American Chamber of Commerce of the Western United States, Inc.
465 California Street, Suite 506
San Francisco, CA 94104
Tel: +1 415 392 22 62
Fax: +1 415 392 13 14
E-mail: gaccwest_sfo@compuserve.com
Website: www.GACCWEST.org
Contact: Lawrence A Walker

Washington

Representative of German Industry and Trade
1627 I Street, N.W., Suite 550
Washington, D.C. 20006
Tel: +1 202 659 47 77
Fax: +1 202 659 47 79
E-mail: 104075.1540@compuserve.com
info@rgit-usa.com
Contact: Jacob Esser

UZBEKISTAN

Repräsentanz der Deutschen Wirtschaft
ul. Murtasaeva 6, 82-83
700 000 Tashkent
Tel: +998 712 34 99 89, 711 39 13 05/
1, 711 20 66 86
Fax: +998 712 34 16 24, 711 20 64 24
E-mail: ahktasch@naytov.com
Contact: Jörg Hetsch

VENEZUELA

**Cámara de Comercio e Industria
Venezolano-Alemana**
Apartado 61236
Caracas-1060 A
Tel: +58 2 267 14 11, 267 08 52, 267 16
    30, 267 19 45
Fax: +58 2 266 63 73
E-mail: 102213.22@compuserve.com
Website: www.cavenal.com
Contact: Gerd Wilhelm Petersen

VIETNAM

**Delegate of German Industry and
Commerce Hanoi**
41 Ly Thai To
Hanoi
SR Vietnam
Tel: +84 4 825 14 20
Fax: +84 4 825 14 22
Contact: Ekkehard Goetting
(Please direct questions to Hong Kong
office)

* Members of the German Regional Chambers of Industry & Commerce for
Central America and the Caribbean.

Appendix 4

Contributor Contact Details

Eversheds
Senator House
85 Queen Victoria Street
London EC4V 4JL
Tel: 020 7919 4500
Fax: 020 7919 4919
E-mail: carlm@eversheds.com
Contact: Dr Michael H Carl

Federal Center for Foreign Investment in Germany
Federal Ministry of Economics and Technology (BMWI)
Scharnhorststrasse 34–37
10115 Berlin
Germany
Tel: +49 30 2014 9
Fax: +49 30 2014 7036
Website: www.business-in-germany.de

Federal Institute for Vocational Training
Bundesinstitut für Berufsbildung (BIBB)
Hermann-Ehlers-Strasse 10
53113 Bonn
Germany
Tel: +49 228 1070
Contact: Dr Lazslo Alex

German-British Chamber of Industry & Commerce
16 Buckingham Gate
London SW1E 6LB
Tel: 020 7976 4100
Fax: 020 7976 4101
E-mail: legal@ahk-london.co.uk
Website: www.ahk-london.co.uk
Contact: Angelika Baumgarte, Ulrich Hoppe

HSBC Private Equity Limited
Vintners Place
68 Upper Thames Street
London EC4V 3BJ
Tel: 020 7336 9000
Fax: 020 7336 9961
Contact: John Harper

LCT Consultants
Adam-Kraft-Strasse 45
90419 Nuremberg
Germany
Tel: +49 911 397702
Fax: +49 911 331477
E-mail: ericlynnlct@compuserve.com
Contact: Eric Lynn

Lehrstuhl für Volkswirtschaftslehre
Wirtschaftstheorie
Universität Bayreuth
95440 Bayreuth
Germany
Tel: +49 921 55 2880/1
Fax: +49 921 55 2886
Contact: Prof Dr Peter Oberender

New German Länder Industrial Investment Council (IIC)
Charlottenstrasse 57
10117 Berlin
Germany
Tel: +49 30 2094 5660
Fax: +49 30 2094 5666
Website: www.iic.de
Contact: Catherine McDowell, Dr Hans Christoph von Rohr,
    John M Zindar

PricewaterhouseCoopers
Southwark Towers
32 London Bridge Street
London SE1 9SY
Tel: 020 7213 1005
Fax: 020 7804 3913
E-mail: jens.roennberg@uk.pwcglobal.com
Contact: Jens Roennberg

PricewaterhouseCoopers
1 Embankment Place
London WC2N 6NN
Tel: 020 7213 5453
Fax: 020 7213 2415
E-mail: adrian.t.yeeles@uk.pwcglobal.com
Contact: Adrian Yeeles

PricewaterhouseCoopers
Corporate Finance Beratung GmbH
Gervinusstrasse 17
60322 Frankfurt
Germany
Tel: +49 69 1520 40
Fax: +49 69 9585 6533
E-mail: firstname.surname@de.pwcglobal.com
Contact: Anita Davisson, Wolfram Schmerl, Astrid Schmidt

PwC Deutsche Revision AG
Bockenheimer Anlage 15
60322 Frankfurt-am-Main
Germany
Tel: +49 69 95 85 0
Fax: +49 69 9585 1000
Contact: Dr Andreas Freiling, Frank Viecens

PwC Deutsche Revision AG
New-York-Ring 13D
22297 Hamburg
Germany
Tel: +49 40 6378 1649
Fax: +49 40 6378 1035
E-mail: firstname.surname@de.pwcglobal.com
Contact: Morag McLean, Sven Rosorius, Wolfgang Suchanek

PricewaterhouseCoopers
1301 Avenue of the Americas
New York
New York 10019
USA
Tel: +1 212 259 2459
Fax: +1 212 259 2290
E-mail: christoph.schreiber@us.pwcglobal.com
Contact: Christoph Schreiber

Jonathan Reuvid
Little Manor
Wroxton
Banbury
Oxfordshire OX15 6QE
Tel: 01295 738070
Fax: 01295 738090
E-mail: jr.wroxton@ndirect.co.uk

Schulze & Braun
Kaiserstrasse 231-233
76133 Karlsruhe
Germany
Tel: +49 721 91957 0
Fax: +49 721 91957 11
E-mail: cschiller@schubra.de
Contact: Dr Christof Schiller

Schulze & Braun
Postfach 1406
77845 Achern
Germany
Tel: +49 7841 708 0
Fax: +49 7841 708 301
E-mail: ebraun@schubra.de
Contact: Dr Eberhard Braun

Walter Tacke
Sindmuhlenweg 20
33605 Bielefeld
Germany
Tel / Fax: +49 521 25779

University of Duisburg
(Gerhard-Mercator Universität Duisburg)
Fachbereich 2 Erziehungswissenschaften
Lotharstraße 65
47048 Duisburg
Germany
Tel: +49 203 3790
Fax: +49 203 379 2078
Contact: Dr Hermann Schmidt

Wirtshafts- und Sozialwissenschaftliches Institut (WSI)
Hans-Böckler-Stiftung
Bertha-von-Suttner-Platz 1
40227 Düsseldorf
Germany
Tel: +49 211 7778 0
Fax: +49 211 7778 210
Contact: Dr Wolfgang Lecher

Wissenschaftszentrum Berlin für Sozialforschung (WZB)
Market Processes and Corporate Development
Reichpletschufer 60
10785 Berlin
Germany
Tel: +49 30 254 91 0
Fax: +49 30 254 91 431
Contact: Prof Dr Horst Albach

Index

Index of Advertisers

Doing Business with
Germany

The introduction of the euro has brought about many changes to Germany's economic outlook. In addition, the recently elected centre-left coalition government – the first in 16 years – has altered the German political framework and is showing resolution in tackling the structural weaknesses of the economy. These changes are greatly influencing business dealings both in and with Germany, and will do so for many years to come.

Doing Business with Germany highlights and examines these changes, providing information and best practice advice from leading commentators and professional firms.

Topics covered include:

- the euro and the Euro-zone
- financial incentives and investment opportunities
- the private equity market
- economic and business conditions
- competitiveness
- the political climate
- legal issues
- the tax regime
- business culture

Published in association with the German-British Chamber of Industry & Commerce, PricewaterhouseCoopers and Eversheds, *Doing Business with Germany* is an authoritative guide, which is invaluable for those wishing to establish trade links and expand business activities in Germany.

£24.95

Kogan Page
120 Pentonville Road
London N1 9JN
www.kogan-page.co.uk

ISBN 0-7494-2951-8

9 780749 429515